Political Economy of Communications in India

Political Economy of Communications in India

The Good, the Bad and the Ugly

Pradip Ninan Thomas

SAGE www.sagepublications.com
Los Angeles • London • New Delhi • Singapore • Washington DC

First published in 2010 by

SAGE Publications India Pvt Ltd
B1/I-1 Mohan Cooperative Industrial Area
Mathura Road, New Delhi 110 044, India
www.sagepub.in

SAGE Publications Inc
2455 Teller Road
Thousand Oaks, California 91320, USA

SAGE Publications Ltd
1 Oliver's Yard, 55 City Road
London EC1Y 1SP, United Kingdom

SAGE Publications Asia-Pacific Pte Ltd
33 Pekin Street
#02-01 Far East Square
Singapore 048763

Published by Vivek Mehra for SAGE Publications India Pvt Ltd, typeset in 10/12pt Minion by Tantla Composition Pvt Ltd, Chandigarh and printed at Chaman Enterprises, New Delhi.

Library of Congress Cataloging-in-Publication Data

Thomas, Pradip Ninan.

Political economy of communications in India : the good, the bad and the ugly / Pradip Ninan Thomas.

p. cm.

Includes index.

1. Mass media—Economic aspects—India. 2. Mass media—Political aspects—India. 3. Mass media policy—India. 4. Communication policy—India. I. Title.

P96.E252I88 302.230954—dc22 2010 2010014829

ISBN: 978-81-321-0449-0 (HB)

The SAGE Team: Rekha Natarajan, Aniruddha De, Anju Saxena and Trinankur Banerjee

For

Preetha, Nitin and Prianka

Another World is Possible

Contents

List of Abbreviations

AIADMK	All India Anna Dravida Munnetra Kazhagam
AICC	All India Congress Council
AIR	All India Radio
AITUC	All India Trade Union Congress
AP	Andhra Pradesh
APAI	Animation Producers Association of India
APC	Association for Progressive Communication
APEC	Asia-Pacific Economic Cooperation
AV	Audio-visual
BJP	Bharatiya Janata Party
BMG	Bertelsmann Music Group
BPO	Business Process Outsourcing
BSA	Business Software Alliance
BSP	Bahujan Samaj Party
CAMERA	Committee for Accuracy in Middle East Reporting in America
CBN	Christian Broadcasting Network
CEAC	Copyright Enforcement Advisory Council
CEO	Chief Executive Officer
CITU	Centre for India Trade Unions
CJ	Citizen Journalism
CMCR	Centre for Mass Communication Research
CMs	Christian Ministries
CPIM	Communist Part of India (Marxist)
CR	Community Radio
CRIS	Communication Rights in the Information Society
CS	Civil Society
CSI	Church of South India
DD	Doordarshan
DMCA	Digital Millennium Copyright Act
DMK	Dravida Munnetra Kazhagam

DNA	Deoxyribonucleic Acid
DRM	Digital Rights Management
DSNGS	Digital Satellite News Gathering Scheme
DTH	Direct-to-home
DVD	Digital Video Disc
ELCOT	Electronics Corporation of Tamil Nadu
EMI	Electric and Musical Industries Ltd
EST	Expressed Sequence Tag
EU	European Union
E&M	Entertainment and Media
FCC	Federal Communications Commission
FCRA	Foreign Contributions Regulations Act
FDIs	Foreign Direct Investments
FEBA	Far Eastern Broadcasting Association
FICCI	Federation of Indian Chambers of Commerce and Industry
FOSS	Free and Open Source Software
FYPs	Five Year Plans
GATS	General Agreement on Trade in Services
GATT	General Agreement on Tarrifs and Trade
GBN	Global Broadcasting News
GDP	Gross Domestic Product
GFA	Gospel for Asia
GNP	Gross National Product
GPL	General Public License
GSP	Generalised System of Preferences
IAMCR	International Association of Media and Communication Research
IAS	Indian Administrative Service
I&B	Information and Broadcasting
ICANN	Internet Consortium for Assigned Names and Numbers
ICDS	Integrated Child Development Services
ICS	Indian Civil Service
ICT	Information and Communication Technology
IFE	International Family Entertainment Inc.
IIPA	International Intellectual Property Alliance
IKS	Indigenous Knowledge System

IMF	International Monetary Fund
IMG	Indian Media Group
IMI	Indian Music Industry
INC	Indian National Congress
INCP	International Network on Cultural Policy
INGO	International Non-governmental Organisation
IP	Intellectual Property
IPC	Intellectual Property Committee
IPR	Intellectual Property Rights
IPRS	Indian Performing Rights Society Limited
IPTA	Indian Political Theatre Association
IPTV	Internet Protocol Television
IT	Information Technology
ITA	International Trade Administration
KAP	Knowledge, Attitude, Perception
KIADB	Karnataka Industrial Areas Development Board
MBPL	Music Broadcast Pvt. Ltd
MFN	Most Favoured Nation
MIT	Massachusetts Institute of Technology
MKSS	Mazdoor Kisan Shakti Sangathan
ML	Marxist-Leninist
MNC	Multinational Company
MOI	Ministry of Information
MOU	Memorandum of Understanding
MPA	Motion Picture Association
MPAA	Motion Picture Association of America
MRTP	Monopolies and Restrictive Trade Practices
MSO	Multi-system Operator
NAFTA	North American Free Trade Agreement
NASA	National Aeronautical and Space Association
NASSCOM	National Association of Software and Services Companies
NCEUS	National Commission for Enterprises in the Unorganised Sector
NGO	Non-governmental Organisation
NRCFOSS	National Resource Centre for Free/Open Source Software
NREGA	National Rural Employment Guarantee Act

NREGS	National Rural Employment Guarantee Scheme
NRI	Non-resident Indian
NTIA	National Telecommunications and Information Administration
OFCOM	Office of Communications
OSSRC	Open Source Software Resource Centre
PACS Programme	Poorest Area Civil Society Programme
PBS	Public Broadcasting Service
PDS	Public Distribution System
PIO	Public Information Officers
PPL	Phonographic Performance Limited
RCA	Radio Corporation of America
R&D	Research and Development
RFC	Ramoji Film City
RIAA	Recording Industry Association of America
RMI	Rights Management Information
RSS	Rashtriya Swayamsevak Sangh
RTI	Right to Information
SAGIT	Sectoral Advisory Group on International Trade
SAGs	Social Action Groups
SAPs	Structural Adjustment Programmes
SCRIPT	Society for Copyright Regulations of Indian Producers for Films and Television
SISWA	South India Soul Winner's Association
SITE	Satellite Instructional Television Experiment
SLBC	Sri Lankan Broadcasting Corporation
SNPs	Single Nucleotide Polymorphisms
SP	Samajwadi Party
SPACE	Society for Promotion of Alternative Computing and Employment
TBN	Trinity Broadcasting Network
TCIL	Telecommunications Consultants India Ltd.
TCS	Tata Consultancy Services
TDP	Telugu Desam Party
TISCO	Tata Iron and Steel Co. Ltd
TPM	Technology Protection Measure

TRAI	Telecom Regulatory Authority of India
TRIPS	Trade-related Aspects of Intellectual Property Rights
T and V system	Training and Visit System
TWR	Trans World Radio
UDHR	Universal Declaration of Human Rights
UNDP	United Nations Development Program
UNESCO	United Nations Educational, Scientific and Cultural Organisation
UNICE	Union of Industrial and Employer's Confederation of Europe
UPA	United Progressive Alliance
UPOV	International Union for the Protection of New Varieties of Plants
USA	United States of America
USAID	United States Aid
USIBC	US-India Business Council
USPTO	United States Patent and Trademark Office
USTR	United States Trade Representative
VCD	Video Compact Disc
VCR	Video Cassette Recorder
VEW	Village Extension Worker
VHP	Vishwa Hindu Parishad
VSNL	Videsh Sanchar Nigam Limited
WACC	World Association for Christian Communication
WCFCG	World Council for Corporate Governance
WCT	WIPO's Copyright Treaty
WIPO	World Intellectual Property Organisation
WPPT	WIPO's Performances and Phonograms Treaty
WSIS	World Summit on the Information Society
WTO	World Trade Organisation
ZEEL	Zee Entertainment Enterprises Ltd

Foreword

As we enter the second decade of the twenty-first century, India has emerged as one of the world's fastest growing economies, a fact also reflected in the exponential growth in its media and communication sector.

With 70 round-the-clock television news channels—unrivalled in any other country—India boasts of the planet's most linguistically diverse and differentiated media landscape. Sale of newspapers is booming: every day nearly 100 million copies are sold in the country. FM radio is mushrooming as are community and online media outlets. The revolution in telecommunications, especially mobile telephony, has touched almost every aspect of people's lives—economic, political, social and cultural. India is now acknowledged as an information technology giant and a major hub within the global outsourcing industry.

The scholarship on Indian media and communication has scarcely kept pace with the extraordinary changes that have transformed the media and communication sphere in the world's largest democracy. Part of the reason for this has been that, with a few exceptions, most universities have not yet grasped the importance of media and communication in our political, economic and cultural interactions, as well as our globalising experiences.

Though there has been a proliferation of media institutes in recent years, these are primarily oriented to the vocational aspects of the mass media. More often than not, these are private institutions established sometimes by media houses themselves to groom trained workforce for the bourgeoning industry. For a fast growing creative and cultural industry in India, such institutes have an important contribution to make. However, more grounded and rigorous academic work in media and communication has yet to emerge in a systematic manner, though such entities as the Centre for Culture, Media and Governance at the Jamia Millia Islamia are embarking on intellectually ambitious research.

Pradip Ninan Thomas's latest book fits neatly in the latter category. Pradip has lived and worked for many years outside India—first in the UK and now in Australia—and the academic and activist in him has kept a close watch on the rapidly evolving situation in the country of his birth. In this timely and extremely topical book, Pradip breaks new ground in the study of media and communication in India, bringing in new strands of politics onto the communication research agenda. He expertly guides the reader through the exceptional growth and development of India's communication hard and software. The contemporary trends in the media and communication scene are contextualised in a historical framework. Important questions about media and empowerment; information rights and responsibilities; copyright and commodification of cultural industries; bioethics and religious fundamentalism, are tackled with alacrity, great insight and aplomb.

I have always admired Pradip's work. He is one of the best scholars of his generation: committed, conscientious and cosmopolitan. These virtues have ensured that he is a member of the distinguished international advisory board of the India Media Centre—the world's first academic centre dedicated to the study of media in India and its globalising tendencies—which we have recently set up at the University of Westminster in London, in recognition of the important role of Indian media in the world today.

Pradip's book is a major contribution to the study of media and communication in India and indeed to the broader scholarship in the field of political economy of communication. I very much commend its publication and hope that the book will generate greater interest in analyses of the changing contours of media and communication institutions, structures, production processes and audiences in what is likely to become one of the most intellectually exciting and empirically rich fields in this area of research.

Dr Daya Thussu
Professor of International Communication
Co-Director, India Media Centre
University of Westminster, London

Preface

The seeds for this book were sown many moons ago. I remember that the very first article that I wrote, soon after completing an initial draft of my doctoral thesis that I had got rather weary of writing, was on the Gramscian theory of hegemony and state monopoly broadcasting in India. That was way back in 1987. Two decades later, the various trajectories of a critical political economy of the media continue to intrigue me.

To a large extent, my interest in the subject was spurred on by introductory lectures on the political economy of communications given by Peter Golding and Graham Murdock at the Centre for Mass Communication Research (CMCR), University of Leicester, between 1982–1983. I was a student in the MA course before becoming a doctoral candidate at the Centre. Their critical approach to the media and society and the readings that I encountered and required ploughing through, including classic texts such as Marx and Engels' *German Ideology,* certainly helped me imagine India in a new light during and after my fieldwork. My interest in this area was furthered during a longish stint of working at the World Association for Christian Communication (WACC), London, where, as Director of Research, I was responsible for organising a number of international workshops on a range of issues—media ownership and control, intellectual property, media resistance, poverty and the media, involved in co-editing the journal *Media Development* and in global media advocacy such as the Communication Rights in the Information Society (CRIS) Campaign. By this time, I had become a member of the International Association of Media and Communication Research (IAMCR) and frequently attended the political economy section—a watering hole for a great many critical political economists of the media.

I have met and learned from a number of critical political economists, some of whom I count as sage counsels and close friends of mine—Cees Hamelink, Dan Schiller, Yuezhi Zhao. There are a number of other old and new acquaintances whose contributions I value—Manjunath Pendakur, Andrew Calabrese, Robert McChesney, Daya Thussu, Keyan Tomaselli, Roberto Verzola, Hopeton Dunn, Colin Sparks, Lawrence Liang among many others. I also value the insights of a number of scholars from India, including Sevanti Ninan, Vibodh Parthasarthi, Ammu Joseph among others.

My intellectual horizons were immeasurably expanded in the company of my close friends—the Leicester mafia, consisting of Zaharom Nain (Rom), Francis Nyamnjoh, Chien-San Fang, Roderick Salazar, Ubonrat Siriyuvisak, Kim Seung Soo, Muhammed Musa and others, some of whom I continue to collaborate with to this day. Rom, in particular, introduced me to some of the key debates in political economy that we discussed over copious quantities of cheap wine and ale, in a variety of student digs located in the vicinity of the CMCR. While some of these debates, with the benefit of hindsight, were not terribly consequential, my world would have been poorer for not having encountered the thoughts and ideas of a highly variegated cast of characters from the annals of critical political economy. Incidentally, Rom and I co-edited the volume *Who Owns the Media: Global Trends and Local Resistances* (2004).

The University of Queensland has provided an excellent base for this particular study. I have made use of the library resources, tried out ideas in class and valued conversations with a number of my colleagues—Zala Volcic, Michael Bromley, Levi Obijiofor, Martin Hadlow, Elske van de Fliert, Rhonda Breit, Nic Carah, Eric Louw and others.

The ever changing media scene in India has been my bread and butter for many years and has opened me to a range of research interests, some of which I have enjoyed exploring. I have always maintained that it is necessary to strike a balance when reporting globalising India and have tried consistently to deal with its other, less wholesome sides, that international cheer leaders of India Inc. along with most Indian journalists and media academics have chosen to ignore. Arvind Adiga's novel *White Tiger*, the film *Slum Dog Millionaire*, the Indian journalist Sainath's consistent exposes of poverty and the scandal at Satyam Computers reveal that not everything is well at India Inc. and that it will take more than technology to redeem the image of 'India Shining'. India has, for sure, made significant advances in science and technology and in communications. The great variety of regional and national channels and media is quite astounding especially when compared to the strictly limited media environment in Brisbane, Australia, where I currently reside. However, in spite of these achievements, India does face significant issues related to poverty and human development, with poor governance and state and private media monopolies that have developed at the expense of its many marginalised communities. I hope that this book throws light on issues and concerns that are often forgotten in the context of the general euphoria with India's satellite days and cable nights.

A critical political economy-based approach can be used to throw light on the impact of 'structures', power and ideologies in other areas of communication research—communication and social change, religion and the media and alternative media. Critical political economy has given me a tool-box, consisting of resources, ideas, texts and conversations that I have frequently used to illumine the key deficits and blind spots in the media in India. I have deliberately chosen not to deal with the major controversies that have dogged the political economy tradition, in particular the debates with those in cultural studies over the base/superstructure, although, having said that, I cannot resist adding the following. While culture certainly plays an important role in the structuring of identity and choices that consumers make and needs to be studied for its complexity, its role in mediation and the making of social relatedness and meanings, the dog's breakfast that some expressions of contemporary cultural studies has morphed into and the widespread lack of critique linked to this tradition is not in anybody's interests, except global capital. I am quite content to concur with Murdock and Golding's (2005: 62) views that since production happens prior to consumption, that is an obvious place to start one's analysis from. '…we can think of the economic dynamic, *as playing a central role in defining the key features of the general environment within which communicative activity takes places*, but not as a complete explanation of the nature of that activity' (emphasis mine; Murdock and Golding 2005).

What does this book cover? This book primarily deals with the politics of media structures, policy and processes related to the political economy of communications in India, in the context of convergence. The canvas for this exploration is intentionally both local and global. What I have tried to explore are numerous vantage points, pegs that can be used as an entry point for exploring a political economy perspective. It presents a critical perspective and includes a section on resistance to this dominant political economy of communications. *What is not covered in the book*? It does not deal with the intricacies of mediation per se or with audiences. While I do concur that what people do with media is an important aspect of understanding the media, that calls for another approach that includes the business of 'meaning making' and I would certainly hope that there will be studies in the future that throw light on the complex interactions between media and audiences in India. The book is also not a study of specific genres and associated structures such as satellite news channels (See Nalin Mehta's (2008) *India on Television* for an analysis of satellite news channels), specific media empires in India (for which there is a crying need for studies) or of the media seen strictly as a business. There is an excellent book by Vanita Kohli-Khandekar (2006, ed.), *The Indian Media Business*, that provides adequate coverage of this area.

I have, over the years, contributed a number of articles on the political economy of communications to journals such as *Gazette: The International Journal for Communication Studies, Telematics and Informatics, Economic and Political Weekly, Media Development* and to edited books. While I do allude to some of these texts, the chapters in this volume are based on research that I have carried out over the last decade. I strongly believe that students of the media located in India and elsewhere need to be exposed to perspectives that go against the grain and that are based on a critique of the dominant systems and practices of communication.

I am grateful for the support given by the Sage team involved in the production of this book, especially Rekha Natarajan and Aniruddha De. My special thanks to friends and family in India for their no holds barred hospitality—my dear Ammama, Daddy and Mummy, Prem and Beena, Sneha and Shruthi, who in equal measure, have for years, tolerated the ways of an itinerant; my wife Preetha, whose very pragmatic and grounded outlook on life has helped me understand the possibilities and limits of theory, and children Nitin and Prianka who have let me get on with writing, when I am sure they would rather have preferred that I drive them to the Sunshine Coast or play cricket at the Bellbowrie nets.

Pradip Ninan Thomas
February 2009
Brisbane

References

Kohli-Khandekar, Vanita. 2006. *The Indian Media Business*. New Delhi/Thousand Oaks, London: Response Books/Sage.

Murdock, G. and P. Golding. 2005. 'Culture, Communication and Political Economy', in J. Curran and M. Gurevitch (eds), *Mass Media and Society*, 60–83. London: Hodder Arnold.

Mehta, N. 2008. *India on Television: How Satellite News Channels Have Changed the Way We Think and Act*. New Delhi: HarperCollins Publishers India/India Today Group.

Thomas, P. N. and Z. Nain. 2004. *Who Owns the Media: Global Trends and Local Resistances*. Penang: Southbound; London: ZED.

Section 1
A History of Structures

This section includes four chapters. It begins with an introductory chapter that explores key concepts in the political economy approach followed by three chapters that explore the history of the media from a political economy perspective during three distinct periods—colonial, post-colonial (1948–1985) and the new India (1986 to the present), the latter characterised by the country's increasing intermeshings with economic and cultural globalisation. These chapters reveal the varying impact of politics and economics on the media, the uses and abuses of media power and the ways in which the media in India have essentially remained monopolies at various times—at the behest of its colonial rulers, the State, and, in the context of twenty-first century India, the State and a small but influential set of media conglomerates and industrial power houses.

1

An Introduction to the Political Economy of Communications

Why is there a need for a critical political economy of communications? For the simple reason that the media are doubly significant. Not only are media sectors responsible for the generation of sizeable revenues, these industries are crucially involved in the production and circulation of symbolic goods and services—products that, unlike toothpaste and biscuits, have the capacity to influence the choices that we make and the decisions that we take regarding life's small and large quandaries—be it the brand of milk that we buy, the investments that we make or our understanding of the rightness or wrongness of the war in Iraq and, closer to India, the war in Kashmir. This is what makes the media unique and why it is necessary to study them. Changes in the media terrain in India, the emergence of domestic media czars, external and internal policies that have led to media liberalisation, India's attempts at harmonisation of its copyright laws with global rules, its position on trade in audio-visuals, the technocratic vision of lobbies such as the National Association for Software and Services Company (NASSCOM), the changing nature of labour in communications along with the significant media disjunctures in India—for instance, the media's treatment of poverty, and resistance by civil society to the dominant media and their representations are significant aspects that together make up the larger picture related to the political economy of communications in India.

The media play an increasingly important role in the lives of people throughout the world. It has become a primary source for information, education and, in the case of India, entertainment. In spite of its ubiquity, it remains rather paradoxically a scarce resource, increasingly owned by large business houses. Despite the government-supported liberalisation of the media sector in India, doubts remain, and the Telecommunication

Regulatory Authority of India's (TRAI) 2008 Consultation paper on media ownership articulates some of these doubts. Predictably though, the corporate response to this paper suggests that media ownership is a non issue, given fragmented media markets and diverse audiences in India. That selective reasoning can be contested. Rupert Murdoch's New Corporation and the Sun TV network owned by the Marans may be different in terms of their scale of operations but are similar when it comes to their mixing of business with politics. Both are rent-seeking monopolies and the owners of both have used their political connections to enlarge their media empires. Just as the Fox Network in the US has played a significant role in legitimising neo-conservative policies linked to the Bush administration, so, in the context of Sun TV's on and off alliances with the ruling Dravida Munnetra Kazhagam (DMK) party in Tamil Nadu, and the significant involvement of one of the scions of the Sun TV dynasty, Dayanidhi Maran, as a Union Minister involved in the making of communications policy, there have been substantive political investments in assuring Sun TV's corporate, inter-sectoral media dominance.

While there is certainly an argument to be made about the extensive nature of media choice in India today, one can also argue that this choice is circumscribed by the politics of media ownership. The most dramatic example of the links between media ownership and politics is that of Rupert Murdoch whose world-wide media empire News Corporation remains a steady supporter of all causes conservative—from the war in Iraq to right-wing politics. The cultural industries, in other words, play a vital role in reinforcing and legitimising capitalism and mainstream politics. It is also a primary means of reinforcing power and making profit. The exploration of these two aspects of media ownership and control—power and profit—are among the central aims of a political economy of communications. How power is reinforced by and for whom, and how profits are made in national and global contexts characterised by competition, deregulation and the need for ever larger audiences is an essential aspect of the narrative of a political economy of communications. In the Indian context, it is also the story of the success of cable and satellite television and FM radio but not, as yet, of community radio. A critical political economy of communications deals with both the spectacular success of certain cultural industries and the containment of other industries that are not consumer-driven. It asks the question—why are consumer-driven media projects privileged at the expense of citizen-driven projects—and also explores the nature of resistance and civil society-based attempts to create a level media playing field.

The media are not benign institutions. The DMK party in Tamil Nadu promised one television per household in their electoral manifesto prior to the 2004 local elections—a promise that they have striven to fulfil. That could be seen as a case of populism, which it certainly is, although it also needs to be seen in terms of a politics that understands the role of the media in the shaping of attitudes, identities, choices and aspirations. What better than a captive audience fed by a fraternal network (Sun TV) that not only has extensive interests in cable television, but also a monopoly hold over access to cable and satellite signals in Tamil Nadu, and significant interests in both FM radio and the press.

However, a critical political economy also recognises the fact that the media are by no means independent players but that they are critically linked to and part of on-going political and economic processes, negotiations and contestations at both national and international levels. In other words, while there certainly is a need for an analysis of the specificity of media, a critical political economy of communications will necessarily need to deal with its larger stage, de-centre its focus on the media per se and focus on the many elements that shape the media and make it what it is. As Vincent Mosco describes it in his classic text *The Political Economy of Communication*:

> Decentring the media means viewing systems of communication as integral to fundamental economic, political, social, and cultural processes in society...The point is that the political economy approach to communication places its subject within a wider social totality...Both political economy and communication are mutually constituted out of social and cultural practices. Both refer to processes of exchange which differ, but which are also multiply determined by shared social and cultural practices. (Mosco 1996: 71–72)

Decentring however does not mean marginalising the analysis of the media. Rather, the media and political economy need to be seen as 'mutually constitutive', distinct but also co-terminus, synergistically related and as two sides of the same coin.

The Larger Context of a Political Economy of Communications

The globalisation of cultural goods and services, which in itself is a by-product of economic liberalisation, has been accompanied by the removal of trade barriers, deregulation and privatisation and hastened by convergence. There has been a transformation of global, regional, national and local cultural markets, a deepening of ties between these levels and to an increasing complexity in the relationship within and between cultural markets. The emergence of complexity in the relationships between and within the 'production-distribution-consumption' axis aided by multi-sectoral flows is cited by liberal theorists as an indication of changes to the vertical power dynamics that informed struggles over the New World Information and Communication order and that structured the debates around media and cultural imperialism. The growing influence of regional and national hubs of cultural production—be it TV Globo in Brazil, Nollywood in Nigeria, Bollywood in India, Chinese television production and the Qatar-based Al-Jazeera news service along with the many adaptations and 'localisations' of culture would seem to indicate that, indeed, Herman and Chomsky's (2002) classic treatise on media, power and propaganda '*Manufacturing Consent*' is dated and in need of revision. Power, the liberals say, has been flattened, and has resulted in an even dynamics that can no longer be explained with sole reference to US cultural and economic imperialism. An example of this flattening is contained in the annual Federation of Indian Chambers of Commerce and Industry (FICCI)/PricewaterhouseCoopers (July 2009) report 'Indian Entertainment and Media Industry Outlook'. After five years of exponential growth in local television, filmed entertainment, radio, music, live entertainment, the entertainment industry, print media, out of home advertising and internet advertising growth in 2008 was down, reflecting the overall global economic climate along with domestic uncertainties. With the exception of online advertising that showed an astounding 85.2 per cent growth from 2007 although it still had a limited market share of 2.3 per cent of the total advertising pie, growth had declined in all entertainment and media sectors along with mainstream media advertising. However, and in spite of slower media growth rates, all evidence points towards greater intermeshings of Indian media with global media and a tiered ownership structure in the domestic media market. Reliance Anil Dhirubhai Ambani Group (Reliance ADA) Group's 50 per cent stake in Spielberg's DreamWorks co-productions, Bennett Coleman Group's acquisition of Virgin Radio Holdings, Walter Disney's acquisitions of 60 per cent of UTV and the Star Group's picking up of 45 per cent of Jupiter Ventures along with major foreign investment flows from Mauritius for a host of Indian companies indicates the robustness despite the downturn of the entertainment and media (E&M) market (PricewaterhouseCoopers 2009: 19). While 2008 advertising revenues in the region of Rs 18,500 crores accounts for 70 per cent of broadcasting and 80 per cent of print media revenues, the announcement by one of India's largest media houses Zee Entertainment Enterprises Ltd (ZEEL) that subscription revenues had begun to surpass advertising revenues does suggest that there could be a subtle shift in media business models (Ajwani 2009). However, despite the cautious enthusiasm of the most recent FICCI/PricewaterhouseCoopers surveys of the entertainment and media (E&M) market in India, its key descriptors of the market are 'buoyancy' and 'opportunities' for growth. Growth projections remain projections and industry watchers such as Gurbir Singh (2008) paint a darker picture—of falling advertising budgets by 35–40 per cent and curtailment of funds from capital markets resulting in a lack of investment, employment cut-backs, salary freezes, cost cutting schemes, delays in the launch of new media ventures, and even a drop in regional language print readership after years of steady growth.

How does all this relate to the success story of the Indian media consumer? One can argue that the availability of a vast array of consumer technologies and value added services has certainly widened consumer choice in India. However, access and use does not necessarily make sovereign consumers. Henry Jenkins in his book *Convergence Culture* concludes with the following lines:

> Welcome to convergence culture, where old and new media collide, where grassroots and corporate media intersect, where the power of the media producer and the power of the media consumer interact in unpredictable ways. Convergence culture is the future, but it is taking shape now. Consumers will be more powerful within convergence culture—but only if they recognise and use that power as both consumers and citizens, as full participants in our culture. (Jenkins 2006: 258–259)

Jenkin's concluding remarks suggest that for the first time in the history of mediated publics a flattening is taking shape. This flattening is as much a consequence of convergence as it is about the unpredictable ways in which convergent technologies are being used by consumers and 'prosumers'. The current exploration of the many uses of mobile phones in the extension of citizenship does seem to indicate that the appropriation of technology, its availability and to a lesser extent, its modifiability is a key aspect of convergence culture. Having said that, Jenkins' understanding of the manufacture, flow and exercise of power in contemporary society is problematic precisely because both consumers and citizens are the products of structures and their actions are to a large extent determined by their place in society. I am not suggesting that the relationship between agency and structure is set in stone. Rather I am suggesting that what one consumes and how one enacts one's citizenship is often conditioned by a number of factors—economic, social and political. After all, in the context of Australian society, how an Aboriginal Australian consumes or enacts his/her citizenship with or without the mediation of technologies, is bound to be very different from how an average White middle class Australian male consumes or exercises his citizenship. Or to take another example, while it is widely recognised that SMS texting facilitated the mobilisation of anti-Estrada demonstrators in the Philippines that led to the resignation of the President of the Philippines, that act in itself did not affect the feudal constancy of Filipino politics. While this certainly was an exercise of citizenship that was rather dramatically mediated by a new technology, its consequences did not include more than a change in leadership within an over-determined political system. While there are major investments today in the use of health texting for social change in Africa—the agency or the capacity of an ordinary South African miner to translate a health message, say, related to HIV prevention, into action is fundamentally related to his position within an enabling environment. Anti-retro viral drugs are not universally available and policies that support sustainable, accessible, affordable good health environments are certainly not given the same policy weight in the world today as are policies that enable local and global connectivities. In other words, while the new possibilities of consumer digital technologies certainly are extensive, to be 'a full participant' in any culture involves a lot more than access to or the use of consumer technologies. It is clear that in the Indian case, limited forms of interactivity are being described as the revolutionary participation of active audiences. The cultural theorist Mark Andrejevic's (2008: 47) observations on the limits inherent in the notion of consumer sovereignty make particular sense in the context of our understanding of media use in India. 'Consumer sovereignty, in framing tastes as individual and given, partakes in a fundamental misrecognition of our relationships to one another; an inversion whereby that which is constructed through relations with others is assumed to emerge from the depths of isolated individual consciousness.'

While change certainly is in the air, the tradition of a 'revisionist' political economy of communications that celebrates the end of old cultural power and the beginning of new empowerments related to user-generated content and multi-directional global cultural flows has become influential in academic and policy circles. But what quality of empowerment have these changes brought about and has power really become flattened? Whereas complexity needs to be accounted for and the emergence of regional, national and local cultural industries and localisations of culture explored on their own right, the analysis of the global economy in the structuring and restructuring of cultural production cannot be sidelined, simply because there is a sense in which the inter-dependence and inter-connectivities of globalisation, the movements of capital and culture are a response to a logic that emanates from the world's dominant economies and their structuring processes, the US in particular. In other words, the structuration of international economics and politics remains key to the understanding of a global and local political economy of communications. The animation industries in India, that consist of numerous independent entities, can also be considered as off-shore outshoots of the dominant animation industries, in particular those connected to Hollywood that are only too aware of the price advantage of production in India—USD 15–25 million per film as against USD 100–175 million in the US. For all the extraordinary growth in mobile telephony in India during the previous decade, Rajendran's writing in *Business World* has described a major disenchantment with telecom stocks, reflected in a fall in market capitalisation of the major telcos (Bharti Airtel, Idea Cellular and Reliance Communications), the deterioration of cell phone services, the mismanagement of spectrum, the lack of investment in valued added services, clumsy attempts at regulation and in the context of this uncertainty and cash-crunch, moves by the telecom majors in India to sell equity to foreign firms.

> With most Indian telcos, including RCom, Idea, the six new entrants (for the provision of 3G services) and even Tata Teleservices, looking to offload equity to foreign buyers, and BSNL shackled by the government, it looks like foreign companies (such as Vodafone) will soon dominate India's telecom market. (Rajendran 2008)

While the experience of outsourcing has been of benefit to the local market, in the context of the current economic recession, it is arguable as to whether the domestic market is in a position to cushion the downturn and support this industry. It is a fact that outsourcing, irrespective of its financial success, reinforces the centre-periphery logic and has tied in software hubs such as India to the export market at the expense of its own domestic market. The exploration and analysis of such unequal relationships have been central to a critical political economy of communications.

A history lesson on the murky beginnings of the global intellectual property project suggests that contemporary enclosures around the knowledge economy are based on a script that was written in the 1970s. Vandana Shiva, a foremost critic of the proprietorial global economy, has observed that the Trade-Related Aspects of Intellectual Property Rights (TRIPS) regime, that accentuated the globalisation of IP laws, was not formed on the basis of democratic negotiations. Rather, it was an imposition by three organisations.

> ...the Intellectual Property Committee (IPC), Keidanren, and the Union of Industrial and Employer's Confederations (UNICE). IPC is a coalition of 12 major US corporations: Bristol Myers, Du Pont, General Electric, General Motors, Hewlett Packard, IBM, Johnson & Johnson, Merck, Monsanto, Pfizer, Rockwell and Warner. Keidanren is a federation of economic organisations in Japan, and UNICE is recognised as the official spokesperson for European business and industry. (Shiva 1998: 85)

Similarly, the involvement of the mainly Anglo-Saxon players in the conflict in Iraq is closely tied to neo-conservative politics in the US and the hegemonic ambitions of that country.

While such readings may strike one as overtly deterministic, exercises of power by dominant political and economic regimes are by no means extraordinary. While it is to some extent true that the operationalisation of this imperial logic has, of late, been selectively resisted by the stronger economies in the South—China, South Africa, Brazil and India—these resistances tend to be episodic and not consistent. There have been occasions when the strength of moral values has been used by countries in the South to weaken the power of multinational corporations and governments in the developed world. For example, strong lobbying in support of the manufacture of, and South-South trade in generic antiretroviral drugs by large developing nations at the Doha round of trade talks, resulted in the major pharmaceutical companies backing down from their earlier position against generic drug manufacturing in the South. The move by the Communist Party of India (Marxist), an important, one-time coalitional ally of the ruling Congress government, and the opposition Bharatiya Janata Party (BJP) to contest the Henry Hyde 123 agreement between the US and India on nuclear and military cooperation and the unwillingness to downgrade trade with Iran against the wishes of the US, would seem to signify the growing clout of local politics against the requests of the hegemon (*Hindu Online* 2007).

Notwithstanding these important dimensions of change in international politics and the growing clout of certain countries in the developing world, key events in the twenty-first century—the war in Iraq, economic liberalisation and the globalisation of the knowledge economy are predominantly projects that evolved from an imperial logic—that was legitimised as projects related to the extension of freedom, democracy, choice, the free market and global access to knowledge. The denouement of these projects in various parts of the world has certainly not been uniform and one cannot deny the fact that along with a variety of negative effects, there have also been positive effects including the radical overhaul of long-atrophied institutions, processes and habits. One cannot deny the fact that the strengthening of the market in India and the curbing of the 'license raj' has resulted in numerous 'efficiencies' in the provision of popular access to a range of private goods. The market now competes with a state monopoly that once had significant powers in the provision of both private and public goods from television sets to telecommunications. However, it is clear that the dominance of the market has disproportionately impacted on certain sectors in society. While the middle classes have certainly benefited from this growth, and trickle downs such as cheap mobile hand-sets have also accrued to the lower middle classes, economic growth and the cultural industries that sustain this growth—cable and satellite television, advertising, leisure, cultural consumerism—remain disconnected from the lives of the absolute and real poor numbering in the region of 300 million or more. As Dreze and Sen (2002: 308) point out, it is this paradox that is at the core of the growth story in India. 'The growth rates of GNP and GDP can, quite possibly increase further than they have already done in the 1990s but the country remains handicapped economically and socially by its overwhelming illiteracy, backwardness in health, debilitating social inequalities and other crucial failures.'

The fruits of development, in other words, are yet to be fairly distributed. And the state, that had traditionally played a role in provisioning its citizens, has, in the context of structural adjustment policies and its involvement in multi-lateral trade, made significant retreats from its welfare commitments. Loudon (2007a: 16) writing in *The Australian* reports on a 2007 study conducted by the Indian Government affiliated National Commission for Enterprises in the Unorganised Sector (NCEUS) that reveals '…that a staggering 836 million people, or 77 per cent of the population, live on less than 20 rupees (58c) each day.' The most vulnerable populations are those who belong to the Scheduled Tribes, Scheduled Castes and Indian Muslims. The report also adds that 394.9 million Indians work in the unorganised sector, almost all, in difficult conditions. While poverty statistics are routinely contested in India, what cannot be contested is that vast numbers of the Indian population do live in poverty.

So how does one conceptualise the political economy of India today? Is India an emerging power as it is routinely described in the global media? Or is this descriptor based on the rather singular success of its IT industry and the consumer boom? Are we seeing the emergence of an independent economic power house or is what we are seeing a case of dependent development, given that, for instance, the software export market is umbilically tied to the US market and is one in which export revenues account for 80 per cent of total revenues? Are we talking of a mimesis or is there a far deeper, stronger, rooted economic development that is unfolding in India? And how far has economic liberalisation led to the making of qualitatively different media sectors to what they were two decades ago?

A Critical Political Economy of Communications in India

The foregoing preamble offers an entry point to a critical political economy of communications in India. While the focus of this study will primarily be on the political economy of the cultural industries in India, the analysis of these industries—both private and state—needs to take into account not only their distinctiveness as domestic industries, but also their location as industries that are tied into and part of global cultural industries that are significantly involved in extending the logic of capital.

So what are some key issues in a contemporary political economy of communications? I have, in the following pages, highlighted six key areas of concern in a contemporary political economy of communications. These are:

1. Media Concentrations
2. Commodification
3. Intellectual Property
4. Media Policy and Governance
5. Audio-visual Trade
6. Informationalisation and the Cross-Sectoral Digital Economy.

These by no means exhaust the range of issues that relate to a political economy of communications that also include media distribution and issues related to labour in the communication industries. The areas that I have highlighted offer an entry point to an understanding of a critical political economy of communications. These areas have been analysed further, either partially or in-depth, in subsequent chapters in this volume.

The tradition of critical political economy of communication was a reaction and response to the dominant, prevalent tradition of media research in the 1950s and 1960s that focussed on narrow media effects and on the media as entirely self-sufficient institutions involved in offering a benign set of services to the public. The focus on administrative research and research that merely extended consumerism and the culture of contentment (Galbraith 1992) became a prime focus of critique. In fact, one of the doyens of the critical tradition, the Canadian scholar Dallas Smythe (1981), put forward the provocative idea that the media are not only involved in the production of commodities but primarily involved in the production of audiences for advertisers. In Smythe's words, 'the work which audience members perform for the advertiser to whom they have been sold is learning to buy goods and to spend their income accordingly...they work to create the demand for advertised goods which is the purpose of the monopoly-capitalist advertiser.' Golding and Murdock (1997: xvi) have observed that critical political economy is historical, holistic, adopts a realist materialist epistemology, is based on moral-philosophical foundations and deals with the distributional consequences of the media. In a later article, Murdock and Golding (2005: 64) outlined key areas of focus in a critical political economy of communications. 'Five historical processes are particularly central to a critical political economy of culture: the growth of the media; the extension of corporate reach; commodification; the universalisation of citizenship; and the changing role of state and government intervention.'

Media Concentrations

Marx and Engels, in their book *The German Ideology* (1938), include a much-quoted passage that highlights the connections between the dominant class, who by their control over the means of material production also control the means of mental production.

> The ideas of the ruling class are in every epoch the ruling ideas, i.e., the class which is the ruling material force in society, is at the same time its ruling intellectual force...The ruling ideas are nothing more than the ideal expression of the dominant material relationships...Insofar, therefore, as they rule as a class and determine the extent the compass of an epoch...they do this....also as thinkers, as producers of ideas, and regulate the production and distribution of ideas of their age: thus their ideas are the ruling ideas of the epoch. (Marx and Engels 1845)

While this passage did make sense in the context of nineteenth century Europe, there is, as a number of critics have observed, the need for circumspection when using this passage to make sense of contemporary media power. However, and despite limitations, this passage does at least indirectly highlight a contemporary reality—that scarce commodities like the media continue to be owned by conglomerates and media moguls and that the power of a blogger is on a slightly different level to the power of a Rupert Murdoch (irrespective of falling circulations and viewership). Murdoch owns a large chunk of the world's most coveted media real estate from influential global newspapers including the *Wall Street Journal* to satellite and cable television, terrestrial television, Hollywood studios and online companies such as MySpace. Having said this, it is necessary to heed Nicholas Garnham's (1986: 16) critique of the 'unproblematic acceptance' of taking for granted the media as tools of ruling class domination and to instead consider the need for an analysis of 'the specificities of the varying and shifting relationships between economic, ideological and political levels within actual concrete historical moments.' While Murdock and Golding (2005) account for both the production of media products and its consumption along with the moment of exchange in a critical political economy of communications, in response to a long-standing debate between proponents of cultural studies and political economy on the place of 'meaning-making' in the context of critical media analysis, for the most part, the latter tradition has rather doggedly defended the need to explore the larger frameworks within which meaning-making takes place, prior to an analysis of consumption and meaning-making.

The perceived and real consequences of media concentration, diversification, conglomeration and internationalisation have been explored by a number of critical political economists including Murdock and Golding (1973, 1977); Thomas and Nain (2004); Bagdikian (2004); Herman and McChesney (1997); McChesney (2000); Schiller (1999); Mattelart and Siegelaub (1979); Wasko (2001); Hamelink (1994); and Cao and Zhao (2008) among numerous others. This approach, based on identifying and mapping media ownership and control, media structures and their involvement in maintaining and reinforcing the dominant consensus has, without a doubt, produced the greatest amount of literature. Focussing on general, nation-specific studies on media ownership and control and specific studies focussed on particular industries such as the Disney empire (Wasko 2001), this approach has explored issues related to the horizontal and vertical integration of media companies and progressively located the study of media and information industries within the context of globalisation, deregulation, privatisation, commercialisation, convergence and informationalisation. The 1990s which was characterised by a rash of mega media mergers, some that were destined to be short-lived such as the Time-Warner-America Online merger, nevertheless led to studies that highlighted the power of media monopolies that had managed to take control of every stage of the media process—from the inception of an idea, to its production, marketing and distribution on a variety of channels and platforms towards maximising the commercial profitability of a product.

Gomery (1989: 48) describes '...Vertical integration...as the expansion of a business enterprise in gaining control of operations, from the acquisition of fundamental raw materials through the sale of the final product.' This control over a media business from the inception of an idea right through to the making and distribution of the media product is a significant source of power. The fact that some of India's most prestigious industrial houses such as Anil Ambani's Reliance, the Birlas and the Tatas have substantial media and IT interests is a reflection of the fact that such industrial houses have the benefit of capital and influence that are necessary for successful media operations. As Graham Murdock (1990: 3) has observed:

> The potential control it bestows over production does not arise solely from specific exercises of power within the corporations directly owned or influenced. It is also a function of pre-existing and enduring asymmetries in the structure of particular markets or sectors, which deliver cumulative advantages to the leading corporations, and enables them to set the terms of which competitors or suppliers relate to them.

There is a significant amount of work that still needs to be done on the growth of media concentrations in India (See Chapter 3). This is all the more necessary because the contemporary structure of media in India is in a context in which the entire edifice of broadcasting regulation is in flux. Various broadcasting policy projects have been debated and promptly shelved. The Broadcasting Bill, the Convergence Bill and other initiatives of a regulatory nature have been still-born and the regulatory oversight of the Telecom Regulatory Authority of India (TRAI) in an era of convergence is being contested by the Ministry of Information and Broadcasting who would also like to play a role in the business of regulation. From the perspective of this study though, the very fact that deals are being made—for instance, the licensing of FM broadcasting and mobile telephony and the carve up of vast media empires across the media, information and telecommunications sectors by traditional media and non-media companies—in the context of a lack of regulatory oversight, is disturbing. Whether or not this is a consequence of inept government oversight or whether non-policy is a deliberate approach is not as conspiratorial a question as it would seem. For, it would make sense in the current climate of media commercialisation in India to indeed allow both private and state media to take control of specific sectors before regulatory policies are brought into force. The task of a critical political economy should be to explore and analyse the gaps between public policy and practice or, for that matter, the lack of policy, as it would seem to be the case in this instance.

The 2006 report from the Federation of Indian Chambers of Commerce and Industry and PricewaterhouseCoopers 'The Indian Entertainment and Media Industry: Unravelling the Potential' (2006: 11) provides the clearest indications yet of the extent of media liberalisation including foreign direct investment across a number of media sectors including advertising, TV software production, cable networks, FM Radio and Print (see Table 1.1).

While data on media ownership in India is in need of constant updating given the constant changes and fluctuating fortunes of firms in the E&M market, it is clear that there are clear ownership tiers in the key E&M industries including television and radio. While the state broadcasters Doordarshan (DD) and All India Radio (AIR) continue to have the major share of the terrestrial market and coverage, the three major general entertainment channels are Star Plus, Sony and Zee TV along with Viacom 18 Groups 'Colors'. The FM radio market is a case study of media concentration. Reliance Adlabs, for example, have been granted licences for 45 stations, the Sun Network 41 licences, ENIL—32 stations and Music Broadcast Pvt. Ltd (MBPL) 20 stations and all indications seem to suggest that both in key metros and key 'D category Centres', a handful of big media companies will continue to corner the FM radio market. To some extent the large licence fee outlay was an obstacle to the entry of smaller media players in the FM radio market. The *Times of India* group, the largest media house in India is involved extensively in FM radio through its Radio Mirchi network. While the government has, on occasion, discussed the need to restrict cross media ownership, most recently in the Draft of the Proposed Broadcasting Services Regulation Bill (2007) that is scheduled to be debated in the 2010 budget session in parliament, it is now more or less certain that the limitations to ownership highlighted in Section 12. Restrictions on accumulation of interest will not be discussed. A report in the IndianTelevision.com (2010), reports that the I&B Minster will avoid controversies 'by steering clear of words that appeared to offend any television channels or appeared to sound like censorship, regulation or control'.

Table 1.1: Select recent illustrations of strategic foreign investments in the Indian E&M industry

Foreign investor	*Indian entity*	*Segment*	*Nature of investment*	*Reason*
Virgin Radio Asia	HT Media	FM Radio	Equity stake**	Entry into the FM radio segment
Financial Times (Pearson Group)	Business Standard	Newspaper publishing-print media	Equity stake**	Expansion and strengthening of operations
Independent News and Media, UK	Jagran Prakashan	Newspaper publishing-print media	Equity stake**	Expansion and strengthening of operations
T Rowe Price International	Mid-day Multimedia	Newspaper publishing-print media	Equity stake**	Expansion and strengthening of operations
AMP Hendersen, UK	HT Media	Newspaper publishing-print media	Equity stake**	Expansion and strengthening of operations
Bear Stearns	Adlabs Films	Film production and exhibition	Equity stake	Expansion of operations
3i (UK Based Private Equity FTSE 100 Company)	Nimbus Communications	Television and films	Equity stake	Expansion and strengthening of operations
Americorp Ventures, Mauritius	Nimbus Communications	Television and films	Equity stake	Expansion and strengthening of operations
Americorp Ventures, Mauritius	Asianet Communications	Television broadcasting	Equity stake	Expansion and strengthening of operations
Dubai Based NRI Group	Yantra Media	Television content provider in South India	Equity stake	Expansion and strengthening of operations in South India and entry into Hindi television content market
New Vernon Bharat, Mauritius-Based	Jagran TV	Television production and broadcasting	Equity stake**	Expansion and strengthening of operations
Reuters, UK	Times Global Broadcasting	Television production and broadcasting	Equity stake**	Expansion and strengthening of operations

Source: PricewaterhouseCoopers research.

Note: **Indicates cases where investment was a consequence of opening of FDI in that particular segment.

While TRAI has recommended that any company that owns 20 per cent or more in a broadcasting company cannot have more than 20 per cent in a media distribution company, cable TV operation, direct to home television and mobile TV, it is anybody's guess as to whether this will be implemented. In fact, the moves by the corporate affairs ministry to wind up the Monopolies and Restrictive Trade Practices (MRTP) Commission that had been set up in 1970 to deal with monopolistic and restrictive policies of companies would seem to suggest that the pendulum has swung from the curbing of monopolies to an environment characterised by very little regulatory control. One of the guiding principles of the Competition Commission of India[1] that has replaced the MRTP 'to be in sync with markets clearly; have good understanding of market forces' indicates the extent of this accommodation with market forces.

This approach to the study of media maps the growth of media monopolies—both private and state monopolies—and in countries where public broadcasting remains in place, the changing relationship of Public Broadcasting Service (PBS) with the state, its growing commercialisation and the larger influences of a political-economic kind that are a basis for its accommodations, re-inventions, its jockeyings for position and credibility in a complex media market. In this regard, the BBC's re-invention, particularly online, points to one future for public service broadcasting although this too is under threat from commercial broadcasters who resent state-support for a commercially successful public broadcaster. James Murdoch's extraordinary attack on the BBC at the Edinburgh Television Festival in August 2009 is an example of such resentment (*BBC Online* 2009). With respect to the changing role of state broadcasting, there is still a need for a comprehensive study of the state broadcaster Doordarshan and All India Radio in the context of their own re-inventions in the light of economic liberalisation and deregulation. DD's attempts to compete with private media, its regionalisation and internationalisation, its attempts to strengthen multiple revenue streams and the commercialisation of its services, requires an extensive study. Despite the nation-wide presence of cable and satellite television, DD continues to have the most extensive national reach and maintains a virtual monopoly over terrestrial television.

Commodification

'Commodification', as described by Mosco (1996: 139), 'is the process of transforming use values into exchange values, and the manifold ways in which this process is extended into the social field of communication products, of audiences and of labour....' While commodification has affected all institutions in society, one can argue that it is the consumer and leisure industries and the media in particular that have witnessed intense accentuations of commodification. The Frankfurt School of theorists, in particular Theodor Adorno and Max Horkheimer, wrote extensively on the commodification of the cultural industries. Adorno used the example of repetitive formulae used in jazz, such as, the style of the big band clarinetist Benny Goodman, and in popular music as examples of the triumph of 'appearance' over vital, creative content. In their *Dialectic of Enlightenment* (1976) they blamed the monolithic cultural industries for standardising creativity and robbing culture of critique. According to them, capitalism in mass society had robbed products of their use value and replaced it with exchange value leading to exchange value taking a life of its own, thus marginalising the use value of commodities. Without a doubt economic liberalisation, the lifting of trade barriers and the advent of digitisation and globalisation of telecommunications networks has led to increased global flows of media products and its availability in multiple formats. The commodification of personal information that is exclusively used by the market, for instance, insurance agencies (Gandy 1993) and the proprietorial control over 'celebrity' information (Coombe 1998) are but two examples of the extensive inroads made by the market into our personal lives. It is no longer just Disney products that are endlessly recycled, packaged, marketed and sold in a variety of formats, on a variety of platforms, DVDs, CDs, electronic games, toys, music downloads over mobile phones, in a variety of contexts from theme parks and shopping malls to fast food environments, but every aspect of celebrity is potentially marketable. As Rosemary Coombes (1998: 90) has observed, the revenue potential for commodification has accentuated enclosures around celebrities. 'It is no longer limited to the name or likeness of an individual, but now extends to a person's nickname, signature, physical pose, characterisations, singing style, vocal characteristics, body parts, frequently used phrases... performance style and mannerisms and gestures...' Organised religion is another arena that has seen intense commodification. The globalisation of neo-Pentecostalism and prosperity theology has been accompanied by an exponential increase in the availability of religious products—from Hillsong CDs to the Left Behind series of books and DVDs that are available online and from Christian bookshops found in the big cities in India. Similarly, the commodification of Hinduism in the context of the project of Hindu nationalism has led to the availability of Hindu Gods, in particular Ganesh, in every texture imaginable, the availability of online sites that facilitate virtual worship in temples of one's choice, stand-alone Hindu cable channels and the emergence of Hindu entrepreneurs/Godmen and women who offer 'art of living' courses linked into a world of religious consumer products.

One of the most up-to-date descriptions of the Hollywood commodity is in Chapter 3 of the co-written volume *Global Hollywood 2* (2005), by Toby Miller et al. They describe the sophisticated, integrated, synergistic nature of the marketing of Hollywood, films, merchandise and services in different parts of the world. The chapter shows how:

> [S]olidarity around commercial interests is cultivated and reproduced through the continuing and extensive business relations of consumer goods and services, the distribution oligopoly and a myriad of marketing operations. That relation is so robust that it creates a value system of its own, in which the quality of a film, apart from technical questions is determined by commercial potential and marketability....This value system is carried through the nexus of pre-production, production, distribution and exhibition.... (Miller et al. 2005: 259–322)

An invaluable, informative account of the commodification of the Indian media industry from an industry perspective is Vanita Kohli-Khandekar's (2006) *The Indian Media Business*. Chadha and Kavoori's (2005) work on global and national media interactions explores the globalisation of formats such as quiz shows, soap operas, talk shows and reality TV along with the domestication of content:

> It includes police drama (C.A.T.S. from Charlie's Angels), sitcoms (Hello Friend from Friends), soap operas (Tara from the Bold and the Beautiful), games shows (Family Fortunes from Family Feud) and news (Aaj Tak from CNN and Headline News and Star Report from the Fox Report). (Chadha and Kavoori 2006)

Intellectual Property

Copyright, in its infancy, might have been a stimulus to invention and innovation and protected the interests of creative artists. But unlike two hundred years ago, when inventors still had property rights to their inventions, the contemporary software programmer who is employed to write codes for Microsoft does not have any proprietory rights over the code. So with writers and musicians—whose copyrights are owned by companies. In the meanwhile, the trade-off that ensured that products would revert to the public domain has been rather ruthlessly diluted through the most ludicrous extensions given to copyright—leading to a situation characterised by copyright in perpetuity. In other words, the original meaning of Intellectual Property Rights (IPR) as a 'Limited Intellectual Monopoly' has been lost. The 11 copyright extensions (1978–2001) given in the US is the most notorious example of this tendency. Ronald Bettig, in an article in the WACC Journal *Media Development*, has commented on the manner in which copyright has been extended just at the moment when works were scheduled to return to the public domain.

> In 1998, Congress offered a quick fix by passing the Sony Bono Copyright Extension Act, often referred to as the 'Mickey Mouse Extension Act' because of heavy lobbying by the Walt Disney Company to protect the mouse whose term was set to expire in 2003. The act extended copyright for an additional 20 years for cultural works, protecting them for a total of 70 years after the death of an individual author or 95 years from publication in the case of works created by or for corporations. (Bettig 2003/1: 6)

The commodification of the media is closely tied to the ever increasing power of the copyright industries be it through the leveraging effected by the Motion Pictures Association of America and the Business Software Alliance, the extension of national support through compliance measures effected by the US Trade Representatives Sector 301 provisions, the IP plank used by multilateral trade lobbies such as the World Trade Organisation and its General Agreement on Trade in Services (GATS) and Trade-Related Intellectual Property Rights, attempts to harmonise national IP legislations in line with international standards set by the World Intellectual Property Organisation[2] (WIPO) and US and EU legislations. IP provides the moral reason for enclosing 'ideas' ostensibly in support of the author and individual creativity although in the era of corporate reach and power over the fruits of creative labour, IP primarily accrues to industry rather than individuals. The cultural and service industries contribute vast amounts of revenues to the national exchequer in countries such as the US. The report prepared for the International Intellectual Property Alliance (IIPA) (IIPA Filing 2008), '*Copyright Industries in the US Economy: The 2008 Report*' (p. 3), indicates that the total copyright industries in the US including the 'core' copyright industries, namely the motion pictures industry, the recording industry, music publishing industry, book, newspaper, journal industry, computer software industry along with others contributed USD 819.06 billion or 6.56 per cent of the US Gross Domestic Product. The report also indicates 2005 foreign sales and exports of these products in the region of USD 110.8 billion and core copyright employment in the same year in the region of 5.38 million workers. It is not at all surprising, therefore, that the US has invested in strengthening its IP writ in the rest of the world, both unilaterally through supporting state and civil enforcement initiatives against copyright piracy and multilaterally through TRIPS and WIPO.

The most recent attempt to enact a policy related to IP with specific ramifications for the broadcast sector was WIPO's Broadcaster's Treaty that was scheduled to be finalised in late 2007, but shelved for lack of support. While the expressed basis for this treaty was the need to prevent 'signal theft', the treaty, if it had been affected, would have granted broadcast organisations perpetual control over broadcast content. For instance, while Article 18 of the Basic Draft Proposal specified that broadcasters have a property right over content for 50 years, it does not clarify whether that term begins with the first broadcast of content or in the 49th year, giving broadcasters the right to an automatic renewal of copyright. Articles 9 and 14 give broadcast companies the rights of transmission 'by any means' including the internet, thus foreclosing options for webcasters and small-scale broadcasters. WIPO's involvement in granting broadcast organisations complete control over content in a digital era includes their Diplomatic Conference on Copyright and Certain Neighbouring Rights Questions (December 1996) during which attempts were made to support copyright restrictions for temporary copies made in the transmission across networks (Browning 1997). Such attempts to extend the remit of copyright are not restricted to inter-governmental agencies such as WIPO or trade lobbies such as the World Trade Organisation (WTO). Private lobbies, for example, the Recording Industry Association of the US whose members account for 90 per cent of the industry, are also involved in pressuring governments to include stricter copyright provisions. As Sanghera (2002: 10) has observed, '...the association controversially tried and failed to insert an amendment in anti-terrorism bill which would have let it enter consumer's computers and delete stolen files. The amendment would have immunised copyright holders for any data losses caused by their hacking efforts that are reasonably intended to impede or prevent electronic piracy.' The Recording Industry Association of America's (RIAA) presence in India and involvement in anti-piracy has been a pretext for members to agree to increase the prices of their products. Parthasarthy (2001: 13), has observed that BMG, Sony, EMI and Universal have '...doubled the price of Western music cassettes...from around Rs 75 to Rs 125–Rs 150 and CDs' to 'Rs 500 a piece for 8–10 songs'.

While the political economy of IP certainly needs to be explored and monitored not only at the international policy making levels but also at national levels, a critical political economy of communications needs to address the vast inroads made by IP, in the Indian case from the first patent given for 'An Efficient Punkah Pulling Machine' granted to George Alfred DePenning in 1856 to the Patents Amendment Act (2005) (Malavika 2006). There is need to understand the consequences of harmonisation of domestic IP laws to international standards, but also the many ways in which international standards have begun to erode the ordinary Indian's access, appropriation and use of knowledge and the way IP in an era of commodification has begun to affect the Indian cultural market. While the copying of storylines is legion in the context of the Indian film industry, attempts to extend copyright over signs and symbols such as the Tamil film star Rajnikanth's attempts to extend copyright over the use of his 'style' and 'pose' in the film *Baba*[3] and the commodification of this pose via merchandise is an example of creeping enclosures in India. There is also need for work on copyright piracy and its links to the informal economy. Mention must be made of the work on cultural piracy and copyright by scholars and activists in India including Lawrence Liang and Ravi Sundaram. Ravi Sundaram (2001: 99) has observed that '... it is the insertion into the non-legal local, cultural commodity chains, and the unintended mocking of the state that "define" pirate cultures in India. It is this mode that opens up a wide spectrum of possibilities, many of which remain unrealised.' The CopySouth dossier[4] available online offers alternative perspectives on the contemporary political economy of copyright and entry points to a critical study of copyrights and wrongs.

Media Policy and Governance

While media policy has been a fertile area of study for scholars, the relationship between policy making and international and national media governance structures and its impact on the structuring of international and national media environments is of particular interest to scholars involved in exploring a critical political economy of communication. Studies of this interface remain, for the most, limited to international and regional dimensions (O' Siochru and Girard 2002; Raboy 2004; Sarikakis and Chakravarthy 2006; Venturelli 1997) while the national dimension remains relatively absent. Recent efforts to offer a post-graduate course on global media governance at the Delhi-based Centre for Culture and Media Governance, Jamia Millia Islamia University, is a welcome and significant effort to encourage thinking and research in this area (Personal correspondence with Vibodh Parthasarthy).

A UNDP definition (1999) states that, 'governance does not mean mere government. It means a set of rules, institutions and practices that indicate limits and offer stimuli for individual's, organisation's and firm's behaviour.' While a government is generally limited to rule-making and power broking within a given territory—after the Second World War and the creation of the United Nations and the Bretton Woods institutions followed by multilateral and bi-lateral trade lobbies such as General Agreement on Tariffs and Trade (GATT), the WTO, North American Free Trade Agreement (NAFTA), Asia-Pacific Economic Cooperation (APEC) and the like, international rule making—for instance, on economic liberalisation, trade or intellectual property has been pursued by a variety of supranational and inter-governmental institutions. WIPO, for instance, administers 23 treaties related to intellectual property, but more importantly, it is involved in creating and to some extent enforcing norms and policies related to IP on a global basis. As is stated on its website:

> WIPO is constantly alert to the need to develop new norms and standards in keeping with advances in technology and business practices, as well as in response to specific concerns such as traditional knowledge, folklore, biodiversity and biotechnology.

In other words, WIPO is involved in the creation, making and crafting of *rules* that can become the foundation for *regulatory* systems—rules that are authoritative, that are enforceable and that can be employed to exercise *control.* Governance is a *process* involving numerous actors. It is based on *negotiation* and *consensus building* that is often *continuous.* While WIPO is not the only global body involved in creating rules related to IP, it remains a primary body. Generally, these rules have been created through inter-state, bi- and tri-sectoral negotiations. Today, given the complex, inter-related nature of life in a globalised world, supranational and inter-governmental institutions have begun to play key roles in the making of global policy on a variety of issues. The World Trade Organisation not only connects to WIPO through its overseeing the TRIPS mandate but is also keenly involved in the liberalisation of trade in services (the privatisation of telecommunications, e-commerce, advocating mobile telephony) and trade in audio-visuals. In other words there has been a reconfiguration of regulation in such a way that decisions taken by extra-state actors have begun to affect national governments and the lives of citizens. This, in hindsight, had to come about simply because of the massive increase in global-local interactions and consequences—from global warming to international terrorism to financial flows that are extra-territorial and, thus, outside the jurisdiction of any given state. While this is the case, we also need to keep in mind that governments (some more than others) are also involved in rule making and that states are continuously involved in negotiating and adapting these rules to their own specific national interests.

Media governance in India remains, for the most part, a state monopoly. The state has played an extensive role in establishing policies related to media regulation and reform and, in the case of broadcasting and telecommunications, attempted to control the operationalisation, services and environment of these media. While the government certainly has had to negotiate with the International Telecommunications Union and the World Trade Organisation in the context of deregulation and its Basic Telecommunications Policy and with the World Intellectual Property Organisation and the WTO in the matter of harmonising Indian IP legislations with global standards and requirements, there is little information available on these negotiations and, in particular, whether the Indian government has been able to maintain the independence and autonomy of these sectors in the context of a variety of pressures from external governance institutions and trade mechanisms. The US government, through its US Trade Representative, has consistently used the provisions of Section 301 to increase Hollywood exports to India and the various industry lobbies related to the major cultural industries have pressurised the Indian government to curb piracy and to further liberalise foreign investments in all media sectors. While the Indian government has, in public, supported the need for multi-stake holder consultancies on media reform, as the Indian media critic Ammu Joseph has observed in the context of the Broadcast Bill and Content Code:

> Unfortunately, although the draft legislation pays lip service to the public it marginalises the public interest. In fact, several provisions in the Bill strongly suggest that its primary purpose is to enable the government to regain control over the broadcast sector—control eroded over the past decade and a half by the emergence of private broadcasters, both indigenous and international, on the media landscape. (Joseph 2007)

A related area of interest to a critical political economy of communications is the role being played by civil society (CS) actors as a third force in global policy making. Examples of CS involvement include the Communication

Rights in the Information Society campaign at the UN World Summit on the Information Society (2003, 2005) and the continuing involvement of CS actors in deliberations at the Internet Consortium for Assigned Names and Numbers (ICANN). Today there are numerous CS interests involved at a variety of levels of global policy making on a number of critical issues—from the economy to the creating of policies related to accountable, transparent national and global governance. At the level of CS there has always been the understanding that global governance cannot be left solely to traditional governance institutions inclusive of the private sector that play an important role in telecommunication, internet and financial policy making. Fundamentally therefore, CS, in general, is keen to democratise global governance, make it more transparent, accountable and participatory. This desire to democratise global rule making systems is yet to bear substantive fruits. For a start the CS culture and commitment to participation, consultation, representation and accountability is alien to what are basically technocratic or state-based forms of decision making. While the CS sector in India did play an important role in lobbying the government to open up the community radio sector, for the most part, the rather convoluted process related to the establishment of this sector was governed by the state.

Audio-visual Trade

Another critical area in the political economy of communications is audio-visual (AV) trade. The overriding aim of economic liberalisation under the WTO is trade in *all goods and services* and this general objective is recognised in GATS Part IV: Progressive Liberalisation, Article XIX: Negotiation of Specific Commitments,

> In pursuance of the objectives of this Agreement, Members shall enter into successive rounds of negotiations, beginning not later than five years from the date of entry into force of the WTO Agreement and periodically thereafter, with a view to achieving a progressively higher level of liberalisation.[5]

The key issue of AV trade is about whether AV products should be treated like any other tradeable goods and services or whether cultural goods ought to be treated differently given that it is a key vector of identity. On one side you have the US and some of its allies—the dominant AV merchants who are keen to liberalise trade in AV, force countries to open up their AV market and stop countries subsidising their AV industries. On the other side you have countries like France and Canada who are keen to protect their cultural industries. United Nations Educational, Scientific and Cultural Organisation's (UNESCO) proposed Convention on Cultural Diversity[6] supports the protectionists although it is doubtful whether the Convention will have the teeth to deal with some key issues including IPR. Nevertheless, Articles 8 and 11 of the UNESCO declaration illustrate this position:

> In the face of present-day economic and technological change, opening up vast prospects for creation and innovation, particular attention must be paid to the diversity of the supply of creative work, to due recognition of the rights of authors and artists and to the specificity of cultural goods and services which, as vectors of identity, values and meaning, must not be treated as mere commodities or consumer services. (Article 8)

[And that]

> Market forces alone cannot guarantee the preservation and promotion of cultural diversity, which is the key to sustainable human development. From this perspective, the pre-eminence of public policy, in partnership with the private sector and civil society, must be reaffirmed. (Article 11)

The Indian AV industry is at an interesting juncture. Having long been a domestic industry, it is now global and is the source for a sizeable export market. From being at the receiving end of Hollywood and Section 301 rulings that attempted to make India a gross recipient of Hollywood fare, the Indian AV industry's exports now have the possibility of impacting on the fortunes of the local AV industry in South Asia and elsewhere. Despite the success of Hollywood–Bollywood productions, it remains to be seen whether this will translate into a sustainable market in countries that have sizeable Indian diasporas. Will the Indian government treat the AV industry primarily as a business or will it also provide space to deal with the 'specificity of cultural goods and services', in other words, in the context of a larger, nation-wide cultural policy?

Informationalisation and the Cross-sectoral Digital Economy

Given that information has become a constituent element in all life processes by virtue of the ubiquity of digital code, it makes infinite sense to explore ethical issues and, for that matter, critical issues in the political economy of communications, from within this macro context characterised by the informationalisation of society. Digital code has hastened marriages between previously separate technologies—IT and Biotechnology, IT and Military Technologies, and so on, and the ethics of convergent technologies and questions related to the nature of power and property relations in this new era are not only fascinating but also deeply worrying. We live in an era characterised by what James Boyle (1997: 3) has called the 'homologisation' of information—almost all information, whether it be of a biological or non-biological kind has been digitised and digital code has become the mother of all productive applications across a number of sectors that were previously characterised by separate technologies, processes, policies and regulatory mechanisms. A familiar example of separateness is the mass media of yesteryear with its separate technologies, policies and regulatory mechanisms. Today, the world over, policy makers continue to grapple with and respond to the many challenges posed by convergent technologies.

Today computers are not merely used by biotechnology firms to store, analyse and retrieve data, it is being used to model, design, simulate and image products and processes, and reprogramme life itself. Without digital technologies it would have been close to impossible to decipher the billions of bits of data being generated on the human genome. The social critic Jeremy Rifkin (1998: 181) has observed that the operational language of the computer is the '....common language that is creating a seamless web between the information and life sciences and making possible the joining together of computers and genes into a single, powerful, technology revolution.'

The more we read, the more we came to the realisation that these new meta technologies unlike the previous generation of technologies, do have the potential to exert a hegemonic influence on society. Not only has there been a colonisation of production by information and the generation of substantive economic value today resulting from information-based applications and processes, but there has also been an invasion and embrace of everyday life—the spheres of work, leisure, the daily rhythms of existence, relationships, understandings of self and the beyond—in subtle and not so subtle ways by information. It is precisely because of the intimate nature, texture and depth of this embrace that we can call these technologies 'hegemonic'. As these technologies flood the market and tighten its embrace on our lives, it is of extraordinary importance that we find the time and space to query, critique and subdue these technologies to the needs of humanity. The use of biotechnologies by the life science industry has implications for food security, survival and the long-term health of people, surveillance technologies—inclusive of the hard varieties used by the military, national security, the state and commercial actors and soft varieties, such as ID and credit cards—makes sure that we are all perpetually X-rayed, categorised and assessed in terms of our credit worthiness or as a security risk and financial technologies linked to commodity markets are involved in the large-scale pauperisation of communities. These technologies affect our lives in more ways than one and there are a number of ethical issues arising from the interfaces between these new technologies and life. The furore over GM seeds in the South and in some parts of Europe and the many ethical questions that these have given rise to—what right do agro businesses have to control the use of seeds in rural environments in the South? What happens when culture is denied nature and vice versa in these environments? Can seed be owned? What are the ethical implications of seed as property, trade in agriculture and Structural Adjustment Programmes (SAPs) in the South? Such questions can no longer be treated as isolated, separate questions precisely because the underlying technologies, proprietorial environments and relationships that are at the core of the agro-business are mirrored in other productive domains. In other words, it is not just the ownership of seed that is at stake, it is also the ownership of genes, of knowledge, of life itself in all its variety.

Given potential revenues and profits, many of the previously plain IT companies have formed their own 'life sciences' division. These include Compaq, Hewlett Packard, Motorola, Sun, Fujitsu, Hitachi and IBM. The top ten US bioinformatics companies including Accelrys, Cognic Corp., Double Twist, IBM Lifesciences, Incyte Genomics, Informax, Netgenics, Paracel Inc., SAS Institute and Thermo LabSystems will remain among key players in the projected USD 6.9 billion market in 2007. And one can argue that informational convergences and a variety of new technology based operations solutions pose a challenge to political economists of communication who have hitherto dealt with the power dynamics implicated in discrete technologies. The canvas for analysis in the context of the informational economy is much larger, deeper and wider.

Conclusion

The foregoing introduction to the political economy of communications offers some vantage points from which to explore this area. Chapters in this volume will explore these areas further. I am of the opinion that as the Indian media industry changes, there is an accompanying need to assess these changes, critically evaluate the new sources of power in the media and explore resistances to this power. We take our media environments for granted most of the time and in the context of globalising India, the trend has been to celebrate the growth of Indian media at the expense of critique. I would like to conclude with remarks from the activist scholar Robert McChesney (2004: 20):

> There are no simple solutions to the question of how best to organise media and communication to promote a healthy economy and democratic values, just as there is no simple answer to how best to structure the global political economy. Moreover, it is clear that the two debates are very closely related, in view of the significance of the media and communication to both capitalism and democracy. That is why it is imperative that the debates on this topic be widespread and held under the light of day...Our job, as scholars, as citizens, as democrats, is to knock down the door and draw some more chairs up to the table. And when we sit at that table we have to be armed with the most accurate understanding of what is taking place and what is possible that we can generate.

I hope that this book, in some measure, lives up to that ideal.

Notes

1. Competition Commission of India. Available at http://www.cci.gov.in/index.php?option=com_content&task=view&id=120 (Accessed on 9 September 2009).
2. World Intellectual Property Organisation (WIPO). Available at http://www.wipo.int/about-wipo/en/what/ (Accessed on 23 May 2009).
3. Baba Logo in Jeopardy. 2002. *The Hindu Online*, 5 August 2002. Available at http://www.hinduonnet.com/thehindu/mp/2002/08/05/stories/2002080501460400.htm (Accessed on 9 June 2007).
4. The CopySouth Dossier. Available at http://www.copysouth.org/portal/ (Accessed on 23 May 2009).
5. WTO Restricted S/C/W/40, Council for Trade in Services, Audiovisual Services: Background Note by Secretariat. Available at http://doconline.wto.org/GEN_viewerwindow.asp? (Accessed on 7 October 2008).
6. Convention on the Protection and Promotion of the Diversity of Cultural Expressions, UNESCO (United Nations Educational, Scientific and Cultural Organisation). Available at http://portal.unesco.org/culture/en/ev.php-URL_ID=33232&URL_DO=DO_TOPIC&URL_SECTION=201.html (Accessed on 9 July 2009).

References

Ajwani, D. 2009. A TV Story, Retold. Business.in.com. Available at http://business.in.com/article/breakpoint/a-tv-story-retold/2892/1# (Accessed on 24 September 2009).

Andrejevic, M. 2008. *iSpy: Surveillance and Power in the Interactive Era*. Kansas: University Press of Kansas.

Bagdikian, B. 2004. *The New Media Monopoly*. Boston: Beacon Press.

BBC Online. 2009. 'Murdoch Attack on Dominant BBC'. 2009. Available at http://news.bbc.co.uk/2/hi/8227915.stm (Accessed on 23 September 2009).

Bettig, R. 2003/1. 'Copyright and the Commodification of Culture', *Media Development*, 1: 3–9.

Boyle, J. 1997. 'A Politics of Intellectual Property: Environmentalism for the Net', pp. 1–23. Available at http://www.wcl.american.edu/pub/faculty/boyle (Accessed on 5 June 2007).

Browning, J. 1997. 'Copyrighters Block', *Wired*, 5(3) March: 66–68, 102–104.

Cao, J. and Y. Zhao. 2008. *The Political Economy of Communication: A Reader*, Vols 1 and 2. Shanghai: Fudan University Press.

Chadha, K. and A. Kavoori. 2005. 'Globalisation and National Media Systems: Mapping Interactions in Policies, Markets and Formats', in J. Curran and M. Gurevitch (eds), *Mass Media and Society*, pp. 84–103. London: Hodder Arnold.

Coombe, R. J. 1998. *The Cultural Life of Intellectual Properties: Authorship, Appropriation, and the Law*. Durham/London: Duke University Press.

Draft of the Proposed Broadcasting Services Regulation Bill, 2007. Available at http://www.kerala.gov.in/broadcast_bill.pdf (Accessed on 11 February 2010).

Dreze, J. and A. Sen. 2002. *India: Development and Participation*. Oxford: Oxford University Press.

FICCI/PricewaterhouseCoopers. 2006. 'The Indian Entertainment and Media Industry: Unravelling the Potential'. FICCI/PricewaterhouseCoopers, New Delhi, pp. 1–19. Available at http://www.pwc.com/extweb/pwcpublications.nsf/docid/be7e56c3ff8e90a6ca257185006a3275/$file/frames.pdf (Accessed on 23 May 2008).

Galbraith, J. K. 1992. *The Culture of Contentment*. London: Sinclair-Stevenson Ltd.

Gandy, O. 1993. 'Towards a Political-Economy of Personal Information', *Critical Studies in Mass Communication*, 10(1) March: 70–97.

Garnham, N. 1986. 'Contribution to a Political Economy of Mass-Communication', in Richard Collins, Philip Schlesinger, James Curran, Paddy Scannell and Nicholas Garnham (eds), *Media Culture and Society: A Critical Reader*, pp. 9–32. London/Beverly Hills/Newbury Park/New Delhi: Sage Publications.

Golding, P. and G. Murdock (eds). 1997. *The Political Economy of the Media*, Vols 1 and 2. Cheltenham: Edgar Elgar Publishing Ltd.

Gomery, D. 1989. 'Media Analysis: Terms of Reference', *Critical Studies in Mass Communication*, 6(2): 46–30.

Hamelink, C. 1994. *The Politics of World Communication*. London, Thousand Oaks, New Delhi: Sage Publications.

Herman, E. S. and N. Chomsky. 2002. *Manufacturing Consent: The Political Economy of Mass Communications*. NY: Pantheon Books.

Herman, E. S. and R. McChesney. 1997. *The Global Media: The New Missionaries of Corporate Capitalism*. London: Cassel Academic.

Hindu Online. 2007. Left 'Unable to Accept' 123 Agreement. 2007. *The Hindu Online*, 8 August. Available at http://www.hinduonnet.com/2007/08/08/stories/2007080858210100.htm (Accessed on 6 October 2007).

Horkheimer, M. and T. Adorno. 1976/1987. *Dialectic of Enlightenment*. NY: Continuum.

IndianTelevision.com. 2010. 'Broadcast Bill May be Introduced in Budget Session', 15 February. Available at http://www.indiantelevision.com/headlines/y2k10/feb/feb113.php (Accessed on 27 February 2010)

International Intellectual Property Alliance (IIPA) Filing. 2008. 11 February. Available at http://www.iipa.com/pdf/2008SPEC301COVERLETTER.pdf The IIPA represents the interests of six associations, Association of American Publishers, AFMA, Business Software Alliance, Interactive Digital Software Association, Motion Picture Association of America, Recording Industry Association of America. (Accessed on 23 April 2009).

Jenkins, H. 2006. *Convergence Culture: Where Old and New Media Collide*. NY: NYU Press.

Joseph, A. 2007. 'Public Missing in Broadcast Bill Debate'. Available at http://www.indiatogether.org/2007/aug/ajo-bcastbill.htm (Accessed on 9 April 2008).

Kohli-Khandekar, V. 2006. *The Indian Media Business*. New Delhi/Thousand Oaks/London: Response Books, Sage Publications.

Loudon, B. 2007a. 'India faces heat over trade with "outlaw"', *The Australian: The World*, August 8, Australian newspaper, p. 12.

———. 2007b. 'As India Booms, Poor Stay Hopelessly Poor', *The Weekend Australian*, August 11–12, Australia's Saturday paper, p. 16.

Malavika, T.V. 2006. 'Intellectual Property? Right!', *The Hindu Magazine*, 9 April.

Marx, K. and F. Engels. 1845. *Ruling Class and Ruling Ideas*. London: Lawrence & Wishart, taken from Mattelart, A. and S. Siegelaub. 1979. *Communication and Class Struggle, Volume 1: Capitalism, Imperialism*. New York/Bagnolet: International General and International Mass Media Research Centre, p. 98.

———. 1938/1987. *The German Ideology*. London: Lawrence & Wishart Ltd.

Mattelart, A. and S. Siegelaub. 1979. *Communication and Class Struggle, Volume 1. Capitalism, Imperialism, Volume 2: Liberalism, Socialism*. NY/Bagnolet: International General and IMMRC.

McChesney, R. 2000. *Rich Media, Poor Democracy*. Urbana: University of Illinois Press.

———. 2004. 'The Political Economy of International Communications', in P.N. Thomas and Z. Penang Nain (eds), *Who Owns the Media: Global Trends and Local Resistances*. London and New York: Southbound, Zed, World Association for Christian Communication.

Miller, Toby, Nitin Govil, John McMurria and Richard Maxwell. 2005. *Global Hollywood 2*. London: BFI Publishing.

Mosco, V. 1996. *The Political Economy of Communication*. London, Thousand Oaks, New Delhi: Sage Publications.

Murdock, G. 1990. 'Redrawing the Map of the Communications Industries: Concentration and Ownership in the Era of Privatisation', in M. Ferguson (ed.), *Public Communication: The New Imperatives—Future Directions for Media Research*, pp. 1–15. London/Newbury Park/New Delhi: Sage Publications Ltd.

Murdock, G. and P. Golding. 1973. 'For a Political Economy of Mass Communication', in R. Miliband and J. Saville (eds), *The Socialist Register*, pp. 205–34. London: Merlin Press.

———. 1977. 'Capitalism, Communication & Class Relations', in J. M. Gurevitch, J. Curran and J. Woollacott (eds), *Mass Communication and Society*, pp. 12–43. London: Arnold.

Murdock. 2005. 'Culture, Communications & Political Economy', in J. Curran and M. Gurevitch (eds), *Mass Media & Society*, pp. 60–83. London: Arnold.

O' Siochru, S. and B. Girard (with Amy Mahan). 2002. *Global Media Governance: A Beginner's Guide*. Lanhom/Boulder/New York/London: Rowman and Littlefield Pub. Inc.

Parthasarthy, A. 2001. 'Napster Case is no Music to Indian Ears', *The Hindu, International Edition*, 24 February.

PricewaterhouseCoopers. 2009. 'Indian Media and Entertainment Outlook 2009 Report'. Available at http://www.pwc.com/en_IN/in/assets/pdfs/PwC-Indian-Entertainment-and-Media-Outlook-2009-2.pdf.

Raboy, M. 2004. 'The World Summit on the Information Society and its Legacy for Global Governance', *Gazette: The International Journal for Communication*, 66 (3–4): 225–32.

Rajendran, M. 2008. 'Tipping Point', *Businessworld*, 28 August–1 September 2008. Available at http://www.businessworld.in/index.php/Telecom/Tipping-Point/Page-4.html (Accessed on 9 October 2008).

Rifkin, J. 1998. *The Biotech Century: How Genetic Commerce will Change the World*. London/New York: Phoenix.

Sanghera, S. 2002. 'Battles of Copyright Crusaders', *Financial Times*, 14 August.

Sarikakis, K. and P. Chakravarthy. 2006. *Media Policy and Globalisation*. Edinburgh: Edinburgh University Press.

Schiller, D. 1999. *Digital Capitalism: Networking the Global Market System*. Cambridge, Massachusetts: Massachusetts Institute of Technology Press.

Shiva, V. 1998. *Biopiracy: The Plunder of Nature and Knowledge*. Devon/London: Green Books, The Gaia Foundation.

Singh, G. 2008. 'The Print Run Slows', *Business World*, 21 November. Available at http://www.businessworld.in/index.php/Media-Entertainment/The-Print-Run-Slows.html (Accessed on 24 May 2009).

Smythe, D. 1981. *Dependency Road: Communications, Capitalism, Consciousness and Canada*. Norwood, New Jersey: Ablex.

Sundaram, R. 2001. Recycling Modernity: Pirate Electronic Cultures in India (93–99), *Sarai Reader 01*: The Public Domain. Available at http://www.sarai.net/publications/readers/01-the-public-domain (Accessed on 23 May 2009).

Thomas, P. and Z. Nain (eds). 2004. *Who Owns the Media: Global Trends and Local Resistances*. Penang/London: Southbound/Zed/WACC.

Venturelli, S. 1997. 'Prospects for Human Rights in the Political and Regulatory Design of the Information Society', in J. Servaes and R. Lie (eds), *Media and Politics in Transition: Cultural Identity in the Age of Globalisation*, pp. 61–74. Amersfoot: ACCO Leuven.

Wasko, J. 2001. *Understanding Disney: The Manufacture of Fantasy*. London: Polity.

2

The Political Economy of Communications in Colonial India: Mass Communication and the Empire

Ever since ancient times, India has provided a fertile base for invaders, explorers, travellers and traders. Kushans and Greeks, Persians and Tartars, Chinese and Mughals and in the more recent past, the Portuguese, French and the British, have, at different periods and places, trundled into and out of India, carrying with them economic wealth, but also leaving behind a legacy of traditions, including communications and culture, some that continue to exist even today. The tools and practices of communications introduced by the British formed another layer over pre-existing traditions of communications in India that were predominantly oral and that included dance, theatre, music, ritual, art, literature and poetry. It is in this sense that one can say that grand narratives of origin and identity that attempt to fix people into an immutable, untranslatable time warp of beginnings are untenable. All persons and cultures have been preceded. And all traditions are always in process. Tradition has it that my ancestors, the St. Thomas Christians, arrived from Persia in the third century AD. They landed on the Malabar coast to find that a small Jewish settlement had preceded them by almost three centuries. When the marauding Portuguese under Vasco da Gama landed on the Malabar coast 13 centuries later in 1600, they too were surprised to see a thriving community of Christians who had preceded them. By then the spice trade had already been established between communities in the Middle East and those resident in the West coast of India. In this sense there is nothing extraordinary about the phenomenon of globalisation that we hear so much of these days. India has always been open to influences from the outside and has, in turn, influenced the destinies of nations in its immediate vicinity. It has traditionally been an accomplice to and a conduit for globalisation. The issue today is of course the pace, tenor and texture of globalisation and whether it can be moulded to achieve distributive justice in the economy and culture and communications. The legacy of modern communication bequeathed by the British has had a lasting impact and although imperial communication primarily aided the imperial cause, its cultures have persisted and those schooled in this tradition have exerted considerable influence in Independent India. Post-colonial consciousness has been moulded by its experience of and entanglements with the media in colonial India.

Mass Communication and Empire

India's tryst with mass communication was forged during the Raj. As Kaul (2006: 4) has observed:

> From the early nineteenth to the mid-twentieth centuries, Great Britain was a supreme communication media power, that is to say, it possessed unparalleled capacity to report and transport news, information and ideas, as well as transport people, soldiers and produce, around the world. Britain was also the predominant imperial power, that is, it controlled and directed their affairs of large parts of the world. These were two distinct states of affairs. Yet there were close and reciprocal links between the two. It was communication media power that helped create and sustain imperial power, and this power in turn reinforced and shaped the development of communication media power.

While there were of course many forms of extant communications—from traditional dance and drama to indigenous postal systems based on 'runners' in some of the princely states, these were by no means national in scope. And it is in this sense that one can argue that the British played an absolutely central role in introducing Indians to the project of modernity via systems of mass communication.

The telegraph, press, radio and film were, in that order, introduced primarily as a means to reinforce and prop up the Empire. However, this introduction was fraught and the project of imperial communication was contested from within and without. For instance, dual government operating from Whitehall and Delhi impacted on the nature of investments in communications such as in telegraphy. And there were concerns, such as that expressed by Charles Bright (1918: 214) for British telegraphy in the context of intra-imperial rivalries to be completely independent given that '….there is great strategic advantage in lines being laid right away from our "European" friends and in deep water—where they would not easily be picked up by a cable ship—with few approaches to land, and landing only on British soil.' While the telegraph resolutely remained a tool for the Empire until Independence, the press in particular and to a lesser extent radio became the means for nascent expressions of nationalism and anti-British sentiment. In fact, the vernacular press played a critical role in advancing the cause of the Congress movement especially among the educated classes. Anti-colonial theatre in vernacular languages also proved to be an efficient means of challenging and mobilising ordinary, illiterate people against colonial rule.

While the imperial and imperious project of Macualay's infamous Minute on English education was certainly directed towards creating a class of servile 'brown sahibs', this project too that was partially based on the extension of 'Enlightenment ideals' unwittingly contributed to the circulation of ideas related to freedom and rights and, subsequently, to the creation of a pro-Independence movement. As Alisdair Pinkerton (2007: 167–169) has observed:

> The development of the railway, the telegraph and uniform postage during the 1850s may have instituted India's 'nineteenth century communication revolution', but it had also helped spark the touch-paper of early Indian nationalism; the improved state of transport and communications allowing latent ideas and attitudes to travel and ferment into broader political movements.

At the very same time, the consolidation of communications in the empire was a slow and fraught process. Not only were there major contestations between Whitehall and the colonial government in India and inter-colonial rivalries, but there were also struggles between the colonial state and commercial forces in the establishment of communications. While the privately owned Reuters controlled the flow and distribution of news within the British Empire, the fact that the corporate giant Eastern Cable Company did not control the Bombay–Madras link which was in the hands of the government-owned Indian Telegraph Department was a source of anxiety for Reuters (Choudhary 2004).

From the perspective of a political economy of communications, a key aspect of British rule was that it laid the foundations for the media in post-colonial India. In fact in terms of laws and regulations, systems of governance, types of media ownership and control shared between the state and the private sector, centralised broadcasting and telecommunications—the legacy has been long-lasting. In fact, the post-colonial elite who took over the reigns of power, preserved this system well into the twenty-first century prompting the erstwhile broadcast mandarin Mehra Masani to offer three reasons for such continuities in broadcasting between the pre-Independence and post-Independence periods.

> The first would credit our former rulers with extraordinary foresight and understanding of broadcasting; the second would reveal our lack of initiative and our incapacity to create appropriate organisations to our needs; and the third would expose the Government's decision to retain, for reasons of expediency, vestiges of our colonial heritage which was neither democratic nor 'progressive'. (Masani 1976: 1–2)

While the cultures of broadcasting have changed in India, the imperial role played by the state monopoly broadcasters, All India Radio first followed by Doordarshan, continues to be a part of the public memory of broadcasting in India.

The Centralisation of Power in Colonial India

India's first encounter with capitalism occurred under the aegis of British colonialism. Traditionally the Indian economy was based on agriculture, was caste and land-based and followed a system of production (*jajmani*) that involved the sharing of produce among the caste hierarchy inclusive of all those who contributed to the production and reproduction of society. This system of agricultural production, particularly its relationship to the ownership of land was inimical to the commercial interests of British colonialism. The industrial revolution in Britain had opened up markets for primary commodities such as cotton and jute and in order to commercialise agricultural production in India, the British introduced the zamindari and ryotwari systems of land tenure in India. These were systems based on the private ownership of land. The enactment of the Permanent Settlement (1793) effectively created a class of private land owners—the zamindar's[1]—who were given the responsibility to raise taxes and produce from a hierarchy of producers. These systems had a deleterious effect on ordinary people. The age-old system of patronage was destroyed and tenants effectively were left with nothing but their labour. The caste system, however, remained intact. The tenant became a 'free man', an unbound landless labourer, who quickly became a prey to moneylenders and exploiters of capital.

Parts of India, for instance, Bengal, soon experienced a rapid decline in the availability of food grains as vast tracts of land were converted into jute, indigo and cotton farms. It was ironic that precisely during the period when Britain experienced the fruits of growth associated with the industrial revolution, Bengal was in the grip of a series of famines that left millions dead. The Indian economist, C.T. Kurien, alluding to this paradox, draws our attention to the search by the British cotton industry for an alternative producer in the light of the loss of cotton from the US, a direct consequence of the Independence struggle and the Civil War between the two countries.

> Demand for cotton from India suddenly shot up; the export of cotton from India to Britain increased from around 500,000 bales in 1859 to close to 1,400,000 bales in 1864...between the last decade of the nineteenth century and the middle of the twentieth, when food production in India declined by 7 per cent, production of commercial crops increased by 85 per cent. (Kurien 1994: 29)

The contemporary food crisis is also partly a consequence of the globalisation of agriculture and the emphasis on cash crops at the expense of subsistence agriculture.

Media Resistance: Some Early Examples

It is not, therefore, entirely surprising to learn that Bengal became a centre for cultural and political protest against colonial policies. The first significant political protest play in India was Dinabandhu Mitra's Nildarpan (1872). It was based on the exploitation of indigo farmers by British planters. This play was pivotal in the history of political theatre in India as it demonstrated the power of theatre to galvanise anti-colonial sentiments among ordinary people. It also demonstrates the fact that in a predominantly oral culture characterised by very low literacy levels, familiar traditions such as theatre had a larger impact on anti-colonial political mobilisation than the press whose readership was strictly limited. In this sense the pro-Independence public sphere in India was to a much greater extent developed through popular participation in oral communication platforms—from theatre, to rallies and other forms of mobilisation. Nildarpan was followed by other productions that were patently anti-British in expression and intent. Bhatia (2004: 2), in a comprehensive study of political theatre in colonial India, points to:

> [T]he formation of numerous theatre companies in 1876 that travelled to various parts of the subcontinent and, through a complex mixture of imagery, state design, and dialogue launched attacks on colonial politics and practices [that led to the] further sharpen(ing) of concerns related to the genre.

This led the government to enact the Dramatic Performances Act (1879) that made it mandatory for any theatre company or individual to submit the final script to a board of censors before the performance. Solomon (1994: 325), in a study of anti-colonial theatre in India, in particular the Marathi playwright Krishnaji Prabhaker Khadilkar's militantly anti-colonial melodrama *Kichaka-Vadha*, has made the following observations on the implementation of Ban Orders against plays considered seditious: 'In the case of Shri Shiv Chhattapati Vijaya (Victory of Shri Shiva Chhatrapati 1898), the Commissioner of Police in Bombay "also confiscated all printed copies of the play"... The Political Agent of the Deccan States similarly seized five hundred copies of Vijaya Toran (Garland of Victory 1909), while in Colaba where the play was staged the District Magistrate "bound over all of the 15 accused (actors of the play) to be of good behaviour[and] execute a bond of Rs. 200 each for one year".'

Colonial Information and Governmentality

There is an abiding relationship between power and knowledge as theorists such as Michael Foucault and Edward Said have demonstrated in some of their writings. Such displays of power are as common today as they were in the past although given the sophisticated nature of 'spin' and common sense in circulation, it is difficult to understand or much less pinpoint the manner in which power manifests itself through everyday practices, thereby affecting life in every detail. All colonial governments have traditionally invested a great deal in trying to understand the cognitive and cultural universes inhabited by their subject populations, the knowledge systems in operation and the languages used to secure identity, precisely to control them. It was often the case that the tools of historiography were employed to translate the subject population into familiar, understandable categories. This process of translation involved the subduing of 'native' language and culture within the categories of the coloniser. In the case of the British in India, the comparative study of Indian languages helped the colonial authorities to streamline the task of administering a continental land mass that was culturally and ethnically diverse. In a review of a book by Bernard Cohn (1997) on the relationship between colonialism and the ordering of knowledge in British India, Mukhopadhyay (1998: 65) highlights Cohn's expose of the ways in which Indian languages were rendered user-friendly, thus, enabling it to be used in the centralisation and administration of British power in India:

> [E]ven Indian grammar could be converted from an Indian form of knowledge into an European object that was lexically knowable and quantifiable in the idiom of English rationality. The close link between knowledge and power was rendered more obvious with some European missionaries bypassing classical linguistic training in Persian and Sanskrit altogether and concentrating instead on the vernacular languages of Bengali and Hindustani, felt to be better harnessed to the simple structures of command on which colonial rule was based.

Every aspect of governing India was turned into published reports, district gazetteers, legal codes, all manner of written documents that were meant to simplify the understanding of India and to reorganise it in terms set by the colonial government. Bayly (1999: 365), in a study titled 'Empire and Information' has argued:

> [T]hat successful intelligence-gathering was a critical feature of the British domination of India…the British took over and manipulated the sophisticated systems of internal espionage and political reporting which had long been deployed by the kingdoms of the Indian subcontinent. One overriding reason why the east India Company was able to conquer India and dominate it for more than a century was that the British had learnt the art of listening in as it were, on the internal communication of Indian polity and society.

In order for the Empire to function, they simply had to have the support of the local literati, potentates and chieftains. These people were cultivated with money and favours and many of them became the faithful eyes and ears of the Empire. The reconversion of traditional knowledge into the categories of Empire has had major consequences in the context of Independent India. In fact, successive governments in post-Independent India have merely followed these traditions leading to a widening of gaps between the rulers and the ruled.

When governments are faced with the 'untranslatable'—traditions and people that they cannot or who refuse to be comprehended—they fall back on coercion and brute power. This has unfortunately been the case in post-Independent India too. Another altogether more effective means used by the British to control the vast, multi-ethnic mosaic of India was through the introduction of writing to a subject community who were hardly literate in the sense of being able to read and write. The British with their records and treaties were able to supplant the value and place of 'oral' authority with that of written authority. This had tremendous consequences for it gave the British the power to control cross-sectorally negotiations with the subject population and manipulate outcomes that strengthened the Empire. Ajay Skaria, in a fascinating account of the ways in which writing was used by the British to subdue *adivasi* (indigenous) communities in the Dangs, has observed:

> While in the early or mid-nineteenth century (and possibly earlier), Dangis saw writing as a powerful plains technology, they did not necessarily regard written agreements as any more binding than oral ones. With the consolidation of the British authority, however, the power of colonial writing came to be perceived to be greater. This was in part because of the extensive colonial use of writing, and because of their political domination and authority, which allowed them to insist on the consistent implementation of written agreements. (Skaria 1996: 18)

Brown Sahibs and Empire

Systematic changes to the traditional agricultural and industrial economies in India were complemented by the cultivation of a class of people who were employed to ease the administrative burden of looking after a country of such continental proportions. The ideological plan was, in the now infamous words of the colonial educational strategist Thomas Babbington Macaulay to create a class of people who 'would be Indian in blood and colour, but English in taste, opinions, values and intellect' (Macaulay 1957: 16). English education became a primary attribute of learning in the light of another one of Macualay's pre-emptory dismissals of oriental learning and literature to the dustbins of history—'I am quite ready to take the oriental learning at the valuation of the orientalists themselves. I have never found one among them who could deny that a single shelf of a good European library was worth the whole native literature of India and Arabia' (p. 175). In time, this English-educated class of people of India took over the reins of power in India to the extent that the entire administrative system in rural and urban India was manned by servants of the state. Take the case of rural administration in Bengal.

> Out of the 790 members in the District Boards of Bengal in 1881–92, 31.5 per cent were government servants, 28.9 zamindars and talukdars, and 26.6 per cent legal practitioners. In the Local Boards, 47.7 per cent were zamindars, talukdars

> or their servants, 23.8 per cent legal practitioners and 12.5 per cent government servants. (Mishra 1983: 211)

In a similar vein, the sociologist Andre Beteille (1967: 233) has pointed out that 'The Indian component of the Indian Civil Service (I.C.S.) of which the Indian Administrative Service (I.A.S.) is the successor, was in its early phase made up almost entirely of members of two or three top castes.' He goes on to say that, 'In Madras between 1892 and 1904 out of the sixteen successful candidates for the I.C.S., fifteen were Brahmins. In Bengal during this period all or almost all Indian members of the I.C.S. were either Brahmins or Kayasths... The position in Bombay was about the same.'

Ironically, the nationalist movement in India, consisted mainly of people who had been through the colonial educational mill, but were influenced by the freedom wave that had begun to cut a swathe through the colonies. Jawaharlal Nehru, the first Prime Minister of Independent India, was in many ways an archetypical liberal democrat and Mahatma Gandhi too was schooled in that tradition, although in the case of the latter, he ended up subordinating the influence of that received tradition to a home-spun tradition. Indian industrialists were conspicuous by their absence in the freedom movement, until the latter period of the nationalist movement, when there was a general realisation of the role played by the colonial government in marginalising the growth of Indian industry. These latecomers to the cause of Indian Independence were to become fervent supporters of the Swadeshi (Independence) movement and were rewarded for their efforts in post-Independent India. It resulted in a situation in which '...an amalgam of social classes, of an agrarian oligarchy and industrial monopolies, of traders and businessmen, of bureaucrats and professional groups...came to dominate state power in post-Colonial India' (Basu 1988: 145). The Tatas and Birlas, who continue to be among the most dominant industrial houses in India were, for instance, involved in drawing up the Bombay Plan (1944) that laid the foundations for Indian industrial policy and that, incidentally, was promoted by the Birla-owned journal the Eastern Economist (Chenoy 1985).

Censorship and Empire

The newly introduced communication system was, without a doubt, intended to remain a handmaiden of Empire. Clarke (1927: 80) describes thus one of the early attempts at the consolidation of communications in India:

> By 1827 the Indian Empire had been consolidated and it was therefore necessary to consolidate the postal service. It was not however until 1837 that an Act was passed establishing the absolute monopoly of the East India Company of the conveyance of letters of hire.

While the colonial state and Whitehall invested in centralising communications, it was close to impossible to maintain this hold given that the press in the UK had begun to contribute to the making of a 'public sphere' and there were a number of public servants and missionaries for whom the press was a natural ally in the project of civilising India. While circulation figures were on the low side, patronage by royalty, the literati, businessmen and government helped the English and vernacular press to survive.

The colonial power used every law possible to censor, outlaw and suppress an errant press. This was the case with the first newspaper that was established in India—James Hicky's the Bengal Gazette on 29 January 1790—as it was with the vernacular nationalist newspapers, some of which were vehemently anti-British in the period immediately preceding the granting of Independence to India in August 1947. In response to a non-compliant press, the state decided to exert its control. In the words of Gupta (1977: 213):

> A unanimous decision of the Viceroy Council was taken on 14 March 1878 to establish a check over the vernacular press in India. This was Act IX of 1878, an act for 'the better control of publications in oriental languages'. It was to control 'seditious writing' in the vernacular newspaper everywhere in the country, except the South. Too much was being written in these newspapers of the injustice and tyranny of the British government, 'its utter want of consideration towards its native subjects' and the 'insolence and pride of Englishmen in India'.

However, the speed with which printing presses evolved in colonial India surpassed the ability of the authorities to ever control its output to the extent to which they desired. The English press, such as *The Times of India* (1861), was to a large extent the handmaiden of the empire and functioned as such. However, by the time of the 1857 Indian Mutiny, there were two distinct press camps—the pro-Empire largely English press and the vernacular press who took up the cause of the nationalist struggle. Although the Vernacular Press Act (1878) was enacted to control the nationalist press, its suppression merely led to the making of a stronger, more diverse vernacular press committed to the cause of freedom from British rule. In fact, as Greenough (1983: 353) has pointed out, the fortunes of the Congress movement was linked to the press so much that 'Of the 72 representatives who gathered in Bombay at the first Congress meeting in 1885, more than dozen were professional journalists.'

Telegraphy and Empire

The 1857 Mutiny was a key moment in the history of British rule in India. While some sections of the British press, in their response, blamed the Mutiny on colonial maladministration and recommended a stronger role for Indians on governance, they were, as Palmegiano (1991: 9) has pointed out, united in their support for the Empire:

> Whether by changing Indian operations or chastising Indians, journalists appeared certain that England would dominate India for a very long time. Indeed, in the millions of words penned about the rebellion was implicit the idea that the entire British Empire, though temporarily unwell, was going to live indefinitely.

The struggles that the British were involved with in India were fought on two fronts:

1. there were the attempts to consolidate their power in India and quell domestic revolts and rebel campaigns waged by local chiefs and kings such as Haider Ali and Tipu Sultan and
2. economic wars for control of the trade in primary commodities that were being fought with other erstwhile colonial powers, most notably the French, Portuguese and the Germans.

In this regard, the advent of the telegraph proved to be as important as that of the railways in the consolidation of the British Empire. It contributed to the centralisation of economics, politics and administration. In fact, the centralisation of telegraphy first, followed by broadcasting, was systematic and deliberate. While the first telegraph lines were laid in 1851, by 1857 there were 6,800 kilometres of telegraph lines. This real and symbolic power of the telegraph to the Empire invited the attention of anti-British forces and it is interesting to know that 1,479 kilometres of lines were destroyed by revolting soldiers during the 1857 mutiny. However, and despite such losses, the telegraph did play a role during the Mutiny and in particular was used to communicate the containment of the Mutiny to Whitehall. Winseck and Pike (2007) have observed that 'The Indian Mutiny shocked the security of the British Empire and galvanised the government's resolve to do whatever it took to establish communication links between London and Delhi as rapidly as possible.' It also became a tool that Whitehall used to control the colonial administration in India and in particular Viceroys who were independent-minded. However it was precisely the issue of security with overland cables that led the British to invest in undersea cables. Not only was there an internal threat to contend with, there were overt and covert wars with old and new colonising powers like the US who were keen to wrest the imperial advantage, including communication that the English had enjoyed for many decades. With the creation of the Electric Telegraph Act (1854), the telegraph became a government monopoly. It was used mainly to maintain the integrity of the colonial administration of the Empire although it was also used for commercial purposes. This was followed by the Indian Telegraph Act (1889), which for all practical purposes continues to remain the key legislation on data transmission and reception in India. This act has of course now been made somewhat redundant by the cable, satellite and IT revolutions and by the reality of convergence, although, rather typically, Delhi has been slow to respond to the need for a new Act. Jill Hills (2002: 43) has commented on the importance of telegraphy to the cause of territorial imperialism.

> India became important as a transit country for lines to Asia. The opening of the line from Madras to Singapore in 1871 was marked by the telegraphy of the results of the Oxford-Cambridge University boat race, and put Singapore in direct contact with London for the first time.

By 1948, there were 118,395 kilometres of telegraph lines and 3,324 telegraph offices (Singh 1999). Centralised communication was also enhanced by cable links that connected the various nodes of Pax Brittanica. The first undersea cable, linking Malta and Alexandria, was laid in 1870, thus enabling London to communicate with India. Both the cable and the telegraph provided the reason for newer, more efficient systems of news gathering. Reuters, the first global news agency, was established in 1851. It concentrated on processing economic information from the colonies unlike the French Havas, which dealt with news and advertising. The French communication theorist Armand Mattelart (2000: 24) in a study on networking, has this to say on the imperial designs of the big three news agencies—Havas, Wolff and Reuters.[2] 'Through a treaty of alliance signed in 1870, this triad carved up the world into territories or spheres of influence, thus marking the birth of an information market conceptualised on a global scale and based on geopolitical interests.'[3] This is a scenario that is very reminiscent of the contemporary domination of communications in some parts of the world, for instance, that of Cable and Wireless in the telecommunications sector in the Caribbean.[4] Reuters, of course had a monopoly over news services in the British Empire. Media cartels were a characteristic feature of communications during the age of the Empire and four wireless firms—Marconi, Compagnie Generale de Telegraphie sans Fil, Radio Corporation of America (RCA) and Telefunken controlled this sector (Winseck and Pike 2008).

Broadcasting and Empire

The centralisation of communications during the British Raj continued with the advent of broadcasting. While it is true that the government did allow private broadcasting, for instance, in some of the princely states, the Times of India/Bombay Posts and Telegraphs broadcasting initiative in 1921 and other private initiatives in Madras and Calcutta, these initiatives did not last and by 1930 broadcasting had become a government-owned affair, a tradition that was subsequently honed to perfection by successive governments in post-Independent India. All India Radio, the national network, came into being in 1936 and became an indispensable medium for propaganda, information gathering and dissemination. In fact, the propaganda was directed at two enemies of the Empire—the nascent Congress movement and the axis powers, Germany in particular. Support for Britain's war efforts in India was not as forthright as the government thought it would be and radio was used to enlist support. When the Indian National Congress became a significant mass movement, the issue of anti-Congress propaganda became a delicate matter.[5] Nevertheless, AIR's role in intelligence gathering continued to be of prime importance. The following excerpt from a directive issued by the Empire Intelligence Service (1940) reveals the connections between radio and intelligence gathering:

> [W]e need our own intelligence organisation on the spot, with headquarters in Bombay, controlled and administered by a specially chosen Indian...It is clear that the co-operation of All India Radio would be essential but there is every

reason to suppose that it would be cheerfully forthcoming. The organisation would also be able to produce a skeleton service of information about Burma.

In spite of AIR's allegiance to the Empire, its role in India was contested from within and Lionel Fielden who presided over the consolidation of AIR between 1930–1940 was keen to create an AIR along the lines of public service broadcasting and in particular the BBC.

Another example of the disconnect within the imperial broadcasting project is that of the rural broadcasting initiative that was popularised by Frank Brayne and others who believed that the aim of broadcasting was rural uplift including strengthening village communities against the onslaught of modernity. This initiative paved the way for the establishment of rural broadcasting and community radio. As Zivin (1998: 718) has observed:

> Through their efforts, a handful of experimental community listening systems were established in the early thirties on the rural outskirts of the Northern cities of Lahore, Delhi, and Peshawar, in Southern Madras, in the water-logged but politically charged Midnapur district of Bengal, and in the Princely State of Hyderabad. As independent systems they were short-lived, subsumed under the expanding Government of Indian controlled All India Radio network by 1937.

It is fascinating to be reminded, precisely at a time when the democratisation of broadcasting in India, including space for community broadcasting, continues to be a significant concern, that the country has had the experience of 'illegal' counter broadcasting, during the heady days leading up to Indian Independence. From 1940 onwards, there are instances of amateur radio operators setting up pro-Congress stations as, for instance, Azad Hind Radio (Free India Radio). The arrest of Gandhi in August 1942 following the All India Congress Committee's decision taken in Bombay on 8 August 1942 to make the British quit India, led to the idea of using radio for sustaining a 'leaderless movement'. It started operations on 26 August 1942 in Bombay on the 41.78 metre wavelength although its operations were moved many times to escape detection. '...the secret Congress radio', as Chatterjee (1989: 16) informs us, 'took up the challenge and disseminated the much needed information to the masses so that a leaderless movement could be sustained and deal the final blow to British Imperialism.' Two amateur radio broadcasters 'Bob' Tanna and Nariman Abarbad Printer played a key role in setting up Congress radio. As Owen Williamson[6] notes:

> Despite sporadic British jamming, the crystal-controlled signal of Congress radio was audible on the then-unoccupied 40-metre band throughout the Indian subcontinent, and as far away as Japanese-occupied Burma. The station

transmitted recordings of the Mahatmas' sermons and his calls for non violence, uncensored news, pro-independence music, instructions for Gandhian activists, and political declarations by the movement' underground leadership....

Conclusion

The British played an important role in establishing the backbone of communications in India. While that backbone was created to serve, first and foremost, the Empire, its institutions, ideas and ways of operation were handed over to the Indian elites who replaced the British at the time of Independence. What is fascinating is that the very same traditions and methods of employing communications to aid the imperial project was used by successive post-Independence Congress governments in particular, to control the people and maintain the hegemony of the Congress. This will be the subject of the following chapter.

Notes

1. The Zamindars had traditionally been tax-collectors under the Mughal rulers. With the Permanent Settlement, they, in effect, became the only legitimate proprietors of land.
2. The importance of Reuters to the Empire is expressed in the following letter 'Infinitely, the most important channel of Indian news to the outside world is Reuters News Agency, which not only supplies newspapers throughout the Empire directly but has exchanges of news arrangements with all the leading national newspapers in the world.' Letter from the Principle Information Officer, Home Department, Government of India—Josselyn Hennessy to A. H. Joyce, Esq., O.B.E., Information Officer, 21 March 1940, Delhi, India Office Library Holdings, London.
3. The carve-up was based on the following formulae: 'Reuters laid claim to the entire British Empire, Holland and its colonies, Australia, the East Indies and the Far East; Havas obtained France, Italy, Spain, Portugal, the Levant, Indochina, and Latin America; Wolff focussed in central and northern Europe....' (Mattelart 2000: 24).
4. 'Cable & Wireless controls telecommunications services in eight English-speaking Caribbean countries and has a 49 per cent stake in another.' One fourth of the groups' profits comes from their operations in this region. See the article by James (2000).
5. A report from the Publicity Conference, 1941 expresses this anxiety—'There was complete unanimity that for the present at any rate it would be bad policy to make any direct attack on the Congress through official propaganda agencies which might have the effect of increasing bitterness' (Second Publicity Conference 1940).
6. Owen Williamson, 'The Mahatma's Hams', http://www.wr6wr.com/newSite/articles/features/mahatmashams.html (Accessed on 23 May 2008).

References

Basu, S. 1988. 'State and Industrialisation in a Post-Colonial Capitalist Economy', *Economic and Political Weekly*, 30, 23 January (10): 143–150.

Bayly, C. A. 1999. *Empire and Information: Intelligence Gathering and Social Communication in India, 1780–1870*. New Delhi: Cambridge University Press.

Beteille, A. 1967. 'Elites, Status-groups and Caste in Modern India', in P. Mason (ed.), *India and Ceylon: Unity and Diversity, Institute of Race Relations*. London: Oxford University Press.

Bhatia, N. 2004. *Acts of Authority/Acts of Resistance: Theatre and Politics in Colonial and Post Colonial India*. Ann Arbor: The University of Michigan press.

Bright, C. 1918. 'Telegraphic Communication during War', *Journal of Comparative Legislation and International Law*, 18(2): 210–215.

Chatterjee, G. 1989. 'Quit India Movement and "illegal" Congress Radio', *Mainstream*, XXVII (46), 12 August: 15–17.

Chenoy, K. M. 1985. 'Industrial Policy and Multinationals in India', *Social Scientist*, 13(3): 15–31.

Choudhary, D. K. L. 2004. 'Sinews of Panic and the Nerves of Empire: The Imagined State's Entanglement with Information Panic, India c. 1880–1912', *Modern Asian Studies*, 38(4): 965–1002.

Clarke, G. R. 1927. 'Post and Telegraph Work in India', *The Asiatic Review*, LXXXVI: 79–108.

Cohn, B. S. 1997. *Colonialism and its Forms of Knowledge: The British in India*. NJ: Princeton University Press.

Empire Intelligence Service. 1940. *Recommendations for an Empire Intelligence Service*, 27 November 1940. War Series File No. 462/57 M, B.B.C. Empire Intelligence Scheme, L/I/1/962, India Office Library Holdings, London.

Greenough, P. R. 1983. 'Political Mobilisation and the Underground Literature of the Quit India Movement', *Modern Asian Studies*, 17(3): 353–386.

Gupta, U. D. 1977. 'The Indian Press 1870–1880: A Small World of Journalism', *Modern Asian Studies*, 11(2): 2134–2135.

Hills, J. 2002. *The Struggle for Control of Global Communication: The Formative Century*. Urbana/Chicago: University of Illinois Press.

James, C. 2000. 'C & W Feels Heat of Caribbean Liberalisation', *Financial Times*, 23 August.

Kaul, C. 2006. 'Introductory Survey', in K. Kaul (ed.), *Media and the British Empire*, pp. 1–19. Basingstoke and New York: Palgrave Macmillan.

Kurien, C.T. 1994. *Global Capitalism and the Indian Economy, Tracts for the Times*, Series 6. Hyderabad: Orient Longman.

Macaulay, Thomas Babington. 1957. 'Minute of 2 February 1835 on Indian Education', *Macaulay, Prose and Poetry*, selected by G. M. Young, pp. 721–24, 729. Cambridge MA: Harvard University Press.

Masani, M. 1976. *Broadcasting and the People*. New Delhi: National Book Trust.

Mattelart, A. 2000. *Networking the World: 1794–2000*. Minneapolis, London: University of Minnesota Press.

Mishra, B.B. 1983. *District Administration and Rural Development*. Delhi: Oxford University Press.

Mukhopadhyay, A. 1998. Review of B. S. Cohn. 1997. *Colonialism and its forms of Knowledge: The British in India*, pp. 65–67. New Delhi: Oxford University Press. In *Seminar*, 465, 'Power Play', May 1998.

Palmegiano, E. M. 1991. 'The Indian Mutiny in the Mid-Victorian Press', *Journal of Newspaper and Periodical History*, 7(1): 3–11.

Pinkerton, A. 2007. 'Radio and the Raj: Broadcasting in British India (1920–1940)', *The Journal of the Royal Asiatic Society*, Series 3, 18(2): 166–191.

Second Publicity Conference, Imperial Secretariat, New Delhi, 16–17 December 1940. Publicity Conference—Summary of Proceedings, Information Officer, No.1686, 1941. India Office Library Holdings, London.

Singh, J.P. 1999. *Leapfrogging Development: The Political Economy of Communications Restructuring*. New York: State University of New York Press.

Skaria, A. 1996. 'Writing, Orality and Power in the Dangs, Western India, 1800s–1920s', in S. Amin and D. Chakrabarty (eds), *Subaltern Studies IX: Writings on South Asian History and Society*, pp. 13–58. New Delhi: Oxford University Press.

Solomon, R. H. 1994. 'Culture, Imperialism and Nationalist Resistance: Performance in Colonial India', *Theatre Journal*, 46(3): 323–347.

Winseck, D. R. and R. M. Pike. 2007. *Communication and Empire: Media, Markets and Globalisation, 1860–1930*. Durham/London: Duke University Press.

———. 2008. 'Communication and Empire: Media Markets, Power and Globalisation, 1869–1910', *Global Media and Communication*, 4(1): 7–36.

Zivin, J. 1998. 'The Imagined Reign of the Iron Lecturer: Village Broadcasting in Colonial India', *Modern Asian Studies*, 32(3): 717–738.

3

The Political Economy of Communications in Post-colonial India: 1948–1985

A critical political economy of communications and culture deals with the media and communication systems as essential institutions in contemporary societies that are broadly determined by key factors in society—namely, economics and politics. In other words, media systems, in this approach, are not seen as independent institutions that produce symbolic goods for individual consumption but as social constructions established by a range of forces and institutions in society. The focus is not on an analysis of individual consumer behaviour (reception) but on a holistic, integrated, historical, materialist analysis (Golding and Murdock 1997) that attempts to understand the production, distribution and consumption of symbolic/material goods within the parameters of global and local capitalism. This includes understanding media within any given context not only with reference to the internal contingencies of its making but also its external contingencies such as the influence of global media policy and global media governance institutions such as the World Trade Organisation, the World Intellectual Property Organisation, the International Telecommunication Union, among other organisations. In the context of India, the media and communication environment has been resolutely shaped by local politics as much as by external forces such as the World Trade Organisation and the World Bank.

While there are a number of definitions of a critical political economy and a critical political economy of communications and culture that range from what may be considered broadly economic determinist to that which includes the need to engage with the 'cultural effect' of media goods and services, Murdock and Golding's (2005: 61–64) interpretation reflects the tenor embraced in this book.

> Critical political economy differs from mainstream economics in four main respects. Firstly, it is holistic. Secondly, it is historical. Thirdly, it is centrally concerned with the balance between capitalist enterprise and public intervention. And, finally, and perhaps most importantly, it goes beyond technical issues of efficiency to engage with basic questions of justice, equality and the public good....

While the state played a pre-eminent role in determining the nature of the media environment in the post-Independent period, that role today is shared with the representatives of domestic and global capital and global media governance institutions.

The Political Economy of Post-Independent India

There are two outstanding features of the political economy of India that characterise the post-Independent period 1948–1985: the hegemony of the Congress Party that was in power for almost the entire period except for a brief interregnum in the immediate aftermath of the Emergency (1975–1977), and a *dirigiste* mixed economy characterised by centralised planned growth and state involvement in a range of productive sectors, including information and communication technologies. In hindsight, this prior involvement in electronics and computing provided the foundations for contemporary growth in these areas. There are other aspects too that need to be factored in and featured in the narrative of the nation in the post-Independent era including India's commitment to non-alignment, the welfare economy, the public sector, nationalisation of key industries, bureaucratisation and what euphemistically has been called 'the license raj' along with a range of affirmative actions and projects related to addressing issues regarding poverty and inequality.

Without a doubt, all these aspects also influenced the growth, development and tenor of the media during this period. While the press and cinema were in the hands of the private sector, they were significantly impacted by a raft of government regulations that were on occasion invoked most famously during the Emergency (1975–1977), to silence opposition to Congress rule. Broadcasting—both radio under All India Radio and television under Doordarshan—were projected as public broadcasters although, in reality, they functioned as instruments of the state that were routinely used by successive governments for explicitly political ends. This was also the era in which the community media sector began to make its presence felt. This sector included a variety of traditions characterised by the leveraging of culture for radical social change including political and popular theatre, media literacy, alternative video and film—by the organised and unorganised Left and social action groups (SAPs). In their entirety these expressions of alternative media can be called the Third media sector. This sector catered primarily to dealing with the deficits faced by the oppressed classes and castes and existed primarily on the margins. The emergence of this sector was a reflection of disillusionment with the state, in particular its inability to effect distributive justice and extend substantive democracy. By the late 1970s,

> [T]he 'universe' of NGOs in India include(d) Gandhian organisations, secular religious organisations, foreign relief and developmental organisations, organisations formed by professionals from the middle class or lower middle class to serve the poor, intermediary organisations [that trained or] offer(ed) consulting services in development, and organisations formed by people disillusioned with the state, electoral politics, and social movements. (Sen 1999: 333)

Industry

With Independence, power was effectively transferred from the colonial government to an Indian ruling class that largely comprised of an industrial and agricultural bourgeoisie. Interestingly enough the industrial elite were not exactly vociferous supporters of the Independence movement. In fact, it was only when they realised that British economic interests were inimical to their own, that they joined this movement and became involved in the Indian National Congress (INC). Both Chenoy (1985) and Ghosh (1983) allude to the initial vacillations of the industrial elite vis-à-vis the Swadeshi movement and their later accommodations. In spite of the strong influence of Gandhians in the INC, the industrial elite and, in particular the Tatas and Birlas, played an extremely important role in creating the blueprint for post-Independent economic growth in India. The Bombay Plan also called A Plan for Economic Development of India (1944) was drawn up by J. R. D. Tata and G. D. Birla and was promoted by the Birla-owned journal the *Eastern Economist.* The Plan supported private enterprise and protectionist policies in support of indigenous capital. However, it was the state that emerged as the key actor in the economic growth of the country.

Under the provisions of the Industrial Policy Statement adopted at the Avadi session of the Congress government in January 1955, basic and strategic industries, including heavy industrial plants and machinery, defence, etc. were exclusively reserved as public sector projects. The Industrial Policy resolution of 1956 also 'reserved telecommunications, broadcasting and defence equipment for the public sector' (Parthasarthi 1988: 7). Self-reliance and import-substitution were adopted as key economic policies of the state and a series of Socialist-style Five Year Plans provided the blueprint for economic growth in the country. While the state did invest heavily in the development of private capital by developing nation-wide infrastructure as, for instance, in telecommunications and the transport system (Sanyal 1988), growth in the public sector was guided by the norms of propriety and social justice rather than an undiluted profit motive. In successive blueprints of Five Year Plans, state intervention was justified to the extent that as Bardhan (1984: 37–38) has observed:

> [The State] had accumulated powers of direct ownership and control in the economy to an extent unparalleled in Indian history, both in the spheres of circulation (banking, credit, transport, distribution and foreign trade) and of production—directly manufacturing much of basic and capital goods, owning more than 60 per cent of all productive capital in the industrial sector...running eight of the top ten industrial units in the country...directly employing two-thirds of all workers in the organised sector, holding through nationalised financial institutions more than 25 per cent of paid-up capital of joint-stock companies in the private sector.

Although various legislations were enacted both in industry and agriculture to prevent monopoly growth—various Land Ceiling Acts, the Industrial Policy Resolution (1948), Industrial Licensing Act incorporated in the Industrial Development and Regulation Act (1951), the Companies Act (1951) and the Monopolies and Restrictive Trade Practices Act (1969), relationships of patronage with the Congress party allowed for the selective interpretation and implementation of anti-monopoly rules and regulations. The feudal constancy of relations of production in agriculture and the unfettered growth of industrial monopoly houses were allowed to continue within the parameters of state-directed planned economic growth. Chenoy (1985: 20) has observed that deregulation and a dilution of the policy of import substitution, industrial licensing and accommodation of foreign capital remained one side of a Janus-faced policy that directly led to the consolidation of the major industrial houses in India.

> [T]he assets of the Tatas house grew from Rs. 54.3 crores in 1951 to Rs. 504.4 crores in 1966, of the Birla House from Rs. 24.2 crores to Rs. 457.8 crores and of the Mafatlal House from Rs. 4 crores to Rs. 92.7 crores over the same period.

This growth in itself was focussed on products and sectors that were most profitable—a trend that has continued and that has, for example, led to the inability of the state to enforce private mobile telephony providers to fulfil universal service obligations related to the provision of rural telecommunications. Much has been written about the inefficiency of public sector enterprises and while there are many enterprises that have been a drain on public funds, the political economy of industrial production in India is a complex story that reveals the growing ascendency and muscle of private capital directing economic growth. In this connection, Bagchi, Ghosh and Dasgupta's (1985: 12) observations are a useful counter to the almost knee-jerk PSU-bashing that is a media staple.

> Comparison is frequently made between the Tatas and public sector steel plants. What is not always realised is that the public sector steel plants were not free to choose their product-mix: they were required by Government to produce low value items (in high demand) in the public interest. The Tatas have long since given up the production of pig iron for sale to foundries; the entire burden falls on the public sector plants. In terms of operating efficiency—physical materials and energy the Bhilai Steel Plant is no worse than Tata Iron and Steel Co Ltd (TISCO), and Bokaro has a more efficient energy balance.

The Politics of Aid

While self-reliant development was a key policy plank of successive Congress governments, internal economic crisis of one sort or another led to a growing dependence on external aid. Given the increasing strength of the pro-capitalist lobby in the Congress, the foreign exchange crisis of 1956 and the dramatic drop in agricultural production, the state, in exchange for foreign capital, relented on its Socialist policies on growth. Both the 1959 Ford Foundation report on 'India's Food Crisis and Steps to Meet it' and the Bell report of the World Bank (1967) laid down clear conditions for the provision of aid. The Bell report objected to attempts at institutional change and the policy of co-operatisation and insisted that aid be given on condition that the policy of development shifts its attention to the concentration and intensive cultivation of districts and people. As Ilchman (1967: 678–679) has observed:

> The Indian Government was restricted in its choices, among many other ways, by loans tied to purchases in the aid-giving countries. In 1961–62, about 80 per cent of the aid was tied to specific projects and programs...These are turnkey

> arrangements that keep the administration of the project, and hence part of its political relevance, in the hands of aid-giver, often denying flexibility in the Indian regime.

Between the First Five Year and Second Five Year Plans, exogenous funding for the plans increased from 9.5 per cent to 31 per cent. Aid played a role in the liberalisation of the economy, to the deregulation of public sector manufacturing and to the opening up of key industries to national and international capital.

The influence of aid was particularly evident in the context of development communications. Along with aid from the US to agricultural universities there also flowed theories, methods and concepts related to the role of communication in development—the diffusion of innovations, knowledge, attitude, perception (KAP) studies and behavioural communications. During the period of the first and second Five Year Plans (FYPs), a large part of US aid through the Technical Cooperation Mission (now USAID), the Ford and Rockefeller Foundations and the World Bank was directed towards financing the growth of technical and agricultural institutions in India. Aid went to the establishment of agricultural universities in Hyderabad, Guwahati, Jorhat, Coimbatore, Hebbal, Uttar Pradesh, Bhubhaneswar and Kanpur among other places and agricultural extension and information projects in Vijayawada, Delhi, Poona, Bengaluru, Pali and other centres. It was via these institutions that the dominant paradigm of development communications with its accent on behavioural change and the diffusion of innovations and ideas became established in India.

The following excerpt from a letter written by the ex-President of the World Bank, Eugene Bell to the then-finance minister of India, T. T. Krishnamachari, illustrates the politics of aid:

> India's interest lies in giving private enterprise, both Indian and foreign, every encouragement to make its contribution to the development of the economy particularly in the industrialised field. We would have to consider the pace and scale of our further loan operation in India from time to time in the light of economic conditions and prospects taking into consideration the economic policies pursued by your government.(Chenoy 1985: 18)

Agriculture

On the agricultural front, an attempt was made to pursue a policy based on growth and distribution. Given the preponderance of the work force in the agricultural sector and the central role played by agriculture in the life of the nation, the Congress government attempted to organise a nation-wide change in agricultural relations and modes of production. One of the first initiatives taken by the government was to abolish the zamindari system and intermediaries and to give share-croppers and tenants tenure and a share in the land. This was complemented with the passing of land ceiling legislations that limited the extent of land ownership. The impact of these major initiatives were, however, restricted given the fact that with one or two significant exceptions including West Bengal, most states in India were unable to implement land ceilings. In most parts of the country this policy merely led to another set of feudal landowners—the *talukdars*—taking over from the zamindars. The *talukdars* were supporters of the Congress party and in return for electoral support:

> [T]he Congress pursued land reforms beyond Zamindari abolition only on a rhetorical level, ignored the possibilities of raising any serious government revenue from agriculture...and set up any number of programmes in community development, rural credit and education that funnelled benefits into the hands of the locally dominant groups, thereby enhancing their position. (Blair 1980: 247)

Low land-man ratios have been the norm all over India and unproductive agriculture led to the creation of a growing population of casual labour as opposed to wage labour. In the words of the economist C. T. Kurien (1987: 6):

> For the period from 1901 to 1961 cultivators accounted for about 53 per cent and agricultural labourers between 14 and 17 per cent. There was a very drastic change in this composition in the decades of the sixties. The share of cultivators came down from 52.3 per cent in 1961 to 42.9 per cent in 1971 while that of agricultural labourers increased from 17.2 per cent to 26.9 per cent which has continued through the seventies as well.

The inability of governments in India to tackle key social issues in rural India including caste and class impacted on their ability to implement radical rural reform. This in turn led the government to focus its agricultural modernisation policies and productivity to the relatively wealthier farmers who had the wherewithal to absorb capital costs related to intensive production. While the Green Revolution certainly increased agricultural production and turned India into a food-grain surplus country, it also reinforced already existing disparities and large-scale agricultural innovation systems such as the World Bank's Training and Visit (T and V) System that were directed towards increasing the productivity of 'contact' farmers who more often than not happened to be the wealthier farmers. In field work that I carried out in the Nilgiris in the mid-1980s it was clear that the T and V system benefited those who had land and who had the means to diversify and implement scientific horticultural production. Furthermore, the system was based on one's ability to negotiate with the local village extension worker (VEW), who apart from being the conduit for information flows also controlled among other assets cabbage seed vouchers. While cabbage seed could be bought in the open market, the quality of such seed was unreliable. While the VEWs personally handed out these vouchers to contact farmers, non-contact farmers were dependent for the vouchers on the whim of the VEW. The T and V system was based on the assumption that poverty is caused by low productivity and that higher levels of productivity will lead to an eventual trickle-down. But this was not borne out in practice and high-tech agricultural revolutions such as the Green Revolution, as has been documented by Griffin (1975), Frankel (1978) and Menscher (1978) among others have widened the gaps between the have and the have-nots.

Not only was the average Indian faced with economic uncertainties, but also with the prospect of negotiating life through a top-heavy bureaucracy. This included the legacy of a nation-wide set of institutions, a vast administrative apparatus along with an administrative ideology. The centralisation of the major public institutions led to the development of a ponderous bureaucratic network, whose vestiges continue to play a formative role in contemporary India as, for instance, the unnecessarily complicated process of licensing for the community radio sector. The political scientist Sudipta Kaviraj (1984: 232) has commented on the complicated journey of each 'decision...in this large and ill-regulated machine, as it journeys from adumbration to policy, through its transmission, decimation and eventual "ironical" implementation, often in unrecognisable forms.'

Politics

The Congress party was virtually the government of India for all but two years between the years 1948–1985. This unparalleled position of strength was established through a variety of means:

1. The post-Independent consensus related to growth based on distributive justice, affirmative action, and public sector interventions within a secular, constitutional democratic order had wide support. 'Modernisation, progress, reform, scientific advance, secularism, egalitarianism, national self-reliance and Indian achievements was written in the narrative of Indian economic nationalism' (Wyatt 2005: 170).
2. The government through constitutional means provided the terms of internal democracy including press freedom, an apolitical civil service and military, support for minority interests and non-alignment in its foreign affairs.
3. Support for a federal system through a syndicated national, regional and state-based Congress apparatus that reached out to India's many villages. This was maintained through the cultivation of regional and local Congress satraps who played a key role in containing dissension and maintaining local Congress rule. Congress also, as Rudolph and Rudolph (1987: 19) have observed, established '... a pluralist basis for support that encompassed a wide spectrum of interests, classes, status groups, regions and communities'.

However, by the late 1960s and in response to the increasing power of local Congress leaders, Mrs Gandhi began what was to become a theme of the 1970s and 1980s—the relentless centralisation of power and the politicisation of key institutions in society including the bureaucracy. As Rangarajan (2007: 35) has observed, 'Having been endangered in office by a powerful Syndicate, she systematically undercut its two founts of power: the party hierarchy and the regional leaders. By 1980, even District Congress Committee heads were being appointed by the president of the AICC' (All India Congress Council). The diffused power structure of the Congress had acted as a bulwark and prevented local crisis from becoming national in scope. The restructuring of political power marked the end of value-based political rule in India. Populist and increasingly personalised politics became the norm and by the mid-1970s it became obvious that an over-centralised government structure could not cope with demands from a pluralist polity or deal with any number of localised crisis. The crisis faced by the Congress party became a crisis faced by the state that manifested itself in the newfound legitimacy and popularity of marginal or suppressed political groups, the emergence of a variety of regional political parties, the surfacing of new movements organised by tribal, Dalit, minority and religious communities, the strengthening of old secessionist movements in North East India and the emergence of new secessionist movements in Punjab and elsewhere. The inability to quell political unrest and the growing demands for 'real' democracy led to the promulgation of the infamous Emergency by Mrs Gandhi during 1975–1977 that resulted in near total press censorship, the outlawing of political opposition and authoritarian rule. The crisis in the Punjab that led to the storming of the Golden Temple and indirectly led to Mrs Gandhi's assassination was a reflection of the failure of dialogue and the failure of force.

The Economy

With the benefit of hindsight it is clear that a mixed economy did bring about mixed results. The state was committed to self-reliance and strengthening the domestic market through import-substitution policies. A vast section of the annual budget was expended on a number of welfare projects in the Five Year Plans. While growth rates between 1947–1985 were certainly limited and is often referred to derisorily as the 'Hindu rate of growth' (averaging 3.6 per cent) as compared to the contemporary 8–10 per cent growth rates that the country has consistently experienced over more than a decade, what must be kept in perspective is that it laid the foundations for future growth, for instance, in the area of satellite technology, computing and software. While private companies were involved in manufacturing, key institutions such as banks were nationalised and there were stringent caps on MNC ownership, foreign currency flows and import taxes. In retrospect, this policy aided Indian industry, both domestic and foreign-owned, as they had to be creative to raise funds that were needed for the expansion of their projects. The issuing of shares to investors through offerings of the Bombay Stock Exchange led to the creation of:

> [A] culture of equity ownership in India on a large scale, because many retail investors were attracted to the opportunity of earning significant returns that were almost assured [and] the process of listing these companies on the Bombay Stock Exchange resulted in the creation of an intermediation and market infrastructure—accounting and auditing professionals, financial analysts, investment bankers and stock-brokers. (Khanna and Palepu 2004: 17)

Nevertheless, the 1960s and 1970s were characterised by a severe fiscal and balance of payment crisis, worsening agricultural crisis and in response to more limits that were set to the ownership of MNC (40 foreign–60 domestic per cent ratios), the exit of foreign capital most notably IBM and Coke Cola in 1975. Without a doubt, the exit of these companies led to the strengthening of domestic capacities and to the establishment of a number of hardware and software companies and soft-drink plants by domestic entrepreneurs.

The Political Economy of Media Ownership

The private sector

For the purposes of this study, I will specifically deal with the print sector and only tangentially with cinema and advertising that were also part of private sector media in India. With the exit of the British in 1947, British owners of newspapers sold their interests to Indian business houses. In the words of Bhaskar (2005: 20–21):

> Seth Ramakrishna Dalmia, a leading industrialist, took over the *Times of India* group, a Chennai businessman acquired *The Mail*... *The Pioneer* of Allahabad, which too was under British ownership went to another industrial house... *The Statesman's* foreign owners also pulled out. They turned their shares to a consortium of Indian industrialists, including the Tatas and the Mafatlals... Towards the end of the colonial period, G. P. Birla, a leading industrialist had obtained controlling shares in the *Hindustan Times*....Ram Nath Goenka.... picked up shares of the Madras edition of the *Free Press Journal* and used it as a launching pad to begin building a newspaper empire under the banner of the *Indian Express*.

We also see in this period the consolidation of a number of private firms with an interest in the media, telecommunications and software. The Tatas, for example, were involved in printing and publishing from 1931, consumer electronics from 1940 and information technology from 1968. In fact, Tata Consultancy Services, which is the premier software company in India today, was established in 1968 by a number of ex-IBM employees. Other family-based business groups involved in the media included the Birlas who owned the *Hindustan Times* along with a raft of vernacular publications, the Goenkas who owned the *Indian Express* along with a number of local-language based publications including the Tamil *Dinamani* and the *Andhra Prabha* and the Mammen Mappillai group in Kerala, who owned the largest circulation vernacular daily, the *Malayala Manorama*, along with other print products. There were also large press houses such as the Bennett Coleman print empire with their flag ship *Times of India* and the Calcutta-based Ananda Bazar Patrika who published the *Telegraph* along with a number of vernacular language products. Big business houses such as the Birlas definitely had an advantage over the smaller firms given their access to financial resources and political connections with the ruling Congress party but also because of the unrivalled economic power that they enjoyed. The Birlas' ownership of the *Hindustan Times* which was the largest circulation English newspaper in North India was complemented with their ownership of pulp estates, pulp-mills, press printing houses and distribution outlets. This multi-layered ownership of the entire process and product chain—from raw material to finished product to the distribution channels, gave the Birlas a competitive advantage over other firms. Monopoly interests were also perpetuated through enduring family links such as between the Goenkas and the Jains and through shared, mutually beneficial representation on the directorial boards of media houses.

The issue of monopoly press ownership surfaced periodically during this period and was discussed at length by two Press Commissions reports that were submitted in 1954 and 1982 and the Inquiry Committee on Small Newspapers. These reports were shelved although there was an occasion when the Minister for Information and Broadcasting, Mrs Nandini Satpathy, did propose the dispersal of shares owned by the proprietors of large newspapers in the hands of public trustees. S. K. Goyal and Chalapathi Rao in a report for the Second press Commission advocated the 'Public takeover of the top eight newspaper establishments because it was essential to delink the press from monopolistic media houses' (1981: 98). The Indian journalist P. Sainath, in an article in the journal Seminar, describes findings from a study on media ownership carried out by the Indian Institute of Public Administration for the Second Press Commission:

> The study found that the commercial interests of the organisations largely controlling the Indian press encompassed an incredible array of industries. Those included—to cite just a few—cement, jute, steel, shipping, aluminium, chemicals, real estate, agro-chemicals, textiles, fabrics, sugar, rubber, tea, coffee, tyres, automobiles, plantations, transport, hotels, electronics, films, trading, excise contracts, finance, machinery, paper, processed foods, gypsum mining and cola. In terms of gross circulation, the study found that over half the industry was either in the hands of big monopoly houses or had strong links with local business and industry. (Sainath 1997: 59)

The relationship between the state and the press was not exactly fraught although there were moments when the tensions were palpable, most noticeably during the lead up to and the period of the Emergency. The government's pro-Socialist leanings were reflected in anti-monopoly acts such as the Monopolies and Restrictive Trade Practices (MRTP) that together with the government's control over newsprint and in its role as a key source for advertising revenue gave it an advantage that was used to control press houses that took an anti-Congress line. The most prominent example of such control was the attempt by the government to control the Goenka-owned *Indian Express* group that, by the early 1970s, bought a quarter of all available newsprint and earned substantial advertising revenues from the state. Press regulations were selectively implemented and this was graphically illustrated during the Emergency when media belonging to pro-Congress and pro-Emergency barons such as K. K. Birla were spared the privations that other media houses had to endure. In the words of Amiya Rao and B. G. Rao (1977: x–xi):

> [E]very newspaper, every news agency had a censor sitting in its premises, red pencil in hand; he would run through every item in the next issue from the beginning to the end, advertisements, news, editorials, other articles except, perhaps, the names of the editor, printer and publisher. His red pencil was the final arbiter of what the people would be permitted to read.

Not only was an attempt made to curb the production and distribution of the *Indian Express* group, but there were attempts to forcibly make this paper an organ of the Congress party.

The public sector

Without a doubt it is the state's pre-eminent involvement in the media—radio first, followed by television—its involvement in telecommunications and computing, its position as a regulatory body, control of the public advertising purse and its capacity and willingness to regulate the private media that defines the media environment in the 1947–1985 period. The centralisation of state media and its expansion were characteristic features of the media best exemplified by the growth in radio first and then television. In 1947, there were only six broadcasting centres in the country involved in both production and broadcasting. By 1983, there were 86 such centres. During the First FYP (1952–1956), radio signals covered just 20 per cent of the population. By the end of the Second FYP (1957–1961) it covered 56 per cent and by 1985, 95 per cent of the population.

The expansion of television however was most dramatic. While television first began on an experimental basis in Delhi in 1959, the institution of a separate TV body—Doordarshan—in 1976 and its overt centralisation in the context of the crisis of the state and Congress party for the most part of the 1980s, led to its country-wide expansion. In fact in 1987, one television transmitter was installed every tenth day (Masani 1986). Radio and television functioned as the property of the Congress government to be used and abused. On occasion, notably the 1966 Report of the Committee for Broadcasting and Information media, known as the Chanda Committee report; the Verghese Committee Report on Broadcasting in India which became the foundation for the Prasar Bharati (Broadcasting Corporation of India) Bill that was debated in the Lower House (Lok Sabha) in May 1979; the Joshi Commission on Software Planning (1983); and the case for a Second Channel for TV and Radio Broadcasting forwarded by the Chief Minister of Karnataka, R. Hegde, in March 1986, issues related to autonomy, independence, de-centralisation and a federated approach based on a concurrent jurisdiction over broadcasting were debated but subsequently sidelined by successive governments in power. Even the Janata government who was in power in the immediate post-Emergency years (1977–1989) and who had pledged to reform broadcasting, failed to implement the recommendations made by the Verghese Committee. During the Emergency, All India Radio under the likes of the then-Information Minister, V. C. Shukla, became a mouthpiece for the Congress party and was systematically censored. As Page and Crawley (2001: 52) have observed, 'During the Emergency, the main purpose of radio and television was to project the personality of Mrs Gandhi and her son, Sanjay. In that two-year period, AIR broadcast nearly 50,000 items about Mrs Gandhi's "decade of achievements" and about her Twenty Point Program.'

The monopoly role played by the state in the production, distribution and regulation of broadcasting and in the setting up of the terms of consumption were the means used by the state to exert hegemonic control over its citizens. Apart from the routine propaganda that accompanied every attempt at centralising power—for instance, in the post-Blue Star environment—the government used radio first and the television as a platform for top-down consensus building. The task of re-imagining India in the post-Independent era was a fraught project for broadcasting because its key controllers were incapable of envisioning an inclusive cultural policy or leverage broadcasting to strengthen unity in diversity. One oft-cited example of what was an obvious disconnect between programming policy and listenership was the change from Lionel Fielden's approach that was broadly supportive of both 'high' and 'low' culture, to that embraced by the Minister of Information and Broadcasting, K. V. Keskar (1952–1961), who was of the opinion that film music was a corrupting influence and that radio ought to be a channel to transmit and nurture Indian classical music traditions. Keskar, however, was more than just a purist. His crusade was also directed towards validating Sanskritic classical music against what he saw as the pernicious influence of low forms of Muslim-inspired music. As David Lelyveld (1995: 57–59) has observed, 'Under partition All India Radio's major political battles had revolved around Hindu-Muslim communal disputes, especially the issue of Hindi versus Urdu versus Hindustani…under Keskar, measures were taken to assure that the "hindu" side would prevail.' Keskar was also against film music. 'The lyrics, aside from being in Urdu, were generally "erotic", and since the late 1940's there were noticeable infusions of orchestration and to some extent rhythm and melody from Western popular music, which Keskar identified with a lower state of human evolution.' This emphasis on Hindu high culture rapidly led to the migration of listenership from All India Radio to Radio Ceylon. All India Radio did recover some of its listenership after it produced programmes such as Vividh Bharathi, although it did miss an opportunity to transmit popular Indian music of the 1950s and 1960s.

This example relates to what remains an unexplored area in the context of understanding broadcasting in India and that is the class/caste composition of senior employees at AIR and Doordarshan. While broadcasting has traditionally been a domain for high caste workers—Brahmins in particular—there is little information available on the caste/class composition of broadcast employees in the post-Independent era. A recent article by Anand quotes a study conducted by Unniyal in *The Pioneer* in 1996 based on an assessment of names in the Accreditation Index of the Press Information Bureau in New Delhi:

> Of the 686 accredited correspondents listed in it, as many as 414 bore their caste surnames and of them as many as 240 turned out to be Brahmins, 70 Punjabi Khatris, 44 Kayasthas, 26 Muslims with as many Baniyas, 19 Christians, 12 Jains and 9 (Bengali) Baidyas. I checked out the caste affiliation of 47 of the remaining 232 correspondents at random. None of them turned out to be a Dalit…. (Anand 2005: 178)

By the mid-1980s, radio had become marginalised in favour of television and the beginning of soaps and serials also saw a dramatic increase in sponsorship and advertising revenues. This captive revenue stream for the state monopoly broadcaster was another reason to not decentralise or privatise broadcasting. Television advertising for the 'Ramayana' series earned Rs 23.7 million. The chief minister of Karnataka, Ramakrishan

Hegde, had, in 1986, submitted A Case for a Second Channel for TV and radio broadcasting in which he had clearly outlined the need for autonomous broadcasting at state level. In Hegde's words (1986: 49):

> A Central Government monopoly in broadcasting is not in keeping with the spirit of the Constitution. The erstwhile princely state of Mysore had its own broadcasting facility called 'Akashvani' and this did not threaten 'the unity and integrity of India….A second radio broadcasting facility is consistent with the idea of democratic decentralisation, the need for which all national leaders from Gandhiji onwards have been stressing'.

It was clear that by the mid-1980s the limits to Delhi and Hindi-centric broadcasting were questioned by regional leaders. A decade later, private cable and satellite television had begun to shape a regional identity for television in India.

The State, Media and Development

While space research began in India in 1962, perhaps the most significant state-based attempt to expand communication was the Satellite Instructional Television Experiment (SITE) that was conducted between 1975–1976. This attempt at satellite-based distance education was among the most ambitious of its kind and involved 2,330 villages in six states. While the satellite used was on loan from the US-based National Aeronautical and Space Association (NASA), the entire complex of ground-level infrastructure was created and maintained through Indian effort and the software produced locally. Much has been written about the impact of the experiment and while it certainly helped in the development of indigenous satellite technology and helped popularise television, its educational impact has been contested. In fact, as Mody has pointed out, the SITE programme was commissioned to further the political objectives of an increasingly unpopular government:

> [T]he most decisive reason was the demonstration of the political advantages of the government controlled communication system that reached villagers in the remotest corners of the country with the official line from the party in power. The daily satellite news program gave the then beleaguered prime minister…. instantaneous monopoly access to voters. In the Indian context of government-owned and operated television, direct broadcast television had proven its power to the chief political force in her time of greatest need. (Mody 1987: 156)

Another critic Murphy (1983: 106–107) has pointed out that the beneficiaries of SITE included indigenous manufactures of satellite equipment, their foreign counterparts that included NASA, Ford Aerospace, General Electric, Hughes Aircraft, Massachusetts Institute of Technology (MIT) and others, and members of the 'international community who were interested to have a general case study of educational broadcasting by satellite'. Without a doubt, SITE strengthened the indigenous space programme and its 'success' played a role in the launch of Aryabhatta in April 1975, Bhaskara 1 in June 1979, Rohini in July 1980/1981, Apple in June 1981, Bhaskara 2 in November 1981 and the INSAT series beginning with the ill-fated INSAT-1A in April 1982 to the INSAT-1B in April 1982 followed by other satellites in the INSAT series.

One of the off-shoots of the SITE project, the Kheda project, remains a testimony to what could have been achieved by the state to democratise broadcasting. Established in Kheda District, Gujarat, this was an attempt to adapt new communication technologies to the requirement and needs of small village communities. It involved the setting up of India's first terrestrial television transmitter that was used specifically to transmit local programmes. The accent was on participatory programme making, the themes were often local and on controversial subjects and for the first time systematic research was carried out on various aspects of the programme. This project, in many ways, sowed the seeds for community media, in particular, community radio. The Kheda project, rather unfortunately, was carried out in splendid isolation from the mainstream and its learnings were not allowed to influence the development and programme trajectory adopted by Doordarshan. In spite of the state's role in limiting its influence, the Kheda project remains to date the most innovative experiment in using communication for empowerment and participatory rural development.

Conclusion

What is interesting about this period is the pre-eminent role of the state in both regulating the media and using it specifically for political purposes. All attempts at making the broadcasting sector a level playing field were shelved and it took an altogether fortuitous event—the satellite broadcast of the war in the Gulf by CNN—to spark the cable revolution in India and bring about a revolution in broadcasting. What it also clearly reveals are continuities between this era and the previous era characterised by colonialism. While the state did embark on a massive national development and welfare project through its five year programmes and did achieve some important successes such as the Green Revolution and space programme, it was less successful in redistributing wealth and providing a minimum quality of life for its teeming millions.

References

Anand, S. 2005. 'Covering Caste: Visible Dalit, Invisible Brahmin', in N. Rajan (ed.), *Practising Journalism: Values, Constraints, Implications*, pp. 172–197. New Delhi, Thousand Oaks, London: Sage.

Bagchi, A., A. Ghosh and S. Dasgupta. 1985. 'Industrial Policy and the Economy', *Social Scientist*, 13(9): 3–15.

Bardhan, P. 1984. *The Political Economy of Development in India*. London: Basil Blackwell.

Bell Report. 1967. 'Indian Economic Policy and the Fourth Five Year Plan', World Bank, Washington.

Bhaskar, B. R. P. 2005. 'Flourishing Press, Floundering Craft: The Press and the Law (19–36)', in N. Rajan (ed.), *Practising Journalism: Values, Constraints, Implications*, pp. 19–36. New Delhi, Thousand Oaks, London: Sage.

Blair, H. W. 1980. 'Mrs. Gandhi's Emergency, the Indian Elections of 1977, Pluralism and Marxism: Problems with Paradigms', *Modern Asian Studies*, 14: 237–271.

Chenoy, K. M. 1985. 'Industrial Policy and Multinationals in India', *Social Scientist*, 13(3): 15–31.

Frankel, F. R. 1978. *India's Political Economy, 1947–1977*. New Jersey: Princeton University Press.

Ghosh, S. K. 1983. 'The Indian Bourgeoisie and Imperialism', *Bulletin of Concerned Asian Scholars*, 15(3): 2–16.

Golding, P. and G. Murdock. 1997. 'Introduction—Communication and Capitalism', in P. Golding and G. Murdock (eds), *The Political Economy of the Media, Vol. 1*, pp. xiii–xviii. Cheltenham, UK/Brookfreed, USA: Edward Elgar Publishing Ltd.

Goyal, S. K. and Chalapathi Rao. 1981. *Ownership and Control Structure of the Indian Press*. Report Prepared for the Second Press Commission, New Delhi.

Griffin, K. 1975. *Land Concentration and Rural Poverty*. London: Macmillan.

Hegde, Ramakrishna. 1986. 'A Case for a Second Channel for TV and Radio Broadcasting', *Seminar*, March: 319.

Ilchman, W. F. 1967. 'A Political Economy of Foreign Aid: The Case of India', *Asian Survey*, 7(10): 667–688.

Kaviraj, S. 1984. 'On the Crisis of Political Institutions in India', *Contributions to Indian Sociology*, 18(2): 223–243.

Khanna, T. and K. G. Palepu. 2004. 'The Evolution of Concentrated Ownership in India: Broad Patterns and a History of the Indian Software Industry', pp. 1–52, National Bureau of Economic Research (NBER) Working Paper Series available at: http://unpan1.un.org/intradoc/groups/public/documents/APCITY/UNPAN019738.pdf (Accessed on 23 May 2007).

Kurien, C. T. 1987. 'Planning and the Institutional Transformation of the Indian Economy', *Social Scientist*, 15(7): 3–29.

Lelyveld, D. 1995. 'Upon the Subdominant: Administering Music on All India Radio', in C. A. Breckensridge (ed.), *Consuming Modernity: Public Culture in Contemporary India*, pp. 49–65. New Delhi: Oxford University Press.

Masani, M. 1986. 'Agitating for an Alternative', *Seminar*, 319, March: 23–28.

Menscher, J. P. 1978. *Agriculture and Social Structure in Tamil Nadu*. New Delhi: Allied Publishers Pvt. Ltd.

Mody, B. 1987. 'Contextual Analysis of the Adoption of a Communications Technology: The Case of Satellites in India', *Telematics and Informatics*, 4(2): 151–158.

Murdock, G. and P. Golding. 2005. 'Culture, Communication and Political Economy', in J. Curran and M. Gurevitch (eds), *Mass Media and Society*, pp. 60–83. London: Hodder Arnold.

Murphy, B. 1983. *The World Wired Up: Unscrambling the New Communications Puzzle*. London: Comedia Publishing Group.

Page, D. and W. Crawley. 2001. *Satellites over South Asia: Broadcasting, Culture and the Public Interest*. New Delhi, Thousand Oaks, London: Sage.

Parthasarthi, A. 1988. 'Informatics for Development', *Mainstream*, 26(40): 15–20.

Rangarajan, M. 2007. 'Reviving the Congress', *Seminar*, 569: 33–36.

Rao, A. and B. G. Rao (eds). 1977. *The Press She could not Whip*. Bombay: Popular Prakashan.

Rudolph, L. I. and S. H. Rudolph. 1987. *In Pursuit of Lakshmi: The Political Economy of the Indian State*. Chicago and London: The University of Chicago Press.

Sainath, P. 1997. 'Amnesia', *Seminar*, 458, October: 58–62.

Sanyal, K. J. 1988. 'Accumulation, Poverty and State in Third World—Capital/Pre-Capital Complex', *Economic and Political Weekly*, 30 January: PE 27–PE30.

Sen, S. 1999. 'Some Aspects of State-NGO Relationships in India in the Post-Independence Era', *Development and Change*, 30(2): 327–355.

Wyatt, A. 2005. '(Re) Imagining the Indian (Inter) national Economy', *New Political Economy*, 10(2): 163–179.

4

The Political Economy of Communications in the New India: 1986 to Present

Making sense of the political economy of communication in India in the twenty-first century is challenging, not least because of the tremendous changes in the Indian mediascape wrought by deregulation, privatisation, economic liberalisation and globalisation. There is a new regime of accumulation in place. The media world in India is expanding in many directions, as globalisation, embourgeoisement and consumerism radically redefines this sector. Industries that were fledgling enterprises two decades ago such as animation and a variety of services related to what has been called 'Business Process Outsourcing' (BPO) are now an established part of the media, information and entertainment sectors in India. The state monopoly broadcasters, Doordarshan and All India Radio, which had existed as sole broadcasters in India for many decades, no longer have the unparalleled power that they had shared for decades. These state broadcasters may still have the largest audience reach in the country although urban audiences with disposable incomes and who are key to the consumer economy have migrated to advertising and subscription funded private media. That monopoly has been broken and today they exist as two important players in a context brimming with media behemoths involved in cable and satellite television, FM radio and convergent media. The formal institution of the Prasar Bharati Corporation in 1997 as the key public service broadcasting organisation in India has arguably brought some form of uniformity to Doordarshan and AIR although critics point out that the net effect has been greater commercialisation rather than public service.

Growth statistics in all media sectors in India during the last decade are impressive. A joint study by PricewaterhouseCoopers and the Federation of Indian Chambers of Commerce and Industry (FICCI) report a 17 per cent growth in the entertainment and media industry in 2007, valued at

USD 12.82 billion up from USD 10.95 billion in 2006. All sectors, with the exception of the music industry, have seen strong growth. Slow growth in this sector is attributed to piracy and to the inability of this industry to adapt to and create online alternatives for downloading music. Even the press in India, unlike the press in the West that seems to be in terminal decline, has seen tremendous growth. Delhi alone had more than 30 daily newspapers including 14 morning dailies in 2007. There were 310 cable and satellite channels in 2007 and over 350 FM radio stations in 2008. While the 2009 FICCI/PricewaterhouseCoopers study does report declines in growth across all entertainment and media sectors with the exception of internet advertising, there is an expressed optimism that the economic recession will end in 2010 followed by renewed growth in this sector. In 2009, there were 450 television channels, over 350 FM radio stations, over 6,000 newspaper and 1,000 movie releases, 80 million pay TV homes and 119 million television households. The media and entertainment sector is turning in healthy profits and it is interesting to note that the most profitable business in News Corporation's Asian portfolio is its Star India network.

However, as D'Costa (2005: 7) has observed, 'Capitalism in India must be seen for what it is, a market system that is evolving in an uneven way, geographically, sectorally, and socially.' And the media, despite all the growth statistics, are implicated in and are a part of this uneven growth, wedded to the middle and upper classes and only tangentially related to large sections of Indian society. There is great diversity in the nature of media penetration in India. While the media, for historic reasons, are ubiquitous in Tamil Nadu, that is certainly not the case in India's largest state, Uttar Pradesh.

The Changing Nature of Politics in India

We begin this chapter, as we began the chapters 2 and 3, with a brief look at the political economy of India. In terms of politics, the key features over the last two decades include the decline of single party rule, in particular that of the Congress party that was in power for most of the post-Independence period, the emergence of the Hindu nationalist Bharatiya Janata Party (BJP), the key roles played by a variety of regional parties including the Samajwadi Party (SP) and the Bahujan Samaj Party (BSP) (Uttar Pradesh), the Dravida Munnetra Kazhagam (DMK) and All India Anna Dravida

Munnetra Kazhagam (AIADMK) (Tamil Nadu), Shiv Sena (Maharashtra), Telugu Desam Party (TDP) (Andhra Pradesh) and Akali Dal (Punjab) among other local and regional parties. While the Shiv Sena is an openly chauvinist language- and local identity-based party, both the Samajwadi Party and Bahujan Samaj Party are caste-based. One of the interesting turns in Indian politics relates to the fact that the decline of the Congress which has been described as '...a broad multi-regional, multi-lingual, multi-religious and multi-caste, in short, a multi-ethnic party' (D'Souza and Sridharan 2006: 18) has been shadowed by the rise of a variety of regional, linguistic, religion and caste-based parties. In addition and just as significantly, in the light of the decline of the Congress party, is the reality of coalitional politics and coalitional governments.

This change in fortunes for the Congress party can be illustrated by the fact that while it was able to muster 70 per cent of the seats in the first Lok Sabha (Lower House) 1952–1957, it managed to get only 27.7 per cent of the seats in the 14th Lok Sabha (2004–2009) (Tumbasek 2007). While Congress did make a remarkable recovery in the 2008 elections at the expense of a number of regional parties and its traditional allies, the Communists, it is still too early to predict as to whether this is the beginning of a long-term trend leading to the renewed ascendance of the Congress party. Taken as a whole, these changes represent the relative decline of the power of the central government and the emergence of a federal system based on power sharing. There has been a resolute vernacularisation of politics in India along with a nation-wide trend reinforcement of dynastic politics. While the Gandhis remain the premier political family in India, regionally powerful political families include that of Karunanidhi in Tamil Nadu, Lalu Prasad Yadav in Bihar, the Badals in Punjab, the Thackerays in Mumbai, Ajit Singh in Uttar Pradesh, N.T. Ramarao in Andhra Pradesh and the Sangmas in Meghalaya among other families.

These regional political families and the identity-based parties that they often represent, are primarily involved in lobbying for and accessing 'public goods' for their constituencies. Banerjee and Somanathan, in a study of the political economy of public goods in India, describe the changes in the allocation of public goods including education and health to communities between 1971 and 1991:

> The most striking difference in our estimates for the two census dates relates to gains registered by the scheduled castes relative to other groups. Higher shares of scheduled castes in 1991 are associated with more high schools, health centres, dispensaries and piped water....By contrast, Scheduled Tribes, Muslims,

> Christians and Brahmans experienced either a decline or little change in access to most goods relative to the control group. (Banerjee and Somanathan 2006)

While there has been some decline in the fortunes of Brahmins in India, relative to their demographics, they continue to play a powerful role in Indian society—be it in the politics of Hindutva, in key industries such as software and in the media, confirming their continuing role in India's old and new economies. Anand (2005: 178) in a study of the caste composition of the press in India, has observed that, 'Out of the 686 accredited correspondents listed in it (Accreditation Index 1996, Press Information Bureau) as many as 454 bore their caste surnames, and of them as many as 240 turned out to be Brahmins...' Caste, in other words, remains a factor in the negotiation of upward mobility. This age-old institution has re-invented itself in the context of Hindutva and new avenues for validation in India's tryst with a global economy.

Politics, Patronage and the Media

The changing nature of politics in India is also broadly reflected in the media. Entire sections of the media—in particular the press and to a lesser extent broadcasting—have taken sides during key events that have defined the nation in modern India. These include the infamous destruction of the Babri Masjid in 1990 and issues related to affirmative action and reservations in the immediate aftermath of the release of the report by the Mandal Commission on reservations in 1989. As Gupta and Sharma (1996: 15) have observed, key English language papers including the *Times of India* and the *Indian Express* and a number of the Hindi newspapers including the *Navbharat Times, Jansatta, Punjab Kesari, Amar Ujjala* have been involved at various moments in legitimising a partisan politics, the status quo and condoning the violent politics of Hindutva.

> In many ways…the mainstream press legitimised the forces of communalism. There is a clear nexus between the two. The tendency to play up tendentious, partisan and provocative statements and to treat accusations as facts appears to be evolving into a normal pattern. The print media manages to manufacture a communal consensus on which the latitude of opinions and attitudes is quite strictly constrained. It does not simply passively and favourably report the actions and opinions of the Hindu Right; it actively contributes to the construction of certain dominant ideologies and a broader consensus about them. (See also Mehta 2006)

The DMK and Sun TV

The relationship between the regional Tamil political party the Dravida Munnetra Kazhagam (DMK) and the Sun TV network offers the most cogent example of the relationship between politics and patronage in India today. The power that accrues from synergies between the media and politics is widely recognised and parties such as the BJP and DMK have made substantial investments in the media. The DMK, of course, has had a close relationship with the film industry ever since its formation in the 1950s and successive chief ministers, including the incumbent, have been associated with this industry. The DMK has been backed by the Sun TV network, one of the largest media houses in the country. This network was established by the Maran family, who are closely related to the present Chief Minister of the state, M. Karunanidhi. Set up as a fledgling concern in 1993, it is one of the largest multimedia concerns in the country today. The former Union Communications Minister in the United Progressive Alliance (UPA) government was the urbane Dayanidhi Maran, during whose tenure the Sun network vastly expanded its operations in a range of media sectors. He has been accused of giving preferential treatment to this network over its rivals and it is widely recognised that the story and fortunes of the Sun network is closely connected to patronage and politics. This network is headquartered within the precincts of the DMK's offices. The Sun network has emerged as the dominant media corporation in South India, with substantive interests in cable and satellite television, a strong monopoly position as a multi-system operator (MSO) involved in distributing satellite signals to thousands of cable operators in Tamil Nadu, a major player in FM radio and with substantive interests in the press including the Tamil daily *Dinakaran*. Sashi Menon, the ex-CEO of Asianet, describes the power of this media behemoth:

> With all round penetration of cable television around sixty per cent of the state, the dominant control by the family of one political group and another large business house effectively meant that they determined the channels that will be distributed and, further, decided which of them will be on prime band and which on the lesser band. The fate of a new channel, even if in Tamil, depended on the whim and fancy of a couple of such multi-system operators...Often new channels seeking distribution were required to pay high carriage costs. Fees down the cable chain, including what must be paid by the last mile cable operator and by the subscriber were stipulated by the MSO. (Menon 2006: 46; see also Sen 1998)

When he was the Union Minister of Telecommunications, Dayanidhi Maran was accused of using his political clout to force the Tatas to give Sun TV a stake in their Tata-Sky DTH venture (*The Hindu Online* 2006). In the recent past, there had been a falling out and rapproachement between the Maran family and the DMK supremo Karunanidhi, who had disinvested his family's holdings in the Sun network and championed the rival Kalaignar TV, Arasu Cable Corporation and Royal Cable Vision. This disinvestment did affect the stock ratings of the Sun network although it is recognised that the network's support is necessary to the electoral fortunes of the DMK. The fact that the larger family is now on talking terms also means that the DMK has the political support of two media networks making it a formidable power in a state that has had a long tryst between politics and the media.

In neighbouring Andhra Pradesh (AP) too, the links between the media and politics are extraordinarily strong. Ramoji Rao, who owns the largest circulation Telugu newspaper *Eenadu*, 12 TV channels, film production including the Ramoji Film City and is involved in manufacturing, finance companies and real estate, has played a key role in supporting the Telugu Desam Party, currently in opposition. The present government in AP, which is Congress based, has been involved in trying to investigate the business deals of the Ramoji Rao group of companies—investigations that predictably have been interpreted as a witch-hunt by the media that belong to this group of companies. As B. P. Sanjay has observed in an article in the online news service, India Together, on government raids on Ramoji's Margadarsi Financers and the freedom of expression argument espoused by their flagship newspaper *Eenadu*:

> The relationship between Freedom of the Press and the capitalist order is problematic especially in the context of the economics of media industry where both cross-media and vertical integration practices prevail. In cases where the interest of the media baron could ostensibly conflict with that of the public and their resources how relevant is the threat to freedom of expression argument... Seen in the light of the raids on the chit fund company, the media's claim to transcend conflict of interest dynamics and posit a public interest dimension is once again under scrutiny. But when political and business interests converge to operate media enterprises, the pretence of public interest is exposed...The poor's right to know is always added as a defence to fight what apparently are the right of wrong practices of a company that is owned by a media baron. (Sanjay 2007)

The relationship between politics, patronage and the media in India varies from state to state. In Kerala, for example, the key political parties, including the Communists and the Congress have traditionally owned and operated media outlets that have been used to further their particular political interests. Kairali TV, We TV and People are channels owned by the CPI (M) (Communist Party of India, Marxist), while Congress owns Jai Hind. However, the relationship between television and politics is not a given and the most interesting example of a politics without television comes from India's most populous state Uttar Pradesh which also ranks among its most backward. Over the last two decades, the rise of the Dalit-based Bahujan Samaj Party and its leader Mayawati has had little to do with the media. This is not surprising given that the media industry in India has traditionally been associated with higher caste interests. These leanings are most graphically illustrated whenever there are anti-reservation stirs in the country when the media generally tends to be anti-reservation rather than pro. Mayawati too, for the most part, has not been covered in a balanced manner. While her foibles have been graphically reported, her achievements have not. Dalit concerns have invariably been under-reported or mis-reported. Given the largely low literacy rates and higher incidence of poverty among Dalits, along with low penetration of television, the BSP has instead focussed on a counter-hegemonic strategy that involves the manufacture of Dalit cultural and political identities around key folk heroes such as the tribal woman rebel Jhalkaribai and the Bhangi caste rebel Mahaviridevi who were both involved in the 1857 mutiny against the British (Loynd 2008). While the BSP does have the support of Dalit newspapers, the fact that it has been extraordinarily successful without the aid of television does suggest that the relationship between television and politics in India is not necessarily cut from the same cloth. As Maxine Loynd (2008: 81–82) has observed:

> The BSP have found success by bypassing the mainstream media and communicating directly with its Dalit and MBC constituency. In doing so it has disengaged from the mainstream media and instead focussed on the cultural messages, symbols and actions familiar to Dalit communities. It has taken these Dalit myths and icons and wrapped around them symbols of equality, self-respect and a rejection of the stigma to empower Dalits and build political support for the party.

The ruling Congress party too has used its power to grant itself special media privileges. In 2005, the Minister of Information and Broadcasting proposed the establishment of an FM radio station in Rae Bareli (Sonia Gandhi's constituency) that would also serve Amethi (Rahul Gandhi's constituency). As Raman (2005: 20) notes, '...the funding for this FM radio station comes from diverting resources from four projects—Digital Satellite News Gathering Scheme (DSNGS), uplinking new state capitals, upgradation of existing satellite uplinking and networking of Vividh Bharati' (Vividh Bharati is the money-spinning commercial arm of the AIR that contributed 23 per cent of AIR's revenues in 2004). Expenses for the transmission tower will be defrayed out of savings from the Tenth and Eleventh Five Year Plans. Such blatant politically-inspired apportionings and appropriations of the media reflect the fact that the state continues to exert significant power in the making of the media landscape in contemporary India.

The BJP, the most media-savvy of the political parties in India, has close links with a number of media institutions and has even been involved in setting up the Makhanlal Chaturvedi National University of Journalism and Communication University in Bhopal. In fact, of all the political parties, it is the BJP that has orchestrated and calibrated media use in the making of Hindu nationalism a pan-Indian project. In hindsight, a key reason for the ascendance of the Hindu Right in India and their allies was their understanding and use of communications—traditional, mass media and the new media. The BJP had a well-thought out media strategy. Diaspora supporters of the BJP have contributed to the media policy and communication strategy of the Hindu Right. In the context of media liberalisation—in particular, the satellite and cable revolution in India—the BJP and its allies have positioned themselves to take advantage of this struggle to win the hearts and minds of middle-class Indian voters through fair means and foul. In parts of Mumbai, for instance, the Shiv Sena, an ally of the BJP, controls large sectors of the cable industry (Anandan 2000). The media has been used to communicate an essential, centralised version of Hinduism, with Lord Rama as its key deity—a departure from traditional Hinduism with its typically de-centralised structure and mosaic of deities and belief systems. In the early 1990s, as a part of their electoral strategy, the BJP embarked on a series of highly symbolic, motorised pilgrimages (*Rath Yatras*) to key centres of Hindu pilgrimage located mainly in North and Central India. These pilgrimages were meticulously choreographed to coincide with Hindu religious festivals. These spectacles were an essential aspect of the cultural politics of the Hindu Right. These highly symbolised and mediated events bolstered the fortunes of right-wing politicians and their politics in India. The motorised chariots were decorated with Hindu symbols (Davis 1996), fiery anti-minority, in particular anti-Muslim speeches were given by hard-line leaders of the Hindu Right during the journeys, cassette tapes of these speeches were freely distributed along the way, anti-Muslim rumours made their rounds and the Hindi language press in Northern India actively acted as foot soldiers for the ascendant Hindu Right. In fact, many of the key Hindi-language newspapers actively supported the destruction of the Babri Masjid mosque in Ayodhya and journalists were seen distributing sweets after that tragic event (Nandy et al. 1995). These anti-minority tirades led to numerous small scale pogroms against minority communities in Central and North India.

Arvind Rajagopal's (2001) Politics after Television offers the most cogent explanations for the role of the media and the rise of Hindu nationalism. Given the synergies between the media and politics, there are examples of conflicts of interest between politics and the media in all states in India. These include political favouritism related to the allocation of cellular phone licensing, the awarding of DTH platforms and, last but not least, the allocation of real estate to this sector.

Financing the Media and IT: Real Estate

The Indian media sector, unlike in the past, now attracts capital from multiple sources. Traditionally, the Indian film industry had a reputation for being bankrolled with money from dubious sources—tax evaders, smugglers and by others in the underground economy in Mumbai, Dubai and other places (Pendakur 2003: 51–56). While the Indian government has tried to regulate what was hitherto an unregulated industry, film financing remains a grey area and is prone to investments that cannot be made elsewhere. As Padmaja Shaw observes of the film industry in Andhra Pradesh, it is controlled by five oligopolistic families:

> The industry is known to be a high risk, high return industry, which absorbs a good deal of the resources from the black economy of the liquor industry, real estate, finance companies thriving in the state. This economic power is used to control political power through direct participation or through proxy control. It was as late as 2000 that the government of India gave the film industry the status of an industry...opening up the possibility of financing films through legitimate means. However, the Telugu film industry continues as an oligopoly.... (Shaw 2008: 6)

India's first dedicated real estate television channel was launched in June 2007 by the real estate Alliance Group. What is perhaps also of concern is that other media sectors, as for instance, FM radio is now flush with funds from a range of sources including real estate. The Hathway

Empire that is involved in publications (*Outlook*, *Intelligent Investor*, *Outlook Traveller*) and cable (Hathway Cable, Datacom and Asianet Satellite Communications) and FM radio, are owned by the Rahejas who are primarily involved in real estate and own more than 14 companies including H and R Johnson, Exide and Prism cement (Kohli 2002). Similarly the Kerala-based Muthoot group, a conglomerate involved in finance, healthcare, education, hospitality and real estate are involved in FM radio. One of India's leading broadcast companies, Zee TV is part of a large network that includes India's leading lottery venture—Playwin—entertainment, packaging and real estate.

Land allotments to the IT sector has not been without controversy. Issues related to real estate and the IT was graphically illustrated by the rise and fall of an iconic software company—Satyam Computers—in late 2008. Its owners, the Raju brothers, were deeply involved in real estate and infrastructure projects. The tens of thousands of acres owned by the Rajus, the owners of Satyam Computers, via their real estate business Maytas Properties, is currently being investigated by the Government of India—a direct consequence of the revenue scam that affected Satyam Computers in early 2009. As Venkateshwarlu (2009) has observed:

> It remains a mystery how Raju managed to acquire 6,800 acres of land, with preliminary reports suggesting *benami* (assumed names) purchases or the floating of a number of companies to circumvent laws...revenue officials are looking at reports that he had bought up large chunks of lands originally assigned by the government to the Scheduled Castes and Scheduled Tribes, some in connivance with a local Congress leader in Ranga Reddy district neighbouring Hyderabad.

A key issue in India is state-sponsored evictions of poor farmers from agricultural land and the conversion of these lands into free trade zones, IT hubs and media centres. The Indian activist-lawyer Lawrence Liang, following a visit to the Infosys Head Quarters in Bengaluru, describes it thus:

> The demands for land by the IT sector are huge, given the requirements of large campus-like spaces. These spaces are built like large US college campuses with in-house malls, mini golf courses, swimming pools, gyms, air conditioned work spaces and well landscaped gardens to provide a comfortable work and play environment for the software engineers, the vast labour pool of the information city. The best example of this is of course the pride and joy of Bangalore, Infosys.... While there, do walk around the picture postcard lawns, and if you do have a chance to chat with the *malis* (gardeners) who take care of the lawns, you

> may be a little surprised to find that these gardeners are often the farmers whose lands had been acquired for the IT city. The founder of Infosys had guaranteed all of them employment in exchange for their land, but unfortunately unlike the other employees at Infosys, these upgraded employees do not benefit from the wealth generating Employee Stock Options Scheme.[1]

The CEO of Infosys, the largest software exporter in India, Narayana Murthy, has been involved in acquiring more than 1,500 acres in Mysore, Mangalore and Bengaluru for Infosys projects including staff accommodation during the tenure of the Congress Chief Minister, S. M. Krishna in Karnataka. Srinivasaraju (2005: 51), writing in the magazine *Outlook*, points out one example of such favouritism:

> The opposition put up in 2002 by Bellandur villagers, outside Bangalore, where Infosys tried to set up a campus on 100 acres of farm land, is well known. The farmers alleged that the land was undervalued—land costing between Rs 45 lakhs and a crore per acre was being sold by the Karnataka Industrial Areas Development Board (KIADB) at Rs 9 lakh per acre.

Hyper-development has disenfranchised large sections of Indians. These marginalised and internally displaced people often belong to indigenous or tribal, Dalit communities and also include poor farmers throughout India. The social activist and writer Arundhati Roy (1999: 61), in one of the best written accounts of development in contemporary India, has observed the dynamics between the exercise of power and powerlessness in India today:

> Power is fortified not just by what it destroys, but also by what it creates. Not just by what it takes, but also by what it gives. And Powerlessness is reaffirmed not just by the helplessness of those who have lost, but also by the gratitude of those who have (or *think* they have) gained.

The New Economics

A number of key events preceded the opening up of the Indian economy in the early 1990s, including, most prominently, a balance of payments crisis that led to a loan from the International Monetary Fund (IMF) amounting to USD 2.1 billion. The government's adoption of structural adjustment measures as part of its New Economic Policy led to economic liberalisation, a process that continues to unfold in India today. The major policy changes that were enforced included deregulation, disinvestment, privatisation, the lowering of tariffs and the ending of what used to be called the 'license raj', the doing away with controls, the devaluation of the rupee and its convertability. It also included the withdrawal of export subsidies and liberalisation of imports, the opening up of sectors hitherto reserved for state involvement to the private sector, the opening up to foreign investment in all sectors beginning with telecommunications but progressively enveloping all media sectors including the press to 75–100 per cent foreign equity, the opening up of agriculture, a key emphasis on exports and the progressive liberalisation of all productive sectors in line with World Trade Organisation (WTO) and General Agreement on Trade in Services (GATS)-related guidelines. This move is also reflected in the gradual withdrawal of the state from its welfare commitments under a planned economy to a *laissez-faire* approach in which state involvement in development is undergirded by the role of the private sector and civil society. All productive sectors including industry, banking and finance, agriculture, labour and the fiscal system have been exposed to reform for over two decades.

What is central to this vision of development that has been articulated by successive coalitional governments in recent years is a belief in India's key role in the global market economy, of 'India Shining' and the mythologising of its economic prowess. The imagined nation of India under the rule of the BJP included the economy as part of its national identity—a process of legitimisation that involved '... constituting nationalist ideology, establishing a basis for this new citizenship, mediating economic "truth" and engineering consent for economic practice' (Wyatt 2005: 165). The success of this economic narrative is best seen in the massive revenues earned by the software and BPO sectors and the exponential growth in these and allied sectors—from animation to acquisitions by Indian companies such as the Tatas of major global icons from car manufacturers Jaguar and Land Rover to Tetley Tea and Corus—leading to a complete turn around from the 'Hindu rate of growth' that characterised the Indian economy until the 1980s.

One can, however, argue that this growth has come at a significant price for vast groups of people in India, particularly the rural and urban poor. Patnaik (2000: 195), for instance, has observed that 'The ratio of development outlay of GDP decreased from 22.16 per cent in 1990–1991 to 18.5 per cent in 1996–1997, while that of non-development outlay remained constant.' The impact of this new economy on the poor and the divides that this economy has wrought between the rich and the poor has perhaps been most clearly articulated by the Indian journalist P. Sainath in his writings in *The Hindu* newspaper, *Frontline* magazine and award-winning book *Everybody Loves a Good Drought* (1996). His stories of farmer suicides in some of the richest states in India, chronic poverty, the death of agriculture, rampant corruption, political indifference and the immiseration of vast populations in India paint a picture of the other side of globalising India that is not consistently reported in both the national and global media. Mehta and Shepard (2006: 23), in a volume on chronic poverty in India, describe this state thus:

> It describes people (individuals, households, social groups, geographical areas, territories) who are poor for significant periods of their lives, who may pass their poverty onto their children, and for whom finding exit from poverty is difficult ... that India has more than one third of the world's chronically poor people using the international $1 day measure....

These people only merit mention in the media when they become the victims of either environmental, social or political violence.

This lop-sided growth is being contested in India by what the writer V.S. Naipaul (1992) has described as a 'million mutinies'. This uneven growth economy based on the government's New Economic Policy that came to effect in the early 1990s, is being contested not only by significant groups in civil society but most seriously by a thriving Maoist movement that is now present in most Indian states but is particularly strong in the South-East and Central India. In a recent article in the *Hindustan Times*, George (2008: 11) has observed that there have been 350 Maoist-related incidents of violence in the state of Chhattisgarh alone, along with hundreds of other incidents in Bihar, Orissa, Andhra Pradesh, Jharkhand and Maharashtra. The current Prime Minister of India, Manmohan Singh, has described the Maoist struggle as the country's number one security concern. The increasing divide between rich and poor is best illustrated by the first world salaries enjoyed by a number of those working in the IT and other allied sectors, the many enclaves of prosperity from Bengaluru in South India, to Noida in North India on the one hand, and the existence of poverty throughout India along with the increasing desperate plight of the rural poor on the other. Sooner than later the government will have to do more than just support poverty alleviation schemes such as the Minimum Needs Programme that is a flag-ship project of the present Congress-led United Progressive Alliance (UPA) government. The travel writer, William Dalrymple (2006: 20), in an article in the *New Statesman*, describes this divide in the following words:

> The grandchildren of Brahmin temple priests may be designing space rockets, but the grandchildren of untouchables are still untouchables...because of the caste system, the hyper-development of India is being driven by a tiny elite section of the population. The tension that this growing inequality will produce can only be guessed at. At the same time as Hyderabad geeks have seized large chunks of the US software writing market, farmers 50 miles to the north have been poisoning themselves in waves of debt-related mass suicides. The militantly Maoist Naxalite movement is spreading out from Bengal and Bihar into the Gangetic heartland of India.

TRAI Consultation Paper on Media Ownership, September 2008

Consultation Paper No. 13/2008 on Media Ownership (TRAI 2008) issued by the Telecom Regulatory Authority of India (TRAI) on September 23rd, 2008 is the clearest indication that issues related to media ownership continues to be of concern, at least at the level of government ministries such as the Information and Broadcasting Ministry and TRAI. The issues flagged in the report include whether or not restrictions are required in the matter of vertical and horizontal media integrations and the consolidation of market share of any medium in a given geographical area (p. 18). Their mandate is described thus in the paper, 'The reference under consideration cuts across the broadcasting sector and the issues of cross-media restrictions are to be addressed in an inclusive manner covering broadcasting services, print media and other miscellaneous ownership within the fold of telecom, information, and broadcasting' (p. 2).

While public consultation on the issue is to be lauded, it is anybody's guess as to how this response will be assessed and whose views will prevail. It is clear from the report that at the moment, the only restrictions regarding media ownership with the exception of the Cable Television Networks Act (1995) are limited provisions and clauses included in licenses given to a range of new television providers and Grant of Permission Agreements given to FM radio licensees. As the paper notes with the exception of FM radio and DTH services, there are currently no restrictions in print, cable TV, Internet Protocol TV (IPTV) and Mobile TV. These provisions and clauses are either based on 'voluntarism' (media houses voluntarily giving up on excess media stock) or retroactive, regulation-based, media-load shedding in response to any future cross-media legislations. Gopalan Ravindran, in a blog on Tamil television, has commented on the largely reactive nature of media regulation in India:

> India's media regulatory framework is a classic case of a reactive one...Media laws come into existence only after the damage to public interest has been done. India had the legislation for regulating cable television long after the cable operators had decided on the profile and rules of the cable television sector. The same (is) true for the cross media ownership of media that has taken a heavy toll on the delivery of choice, content and free media space for the audience. More than a decade after the advent of satellite television and cable television and attendant media sectors, TRAI...started circulating a position paper on the need for cross media ownership laws only in 2009. (Ravindran 2009)

The consultation paper explores three types of restrictions—cross media ownership across electronic and print media, vertical integration within particular media segments and market-share based restrictions. The papers refer to existing cross-media ownership restrictions in the UK, US, Australia, Canada and other countries, although in Section 5.9 (p. 74) it also offers observations on the benefits of media consolidation including economies of scale and scope in news gathering, access to better news management, to overseas capital, improved news gathering and editing and dissemination technologies. What is interesting about this paper are the responses received from 29 major media players including Zee TV (Mohan and Kumar 2008), Star India, Reliance, *Malayala Manorama,* Tata Sky, Bennett Coleman and Co. Ltd (BCCL 2008), FICCI and from five individuals including the media critic Sevanti Ninan (2008). For the most part, the responses from media corporations are either defensive in nature or point to the 'unworkableness' of the proposed solutions. The response from Zee TV, for example, pointedly deals with the ways in which a relatively new company in India, Viacom, that is involved in different delivery platforms including net-based TV, in partnership with local companies such as India's largest Hindi circulation print empire *Dainik Jagran*, has been able to evade the 20 per cent broadcaster cap mooted in the paper. For Zee TV (pp. 26–27), the main issue with Viacom as a competitor to its own media interests is with the problematic nature and operationalisation of Foreign Direct Investments (FDIs) in the media. For our purposes it illustrates the complicated nature of media ownership in the context of convergence and the real difficulties for regulators to lay down the law after the media horse has bolted.

> The question of FDI via multiple entities thus places overseas companies in a differential position vis-a-vis Indian companies. Viacom is a major owner

> of cable networks and the new MSO/HITS platforms are on its agenda. With the alliance between TV18 and Viacom, Post-restructuring, there are 3 listed entities—Network18, TV18 and GBN (Global Broadcasting News). Network18 is the holding company for other unlisted entities such as Studio18 (Film Production), Shop18 (Home Shopping), Setrpo (Cable Distribution) and Web18 (which has some of the popular Internet Verticals—moneycontrol.com, poweryourtrade.com, commoditiescontrol.com, ibnlive.com, tech2.com, compareindia.com, cricketnext.com, yatra.com, jobstreet.com, bigtreeticketing.com, indiaearnings.com, easymf.com—each of the mentioned site catering to respective niche audience).
>
> TV18 has 2 business channels in partnership with CNBC, CNBC-TV18 and Awaaz, while GBN (Global Broadcasting News) has an English news channel CNN-IBN, in collaboration with CNN, and a Hindi news channel in collaboration with Channel 7 (promoted by *Dainik Jagran*—India's Largest newspaper group). The group also has Newswire18 (acquired from CRISIL), announced to venture into e-broking in partnership with Centurion Bank of Punjab and started Web18 Engage, an online real estate venture.
>
> Thus, there is a linkage in terms of the control of *Dainik Jagran* as well in which Viacom FDI has played a role. The present framework therefore presents a scenario of Cross media ownerships with the involvement of FDI. (Mohan and Kumar 2008)

The *Malayala Manorama* group's response makes the point that TRAI does not have the authority to deal with the print sector and that that should be dealt with by the Press Commission of India, an organisation that incidentally is supportive of the interests of the major press groups in the country. The Bennett Coleman Group, which is currently the largest media house in India, uses the 'freedom of expression' argument to state its case for no regulation. As is stated in their response:

> The Cross-Media restriction as sought to be imposed between Press and Broadcasting would therefore amount to imposition of an unreasonable restriction on the right to Press and media to choose or seek an alternative medium and therefore is infringing the fundamental right guaranteed under Article 19 (1) (a) and is not sustainable under Article 19 (2) of the Constitution of India. (BCCL 2008: 12)

The issue of course that needs to be debated is whether the freedom of expression that is largely an individual right can be applied to large media corporations. Other responses point out that India's media market is highly fragmented, that there is media diversity, that there is a lack of empirical information on current media ownership patterns in India, that audiences use multiple platforms, that cross media restrictions would hinder employment generation and that such restrictions cannot guarantee editorial plurality. The major criticism is of course reserved for the public broadcaster, the Prasar Bharati, that is seen by the private industry as the only media monopoly in the country. The media critic Sevanti Ninan, in her response, points to the Sun TV empire as 'the only case for cross media restrictions in the country'.

The limited value of this consultation paper needs to be seen in the context of the 'unworkableness' of the proposed solutions. Voluntarism, ex-post facto legislations and retroactive sanctions directed at curbing dominant media houses are difficult to implement precisely because media houses already enjoy the benefits of being monopolists. The Reliance Anil Ambani group's Adlabs and related companies already have the advantage of vertical integration—with their involvements in production, co-production, post-production, distribution and exhibition in the film industry, major investments in digital cinema, horizontal integration including FM radio operations in 45 circles (Big 92 FM) along with involvement as a direct-to-home (DTH)—Big TV and IPTV operator/provider—not to mention, its major interests in telecommunications. Reliance also owns Zapak, India's leading games portal, and Bigadda, a social networking site, and has plans to launch 20 television channels under its broadcasting arm Big Broadcasting. These initiatives are complemented with Big Motion Pictures, Big Flicks (video on demand and DVD rental), Big Animation, Jump Games (mobile gaming) and Big Music. They are also involved in other leisure sectors including a joint venture with the Great Wheel Corporation who own intellectual property rights (IPR) to the London Eye to set up observation platforms in five Indian cities and a stake in the Mumbai-based amusement park, Esselworld. As Sevanti Ninan (2006: 3) has observed:

> Anil Ambani's trajectory as a future media moghul is to produce entertainment content, put in place a variety of distribution networks, and then leverage the synergies that can be created between the two. Make a film at Adlabs, process it there, distribute it here and abroad...show it in theatres you own, put it on your DTH platform as pay per view, play its music on your FM stations....

Adlabs film exhibition chains are both domestic and external and include more than 200 cinemas across Malaysia and East, mid-West and West Coast US. Their 2006 acquisition of the highly successful domestic television production firm Synergy Communications (producers of the Hindi version of 'Who wants to be a Millionaire') has given them another important stake in domestic television.

Emerging Media Monopolies

Provisions related to curbing media monopolies in the Broadcast Bill had been challenged by industry representatives such as the Indian Media Group (IMG) and, as a result, the government was forced to re-draft this bill. The IMG consists of key players in Indian broadcasting including Zee TV, the *Times of India*, *India Today* and *Dainik Bhaskar* along with others. Moreover, given that mid to maximum foreign direct investment is allowed today in most media including advertising, films, print with the exception of news and current affair newspapers and magazines, and almost all types of broadcasting with the exception of terrestrial television, it would be difficult to implement ex-post facto legislations given the many ramifications of such curbs for global trade. In 2009, Bennett Coleman and Co. was the largest media company in India followed by News Corporation's Star Network. In the space of less than a decade, Network 18 has emerged as one of the top players in the media in India. As Singh (2008) has observed in a story of Network 18's rapid rise to fame, 'It has emerged as the fourth largest media group along with HT Media after the Times Group with estimated revenues of Rs 4,000 crores, Star India Rs 2,500 crores and the Zee companies together clocking Rs 1,500 crores.' While Star's performance in the lucrative Hindi entertainment market needs to be seen in the context of Zee TV and the emergence of a third channel in 2008—Colors, floated by Viacom and Network 18—it would seem that this company has the potential to emerge as India's number one media company. Not only does News Corp. hold 20 per cent in the DTH venture Tata Sky, it also holds 22.2 per cent in one of India's largest cable networks Hathway Cable and Datacom. Star India is one of News Corp's most profitable ventures and 2009 figures indicate that it has done better than both its parent companies News Corp and Star Asia.

FM Radio Monopolies

Already, a handful of big business houses, which have extensive non-media and media interests, have cornered the FM radio market. This includes Reliance Adlabs, who have been granted licences for 45 stations, the Sun Network that has been granted 41 licences, ENIL—32 stations and Music Broadcast Pvt. Ltd (MBPL) 20 stations. The document *List of FM Channels Allocated in Phase II*,[2] which is available online, reveals the extent to which established industry and media houses have been granted FM licences throughout the country. Perhaps this was to be expected since the licence fee range between USD 625,000 for key metro cities and USD 104,166 for the semi-urban 'D category Centres' effectively ruled out small-scale local entrepreneurs from applying for these licences. While point 7.1 of the policy document on FM radio broadcasting stipulates that 'No entity shall hold permission for more than 15% of all channels allocated in the country' (2005) it is more or less silent on cross-media ownership although it does mention (point. 9) expected conformity to the government's guidelines on cross-media ownership as and when it comes into force. Muralidharan, writing in *HimalAsia*, refers to the politics of governmental control in the matter of the allocation of radio spectrum:

> While reluctant to yield their monopoly over the airwaves to any form of community control, New Delhi policymakers showed a greater inclination to treat their trusteeship over the spectrum as a resource to be milked for the greatest profit. Under the tendering principles drawn up, allocations were to be made on the strength of the entry fee offered by each bidder. Moreover, a share of annual revenue would be paid by the operator as a fee for the use of the broadcast spectrum. Advertisements would be the principal revenue source, but there would be no limit imposed on the quantum of advertising that each broadcaster could carry. (Muralidharan 2007)

In contrast to this openess the community radio sector is bound by the strictest of rules regarding raising advertising based revenues.

While the un-shackling of the 'license raj' was perhaps justified in the context of an emergent, market-oriented economy, the rampant deregulation and privatisation of the media and information sectors that began in the mid-1990s seems to have come full circle. From a mixed media regime characterised by regulation to one characterised by little or no regulation is quite an extraordinary turn around and it would seem that the only way forward is for more, rather than less regulation. If there is a single lesson that can be learned from the current global crisis of capitalism, it is that markets can no longer be considered self-regulating mechanisms. It is also the clearest indication that the involvement of civil society in media governance is an absolute must given that both the state and the market have been unable to maintain the health of mediated public spheres.

The theorising of a current political economy of communications in India needs to be seen against the framework of economic liberalisation and the rule of the market, continuing mergers and alliances, cross-sectoral technological convergence as well as institutional convergences between key political players and economic interests. This theorising is done against the background of the lack of a regulatory framework that has effectively enabled the growth of a host of domestic media czars and the closer integration of the Indian media and entertainment industries with the global market.

In spite of the fact that it is not fashionable anymore to propose the existence of media imperialism, media concentrations are a global reality and global media governance institutions such as the Internet Consortium for Assigned Names and Numbers (ICANN) act as conduits for unequal flows of power. Michael Sainsbury (2008: 11), writing in *The Australian*, points out that ICANNs tie-in to the US Department of Commerce through its Joint Project Agreement aligns a global resource too closely to companies located in the US. 'At the moment, a handful of firms dominate the sale of domain names and US companies retain a firm grip on the system.' While the spectre of foreign media ownership and its impact on national sovereignty (with the exception of debates related to foreign news ownership in print media) has receded to the background, clearly there are issues related to domestic media consolidations by media groups such as Bennett Coleman and Co. and the Sun TV group, but also the in-roads into media ownership made by industrial conglomerates in India such as the Reliance group and the Birlas. If media diversity is essential to a democracy, then a level-playing field is absolutely essential. However, the government's support to private media across all sectors as against its grudging support for the opening up of community media stands as a clear indication of its priorities.

Some Features of the Political Economy of Communications in Contemporary India

So what are some of the characteristic features of the political economy of communications in India today?

Privatisation and commercialisation of media

The most striking feature of this period as opposed to the previous period is the new role of the private sector in the entertainment and information industries along with the re-invention of the role of the state as an 'enabler' of processes conducive to the expansion of private media and information markets and the maximisation of the role of the state as a rent seeker rather than as a public service broadcast provider. In less than two decades, the private media have firmly established themselves as the driving force in India's entertainment and information sectors. And in this changed context, the role of the state is now primarily as a regulator of the media, entertainment and information industries. This new role of the state can be seen in its role in the auctioning of spectrum (Jain 2001; Prasad and Sridhar 2008), licensing of cellular phones (McDowell and Lee 2003) and FM radio, and opening up of telecom markets as much as by its role in harmonising copyright laws in line with global trade and industry requirements and providing support for the enforcement of copyright directives by private organisations such as the Business Software Alliance and the Motion Pictures Association. While the state broadcaster Doordarshan remains the only terrestrial television provider with a country-wide reach, it has, for all practical purposes, reneged on its public service agenda and now competes with a number of television platforms, most notably cable and satellite channels. Nevertheless, it remains one of the largest television networks in the world with 31 channels, 66 studios and 1,413 transmitters and access to 128 million households. However, with the exception of DD1, which is a major revenue earner for DD, the other channels that belong to DD do not generate major revenues. As Shukla (2009: 11) has observed, 'Of the Rs 818 crore generated in revenues in 2008–2009, Rs 367 crore was contributed by DD1. Likewise, the channel had contributed Rs 392 crore to Doordarshan's coffers in 2007–2008 when its gross revenues were Rs 893 crore.' Both DD and All India Radio have become gross revenue earners and their business models are similar to that of the private media. The state's disinvestment in public sector units including its long-distance telecommunications carrier, Videsh Sanchar Nigam Limited (VSNL), is another example of privatisation that has affected once dominant public sector firms.

> Forty seven per cent of the shares of VSNL were disinvested to institutional investors and industrial shareholders in March 1999. Of the remaining shares, the government decided that it would sell 25 per cent to a strategic partner and 1.97 per cent to employees. On 5 February 2002, Panatone Finvest, a company belonging to the Tata group purchased 25 per cent in VSNL for Rs. 14.39 billion against the reserve price of Rs. 12.18 billion.... (Dasgupta 2005: 232)

The extent of correspondence between capital and the media is best illustrated by the practice that was first started by the Times Group in 2004, of giving firms that contribute advertisements to the paper favourable coverage. An article in *The Economist* (2008: 80) refers to the possible conflict of interest in a company that has '...120 private treaties of this nature' inclusive of 'accepting payment for ads in the forms of shares in the advertiser's firm'.

Commodification

There has been an intense commodification of mediated products, information and knowledge in India. The ownership of multiple media platforms offers possibilities for re-packaging content—and the common language of the digital has facilitated synergies between different media and products and the targeting of increasingly segmented audiences. Commodification has been supported by a huge increase in advertising revenues over the last decade in India. The advertising industry in India was worth USD 4.9 billion in 2007 up from USD 4.02 billion in 2006.

A contemporary example of the commodification of culture was the attempt to commercialise and copyright Yoga sequences by the Los Angeles-based Bikram Choudhary through a number of mediated platforms. As Allison Fish (2006: 202) describes it:

> Transnational commercial yoga...is a body of essentialised forms that emphasises easily communicated aspects, primarily postures and breathing, selectively drawn from rich South Asian ideological traditions of spirituality and practice. Bikram Choudhary and the franchised purveyors of his choreographed program of 26 postures embody the ultimate commodification of yoga. In this version of practice, students become repeat consumers of a style of yoga that is controlled by a lucrative international structure under exclusive license.

The commodification of media has affected all sectors of the mediascape.

The tying-in of media products within a consumerist paradigm is best illustrated by the fact that there are currently more than 20 cable and satellite channels that exclusively mediate religion and in the process, sell a number of religious products—from evangelical books and CDs on God TV to spiritual well-being products on Aastha. Hindu channels alone include Maharishi Veda Channel, Sanskar, Aastha, Sadhna, Sanskriti and Sudharshan TV. As one report describes it, 'contrary to expectations that this genre of television would invite advertisers of products like incense and joss sticks, researchers were amazed to find branded jewellery, airlines, banks, lubricants, tyres, baby lotion and surgical equipment...' (Televisionpoint.com 2007). The Bengaluru-based Indian guru Sri Sri Ravishankar's 'Art of Living' seminars unabashedly promote health and wealth for the nouveau rich in India. Nanda (2006: 492) on the paradoxes and contradictions of India's tryst with modernity refers to:

> TV programmes selling wild, unsubstantiated health benefits of yoga and Ayurveda, delivered in a heady brew of spiritualism and Hindu nationalism. India's most popular tele-yogi, Swami Ramdev, has massed a fortune selling his Divya yoga on the TV. Interspersed with the swami's calls for awakening '*desh kaa svabhiman*' (national self-respect)...one finds totally unsubstantiated claims about the power of yogic postures, deep breathing and his own Ayurvedic concoctions for every ailment known to humankind including cancer, heart disease, diabetes....

The religious market, therefore, is not just about retailing during key events in the religious calendar of major religions like Diwali and Christmas. Not only has the traditional time-frame of these festivals been extended, as is the case with Christmas, the religious market has become part of the day to day experience of most, if not all the major religions. The commodification of the sacred does have a long history although it is in the context of contemporary capitalism that it has become a ubiquitous aspect of popular culture. While Indian calendars depicting Gods and Godesses have been a part of the religious commodity landscape in India, the hyper-commodification of the Hindu God of success, Ganesh, for example, accelerated in the late 1990s during an era in which the Indian government was supported by a coterie of Hindu nationalist organisations. Even as these religious representations continue to figure prominently in private and public acts of piety, Michelle Caswell reminds us that these representations, outside of the spatial confines and practices of lived Hinduism, run the risk of becoming empty signifiers of meaning, devoid of any spirituality:

> Images of Hindu deities are showing up in trendy boutiques on a huge variety of household objects—even nightlights—but the lunchbox is the most popular. Accoutrements, a Seattle-based wholesale distributor of the 'novelty items', lists the 'Hindu Krishna lunchbox' as its fourth biggest seller and the goddess Kali lunchbox as its fifth biggest seller, right behind the 'wiggly hula girl' and the 'nun punching puppet'. The lunchboxes, which Accoutrements first introduced to the American market in 1998, were inspired by the 'beautiful, bright, and appealing' depictions of Hindu gods on Indian posters, says Heather Conrad, the company's public relations director. (Caswell 2006; see also Thomas 2009)

News too has been commodified. Daya Thussu, in an article on the 'Murdochisation' of news in India, describes the commodification of Star News:

> Star news is leading the way with a news agenda that emphasises metropolitan concerns, with an obsessive interest in glamour, crime and celebrity culture. At the heart of this agenda is the popularisation of news by making it accessible and entertaining, thus expanding the audience base for advertisers as well as promoting synergies among Murdoch's entertainment and news operations in India. (Thussu 2007: 599)

Alliances, mergers, acquisitions and consolidations

The relaxation of its foreign direct investment policy has led to a flurry of alliances, acquisitions and mergers across all media sectors.[3] Table 4.1 indicates the current situation with respect to Foreign Direct Investment in media sectors in India.

While a number of corporate giants from the West have been involved in striking up alliances with Indian companies—Disney with UTV Software Communications Ltd, George Soros with Reliance Entertainment, NBC Universal with New Delhi Television Ltd (NDTV) and Spielberg's Dreamworks with Adlabs—or have been involved in buying up Indian media companies such as the Star Network's take over of Asianet, Indian

Table 4.1: Foreign Direct Investment (FDI) in the Media in India

Serial Number	*Segment*	*Existing limit*	*Recommendations*
1.	Teleport (Hub)	49% (FDI+FII)	74% (FDI+FII)
2.	DTH	49% (FDI+FII) FDI component not to exceed 20%.	74% (FDI+FII)
3.	Satellite Radio	No Policy as on date	74% (FDI+FII)
4.	HITS	No Policy as on date	74% (FDI+FII)
5.	Cable Network	49% (FDI+FII)	74% (FDI+FII)
6.	FM Radio	20% (FDI+FII)	49% (FDI+FII)
7.	Downlinking of TV Channels	100%	Status Quo
8.	Uplinking of TV News Channels	26% (FDI+FII)	49% (FDI+FII)
9.	Uplinking of Non News TV Channels	100%	Status Quo
10.	Mobile Television	No Policy as on date	74% (FDI+FII)

Source: TRAI Consultation Paper on Media Ownership (TRAI 2008: 16).

media firms have acquired stock abroad, as for instance, the takeover by the Times Group of Virgin Radio in the UK and its re-branding as Absolute Radio and Reliance Big Entertainment's investments in Hollywood. The Sky network acquired the Tamil channel Vijay TV, owns 26 per cent of the stake in Balaji Telefilms and has a joint venture in DTH—Tata-Sky. There have been any number of global-local strategic tie-ups in the media including Virgin Radio Asia and HT media and Reuters UK and Times Global Broadcasting. The Times Group also has a tie up with the *Asian Wall Street Journal* and the BBC. The largest media house in India, the Bennett Coleman Group that owns the *Times of India*, 'is considered to be the most vertically integrated media company with several cross media ownerships like mobile advertising under 8888, radio Mirchi, its FM radio operations, and TimesNow, Zoom TV channel, OOH—out of home advertising and also holds media distribution and networks' (Chintala 2008: 1).

Furthermore, there have been moves to both expand and consolidate by market leaders such as Reliance Big Entertainment who have made major efforts to become leading owners of cinema houses in India and have invested in film production in a number of regional languages.

> Acquisitions are expected to play a major role in the expansion of the theatre chain. Adlabs has already grown nationwide this year, from 50 screens in 13 properties in April, to 115 screens in 33 properties in December, the latest being in Meerut on December 21. It has also bought 23 screens in Delhi/NCR, UP, Punjab and Haryana. (*The Economic Times* 2007: 1)

In 2009, Adlabs owned close to 450 screens with the majority in the US, Malaysia and Mauritius. In that same year, it owned 186 screens across 83 cinema halls. Additionally, Adlabs has expanded its FM radio base and currently owns 45 licences. Another feature of the media market in India is investments by regional media companies such as the Sun Network in markets throughout India. Sun TV, for example, holds licences to 45 FM radio stations and has established stations throughout North East India, including Aizawl and Gangtok, the capitals of Mizoram and Sikkim. As the second largest private television network in India, the company also owns 20 television channels and broadcasts in four languages. As the media critic Sevanti Ninan (2007: 2) has observed:

> [One of the] feature(s) of the media consolidation witnessed in 2006 was the way the bidding for FM licenses went. Leading TV and newspaper groups bid for them acquiring licenses in places across the country, away from their traditional territories. The *Times of India*, *Dainik Jagran*, *Rajasthan Patrika* and *Sun TV* have

> all acquired a handful or more of radio licenses each. Cross media empires are growing. Big business is entering the media in DTH, the Tatas are already there, R-ADAG and Sunil Mittal of Bharti have announced their DTH ventures…The Draft Broadcasting Bill was partly aimed at containing cross media expansion, but hasn't been heard of in a while.

A number of foreign and Indian companies have invested in multiplexes, for example, Sony, and also in Bollywood including co-production and investment in studios.

Consolidation is also a factor in telecommunications that began with the 1998 sale of its cellular licence for Mumbai by the Max group to Hutchinson Whampoa. This has been followed by a number of attempts by both local and foreign companies to acquire licences, spectrum, telecommunications infrastructure and networks, customer base and brand value. Four of the six pan-Indian mobile-phone companies today include Airtel, Vodafone, Reliance and Essar Teleholdings.

Trade, Copyright and the Opening up of Indian Media

Another feature of this era is the greater influence of global media governance institutions on the domestic media sector in India. While it is in telecommunications that this accommodation has been most intense, beginning with India's accession to the WTO and involvement in the Basic Telecommunications agreement, it also includes the Indian government's progressive harmonisation of its Intellectual Property (IP) laws, including copyright, with global standards set by international IP regimes like WIPO (See Chapter 6). In spite of what can be termed far-reaching harmonisations between global and Indian IP policy, such accommodations are, by no means, complete. India is neither a signatory to WIPO's Copyright Treaty (WCT) nor to WIPO's Performances and Phonograms Treaty (WPPT). However there are continuous pressures on the government to harmonise its laws—as for instance, the recent moves to amend the Copyright Act 1957 in line with the need to 'introduce anti-circumvention provisions to protect technological protection measures (TPMs) and Digital Rights Management (DRM)' (Chowdhury 2008: 102).

Another issue that has been the focus of debate and advocacy is the consequences of the amendment of the Indian Patent Act to include software patents and the impact of this decision on the Indian software industry. Liang, Sethi and Ayengar have observed that the Indian patent office does not have the capacities, means or experience to assess software patents and this places them at a disadvantage against global firms such as IBM who aggressively patent software. As they note:

> The difficulty in reaching a policy to grant software patents and the impacts of granting these patents in the absence of a policy are indeed far reaching. In the absence of a policy which classified patents on algorithms, techniques, etc. it would take an awfully long time for the patent office to process a claim, searching the 'prior art' which makes the system inefficient and unworkable... IBM was granted a patent on the same data-compression algorithm that Unisys supposedly owned. Such an error could prove lethal for a developing company which has planned its budget meticulously and in consequence of this error would be greatly disincentivised to develop new software.[4]

Interestingly enough, the pressure to liberalise the entertainment sector that has come from private sector lobbies, such as the Motion Picture Associations of America (MPAA), and governments such as the US through its office of free trade—while largely successful—continues to be a point of contention in government circles where the media, at least periodically, is seen as a vector of national identity that needs to be protected. The recent sale of Asianet to the Star network was criticised by the Communist Party of India (Marxist) although not by the government of Kerala (See article in *Gulf Times* 2008).

When multi-lateral trade has not led to liberalisation, bi-lateral political pressure has been applied to open up specific media sectors. A number of US-based trade and policy bodies have been involved in opening up the Indian media market. These include the United States Trade Representative (USTR), the Federal Communications Commission (FCC), the International Trade Administration (ITA) and the National Telecommunications and Information Administration (NTIA). In the 1990s, Section 301 was used by the United States Trade Representative (USTR) against India, ostensibly in retaliation against India's inability to curb video piracy. There were, however, larger trade and security related motives, including the lowering of perceived high tariffs in industrial imports, the opening up of the banking and insurance sector to foreign investment, along with the immediate motive of positioning Hollywood in the Indian film market. While piracy is a reality in India, the International Intellectual Property Alliance (IIPA) has estimated the trade losses of 2002 to the US copyrights industry incurred in India in the region of USD 468.1 million covering book, cable, video, music, business software, internet, retail and entertainment software piracies (IIPA 2003). The infinitely larger prospect of earnings from a potential audience for Hollywood in the region of USD 200 million, plans to carve out 10 per cent of the Indian film market by the year 2000 and opening up the Indian film market was part of the larger game plan. An immediate goal was to pressure the Indian government to lift restrictions on annual Hollywood imports that were restricted to an annual quota of 100 films. While the Schedule of Commitments agreed to by the Indian government on trade in services dated 15 April 1994 under 2D Audio-visual Services rather blandly states that 'ii) Import of titles restricted to 100 per year'(General Agreement GATS/SC/42),[5] the government did, in less than a year in 1995, decide to increase this quota from 100 to 200 films a year to the delight of the Motion Picture Association of America (MPAA). On 29 January 2002, the Government of India, Ministry of Commerce and Industry, Department of Commerce issued a Public Notice No. 64/1997–2002 that announced the end of the quota system— '(i) Import of cinematograph feature films and other films (including film on video tape, compact video disc, laser video disc or digital video disc) shall be allowed without a licence' (Government of India 2000).

The USTR has also imposed sanctions on occasions. 'In April 1992, the President suspended duty-free privileges under the Generalised System of Preferences (GSP) for $60 million in trade from India...Benefits on certain chemicals...were withheld from India, increasing the trade for which GSP is suspended to approximately $80 million' (Office of the United States Trade Representative 1996). The USTR's actions are not only directed towards increasing film quotas, but to systematically opening this sector along with a variety of other trade-related sectors to US investments. It monitors the progress of IPR and AV related domestic legislations, exerts pressure on the government to lift control restrictions, monitors anti-free trade activities and follows through its intent to use bilateral and multilateral means to open this sector to US capital. In the case of motion pictures, the USTR is currently involved in negotiating the lifting of domestic barriers to trade including pre-censorship certification of films, the fees involved, entertainment taxes, the import of film/video publicity material and the ceiling of USD 6 million for remittances by foreign film producers for balance of payment reasons (USTR 1996; for more details, see Thomas 2003). A number of multinational media firms based in the US played a key role in advancing India's liberalisation of its telecommunication market and convergence policy. The methods used included lobbying at congressional hearings in the 1980s and 1990s on a number of issues including satellite broadcasting. Menon has also noted the part played by domestic and international consultants in advancing the cause of liberalisation:

> The Indian government avails itself of many individual domestic and international consultants on an ad hoc basis. However, the institutions that have the most influence are integrated into the government and have the most currency in mass media policy matters, namely Telecommunications Consultants India Ltd. (TCIL) and Broadcast Engineering Consultants India Ltd. (BECIL). (Menon 2005: 40)

The Media Export Industry

The Indian media sector has become a significant exporter of content. This is particularly the case in the context of the Indian film industry that has seen a vast increase in export earnings, successful competition in foreign markets such as in the UK where Bollywood extravaganzas feature in the weekly top 10 list. It is also reflected in cable and satellite channels owned wholly or part-owned by Indian companies such as Zee TV, Sun TV and Asianet. This stands in marked contrast to previous eras when the export of Bollywood was not as organised as it is today. To some extent, this change has been brought about by joint productions between Bollywood and UK and US-based companies although it is also a reflection of the vast market for such products brought about by the Indian diaspora throughout the world and the demand for and consumption of hybrid cultural products such as Indian popular music popularised through MTV and other channels. There has also been a greater salience and recognition of Indian film stars, some of whom have become global icons. What is also a defining feature of this era is the fact that there are multiple flows and influences—with new rock music genres such as Bhangra Rock developing in the West and being exported along with chicken *tikka* to India! Such synergies have undoubtedly strengthened the market for Indian entertainment goods and services. There are, however, caveats. While the software export business has certainly been the source of expanding export revenues, reliance on a single market—the US—can have its consequences, especially in the context of an economic downturn in that country. The software export market earned revenues of USD 31.3 billion in 2006–2007 and this was projected to rise to USD 40.4 billion in the 2007–2008 period. Top software export companies include Tata Consultancy Services, Infosys and Wipro Technologies along with numerous others.

India is fast becoming a hub for global film productions. There are two major sides to this development. The development of animation industries in India is yet to become a focus for academic study although it is fast emerging as a major entertainment sector. Animation companies including Toonz Animation India, Pentamedia Graphics, Maya Entertainment, UTV Toonz, Heart Entertainment, Padmalaya Telefilms, Nipuna Service Ltd, Jadoo Works and Crest Communications have been involved in producing content for clients in Hollywood including Disney, Warner Brothers and Sony. Low costs, coupled with state of the art facilities, have led to the transfer of backend operations in animations and special effects to India. The National Association of Software and Services Companies (NASSCOM report) 'Indian Gaming and Animation 2008' extols the potential in this sector:

> The animation industry in India is estimated to be at USD 460 million in 2008 and set to grow at a CAGR of 27% to reach USD 1163 million by 2012. The market has been defined as animation entertainment (USD 120 million), animation education (USD 53 million) and custom content development (USD 187 million) and multimedia/web design (USD 100 million). The education segment is projected to have the maximum growth rate at about 40% per annum. By the end of 2008, the gaming industry in India is expected to value at USD 212 million expected to reach USD 1060 million by 2012 at a CAGR of 50%. (NASSCOM 2008)

The recent alliance between Steven Spielberg's Dreamworks and Adlabs is one indication of growth in this sector although there are a number of companies that have established operations with production companies in the US and elsewhere. As a result, the domestic market for animation has also seen vast growth. Along with this development is the fact that India has become a destination for pre- and post-production processing of feature films. Skilled labour is cheaper in India although with rising labour costs in India, this is not going to remain a perpetual advantage.

Outsourcing, a major source of revenues for the Indian services industry, is not just limited to call centre operations. Today, outsourcing includes medical and legal services and even religion. A report on *BBC News Online* describes the phenomenon of religious outsourcing—for example, requests for special intercessionary prayers and special masses from Catholics in the West to the Roman Catholic Church in Kerala and similar outsourcing opportunities for other religious communities in India:

> In the Sikh community, the practice of Akhand Path, a marathon reading of the holy scripture of Guru Granth Sahib to bring luck or overcome a problem, has been a boom area. This is gruelling and highly specialised work. A 48-hour reading in a

> Western temple can cost $1,000; in India, the cost is as little as 5,000 rupees ($108). Hindu pujas, a form of prayer that varies from simple home worship to a full temple ritual, is also increasingly being outsourced. (*BBC News Online* 2004)

Labour in the Information and Cultural Industries

While economic globalisation has had a positive impact on the mobility of cultural labour, especially skilled labour, within and outside of India, policies such as deregulation and disinvestment in the public sector along with non-unionisation in the private sector has negatively affected unskilled labour in these industries. One can also include the Business Process Outsourcing (BPO) sector in the group of unskilled labour given the relatively low entry requirements for a job in this sector. There have been moves to unionise labour in the BPO which has been resisted by trade bodies such as NASSCOM. There are more than 350,000 BPO workers, many of them women, in this sector. Over the last decade, a number of concerns related to working conditions, long-working hours, sexual harassment, punitive employment deals, abrupt terminations, high attrition rates, etc. have encouraged the major trade unions including the Communist Party of India-affiliated All India Trade Union Congress (AITUC) and the Communist-led Centre for India Trade Unions (CITU) to demand the unionisation of the BPO sector. The first bi-national (US-Indian) report on the call centre industry 'Bi-National perspective on Offshore Outsourcing: A Collaboration between Indian and US labour' was released on 19 October 2006 (*Business Line* 2006a, 2006b). These initiatives have been complemented by the emergence of new forms of worker activism such as the 'e-union'—the BPO Union which was formed in July 2008. Unlike the strategies employed by mainstream unions to fight management over wages, etc., the e-union plans to, in the words of Sachdeva (2006), 'talk directly to shareholders so that it affects stock prices'. The union believes that 'the fear of a downgraded stock price will force companies to set their operations team and its people in order'. In the words of Vincent Mosco (2006: 788):

> Workers in the less developed world welcome outsourcing because it tends to make jobs available but are less supportive when, as is often the case, their jobs contain none of the regulatory protections that limit hours, set a minimum wage, and provide adequate occupational health and safety standards. The result is a flurry of new forms of workplace resistance which challenge traditional trade unions and give rise to new forms of labour organisations, as well as to new forms of global labour collaboration.

What remains to be seen is whether these new unions will collaborate with, even complement unions such as the BSNL Employees Union and other unions that represent the public telecoms system in India given their often opposed styles of contestation and radically different approaches to collective bargaining.

The situation regarding skilled media labour is a lot better. India has become a magnet for skilled domestic media workers particularly in software and animation. As Miller et al. (2005: 160) have observed, there is a shortage of skilled labour and this is a major issue for trade bodies such as NASSCOM and the Animation Producers Association of India (APAI):

> With the reconceptualisation of Indian labour as a post-production service hub, the continuing development of the graphics business has become a primary concern for technocrats and policy advocates alike. Alarmed that there were an estimated 15,000 people in digital content and only about 1,000 animators in 2000, one advocacy group suggested that India would need 300,000 professionals in the fields of animation and digital context by 2008.

Small Media in the Context of Big Media

The media sector in India not only consists of big and mid-players who dominate every media sector, it also includes a host of local entrepreneurs who are involved in cable TV, software and music production, and the press, along with a range of other activities related to the entertainment sector. Arguably, these small-scale ventures cater to the needs of clients throughout the country. The hand-written Urdu broadsheet *Musalman*, for example, founded in 1927 in Madras (now Chennai), employs three calligraphers (known as *katibs*) and has a print run of 21,000 every day. Whether or not it will survive the technological era, rising overheads and a less discriminatory audience is anyone's guess (Krishnamachari 2007). There are around 60,000 cable operators spread throughout the country. While the large multi-service operators such as Hathway and Sumangali have tried to corner this market and have succeeded to some extent in using their economic and political influence to dictate terms to the many independent cable operators, they have not entirely succeeded in cornering this market. This sector will inevitably be unable to compete with the large players. The entry of DTH and moves to consolidate this platform by groups like the Sun Network, Tata, Bharti, Reliance ADAG and Zee will inevitably impact small scale cable operators (Leahy 2007).

Another sector that will be impacted by big media is community radio that is still in its infancy. Prohibitive copyright costs and restrictive guidelines related to the transmission of copyrighted music can affect the fortunes of this sector.

Consumerism, Poverty and the Media

The media, in the space of two decades, has become the vanguard of consumerism in India. There are around 450 cable and satellite channels today, more than 50 24-hour news channels and around 200 FM radio channels. The media predominantly caters to the needs of the 'chattering middle classes'—reality television, game and quiz shows such as the Indian equivalent of 'Who wants to be a Millionaire' along with endless Bollywood derivatives—at the expense of difficult stories and issues such as poverty, exploitation and the dark sides of globalisation. While one can argue that the great Indian television revolution has fulfilled the need for consumer choice and expanded the televised public sphere, it is fuelled by a ratings game, advertisement revenue and is located at and responds to the demands of urbanity. Nalin Mehta (2008: 185), in a book on India's news channels, explains the reasons for the limited coverage of the agrarian crisis in India by referring to the urban bias of television. 'The structural problems in television's political economy, focussed exclusively on urban India, were a major reason why the problems of rural India were unlikely to be the subject of sustained and focussed news coverage.'

In April 2000, the government acknowledged that large parts of India were in the grip of a severe drought. 12 states in India were affected—in Rajasthan, 26 out of 32 districts and in Gujarat, 17 districts covering 9,421 villages. There were reports of starvation-related deaths of human beings and cattle. After more than a decade during which issues related to 'poverty' had largely been bypassed by the mainstream media in India, media audiences were presented with poverty in all its starkness. It was, as Khare (2000: 1) has pointed out, a rude awakening to an India that had been mesmerised by its growth rates and little else:

> We have been rudely jolted out of our collective reverie about economic abundance, booming stock markets, cyber revolution and venture capitalism. Just when we had thought that we had entered the New Economy's fast lane, we are suddenly being forced to come to terms with evidence of starvation, destitution and deprivation so familiar in the Old Economy.

The mainstream media had, rather conspicuously, embraced the New Economic Policy popularised by the Rajiv Gandhi government in the late 1980s with its accent on economic liberalisation, privatisation and consumerism. Content priorities had also undergone change and satellite broadcasting and the new media were responsible for a new global emphasis—life style, fashion, business, sports, entertainment and personalities at the expense of other concerns, including many that are glaringly visible from the doorsteps and windows of corporate media houses. The rural beat that lacked glamour and has always been seen as a burden by state broadcasters and journalists underwent further downgrading in the context of these new priorities and the accent on targeted viewer and readership. While there has been a quantitative increase in news readership and more pages per issue, including special consumer sections and a variety of entertainment programmes on national television, not to mention cable channels, little or no space is devoted to issues related to how the other half lives and dies in rural and urban India. In fact, one could read the national press and be lulled by the global feel to these papers. In a context characterised by such indifference, the vacuum for poverty news has been filled by statistics churned out by the government's publicity machine.

The central and state governments that had been caught off guard by the drought in the year 2000 responded with classic media management, damage limitation exercises. The cyber- and media-savvy then-Chief Minister of Andhra Pradesh, Chandrababu Naidu, predictably went on the offensive and, as one commentator has remarked:

> The media (we)re inundated with a flood of statistics at regular press conferences and Chandra Babu Naidu himself held weekly video conference sessions with his District Collectors that are open to the public and the press to watch. Government hand outs list(ed) the many 'action plans' that are in the pipeline and endless lists of the quantum of money spent under different heads of expenditure and drought relief. (Menon 2000: 132)

Not surprisingly, media reports tend to regurgitate official statistics—the number of tube wells that have been sunk, the people that have benefited from drought relief, the number who are employed in Work for Food campaigns, the amount of money that has been disbursed for drought relief, the amount of fodder that has been procured, etc. Few journalists have bothered to verify official statistics or to confirm that out of the 280,000 bore wells in Andhra Pradesh, close to 100,000 are defunct or that most of the 25,000 protected water supply schemes are non-functional. But then issues related to poverty are typically dealt with in an episodic manner, fleeting, occasional, event-centred. The Indian journalist, P. Sainath, who is one of the better known journalists who have covered poverty in India, is critical of the priorities of post-economic liberalisation journalists in India:

> We have full-time fashion correspondents, glamour correspondents and design correspondents...11 correspondents covering business in a non-financial daily in a society where less than 2 per cent of the population have investments of any kind. But in all of these beats, you do not have a single full-time correspondent covering poverty. (Sainath 2000: 22)

Very few of these reports provide information on the reasons for drought—environmental degradation, poor life support systems, the destruction of common property resources and the political economy of globalisation as it affects the hinterlands. To be fair though, there has been an increase in the number of journalists who are involved in the investigation of poverty. Having said that, it is only very occasionally that a journalist opts to investigate the larger, long-term reasons for events such as a drought or are inclined to frame poverty as a 'process' rather than as an 'event'. Those who do, paint a grim picture. Parvati Menon, reporting in *Frontline*, one of India's critical news magazines, on the effects of the drought on a little hamlet, Gairangadda, in Andhra Pradesh, has this to say on the cumulative reasons for the drought:

> The drying up of water sources, both for drinking and agriculture has led to crop losses, loss of jobs, increasing levels of indebtedness, distress sale of cattle and other assets, increase in out-migration, a sharp drop in purchasing power, which the recent hike in administered prices has added to and a growing population of the undernourished and the hungry. (Menon 2000: 130)

The world that has been fed on a diet of India on the move, Bengaluru's Silicon Valley, software exports, the number one destination for IT outsourcing projects and Cyberabad, is probably not going to hear of the many reports of the suicides of cotton farmers in Andhra Pradesh, the increased activities of the Marxist-Leninist (ML) Naxalite movement or the recent stories of farmers in this state selling their kidneys as a way of getting out of their indebtedness and poverty (Menon et al. 1997). These stories point to the fact that the real India that exists, simply cannot be wished away or changed with the right infusions of new technologies. Both Arvind Adiga's Booker prize winning book *White Tiger* (2008) and the film *Slumdog Millionaire* portray another side of globalising India that is rarely available for global consumption.

Reporting Poverty

The Indian press is diverse and there are a number of publications that cover issues related to poverty. Most of these publications are either region-specific or cater to audiences who are interested in alternative news. Such publications range from long-standing academic publications such as the *Economic and Political Weekly* and *Seminar* to (Non-governmental Organisation) NGO-based publications such as *Down to Earth*. Perhaps the most edifying and comprehensive account of public journalism committed to the coverage of local issues including poverty in India is contained in the book written by F. Naqvi (2008), *Waves in the Hinterland: The Journey of a Newspaper*. The narrative describes the stories of two publications run by women in Chitrakoot, Uttar Pradesh, the now defunct *Mahila Dakiya* and the thriving *Khabar Lahariya*. Started by a group of poor, rural, low-caste women, it has managed to break down the myths and barriers related to women in journalism and most importantly contributed to the creation of awareness among the doubly disadvantaged Dalit women who occupy the lowest rungs of society in the entire country. Naqvi describes Chitrakoot as the 'war-zone of feudal India' (p. 20) where gender-based violence is common place and caste-based atrocities are everyday. These journalists, as Kalpana Sharma (2008) describes them:

> [H]ave struggled to understand politics, economics, history, have trudged hundreds of kilometres in their districts to see for themselves what is happening on the ground, have learned through mistakes how to double check all the facts before committing to print—in other words, everything that a journalist must learn. The result of all this is evident in the confidence in these women journalists. When we met them in Mumbai, they spoke of the different stories that they investigated, of how they decide each fortnight which story should come on page one, of how district reporters from major Hindi newspapers initially ignored them but now try to steal their information without giving them the credit, of how they have learned to hold their own at press conferences, and why today even district officials, who did not earlier give them the time of day, are willing to speak to them on the phone.

While *Khabar Lahariya* has definite feminist objectives, it is also read by men and has crucially contributed to the empowerment of poor communities and, in particular, women.

> While most local papers continue to portray women either as pin-up girls or, at best, as sorry subjects of the latest sensational rape story, KL is about women and human rights. While mainstream Sankritised Hindi is considered the language

> of the educated and powerful, it chooses to write in a dialect. It writes for people with low levels of literacy when the rest of the world writes for the literate few. Unlike most media products, which even as they go regional and local, continue to cater to a target audience with purchasing power, KL writes specifically for the poorest of the poor...while most publications are written by 'others' for a target audience, KL is written by the target audience itself... (p. 14)

The most important impact of KL is that it has contributed to the creation of 'interpretive communities' within Dalit, Kol, Muslim and lower-caste/tribal households—communities that are habitually ignored and not recognised as people who contribute to the life of the nation. KL has empowered these communities, provided education and created awareness on issues such as governance, transparency, accountability and citizenship. In turn, local exercises of power by empowered communities have led to the recognition of the worth of the narratives that define locality. There has also been recognition of individual identities. As it is noted on the website run by Nirantar,[6] the organisation that produces KL:

> [A]ll the members of the team have become reflective about their gender, class and class identities, and the way in which this moulds their lives and work. Take for example Kavita, who was married at 14. Inspite of much resistance to her studying, and financial constraints, she studied at a residential school and completed her education. After almost ten years of being in a marriage where she had no support or respect, she was able to make the decision to leave and live independently. Shanti, another senior member of the team, is from the Kol community, a scheduled tribe. She had had no access to education as a child, and began to study in her mid-thirties. This had a huge impact on her life: it gave her a confidence she never had before, and allowed her to take up a job, become informed and articulate and give her a mobility that she had never experienced. (Thomas 2010)

Regulation

In the context of this emerging media scenario, regulation has become soft-touch and the grand plan for a single regulatory agency in the context of convergence—such as Office of Communications (OFCOM) in the UK—has not materialised because of continuing turf battles between the Ministry of Information (MOI) and TRAI. The proposed Communications Convergence Bill (2001) was allowed to lapse. The proposed Broadcasting Services Regulation Bill (2007) remains in abeyance—a fate that previous media bills in India have endured. This bill also proposed the establishing of Broadcast Regulatory Authority of India along the lines of TRAI. The following description of the Bill's objectives needs to be seen in the light of its impossible achievability:

> The proposed Broadcasting Services Regulation Bill seeks to achieve the following:[7]
>
> (i) To provide legislative sanction retroactively to Government guidelines on various regulatory aspects such as television channels' Uplinking/Down linking, private FM Radio and Community Radio, DTH, Teleport, etc.
> (ii) To set up a new Broadcasting Regulatory Authority of India and delegate the regulatory functions presently being performed by the Ministry of I&B to this new authority.
> (iii) To incorporate the provisions of the existing Cable Television Networks Regulation Act in the new legislation through appropriate repeal and savings clauses and provide for licensing of cable operators.
> (iv) To make enabling provisions on the following:-
>
> (a) Cross media ownership and restrictions on accumulation of interests to provide for competition and plurality of views.
> (b) Minimum domestically sourced content in foreign channels to promote indigenous media/entertainment industry, particularly in the field of animation and gaming, etc.
> (c) Minimum obligations on all channels for public service broadcasting in their programme and advertising content.

While this Bill has been described both by civil society (Joseph 2006) and the market (Asia-Pacific Broadcasting 2006) as flawed, what needs to be highlighted once again is the near impossibility of implementing retroactive sanctions against economic interests that enjoy the backing of dominant politics in India.

Conclusion

The previous three chapters have attempted to describe the changing political economy of communications in India in colonial, post-Independent and market-oriented, globalising twenty-first century India. While the media in colonial India was characterised by the strong hand of India's imperial masters, the state continued to play a pre-eminent role either by virtue of ownership or as media regulator in post-Independent India. Broadcasting was a state monopoly during post-Independent India. That situation has changed and while the role of the state as a rent-seeker and regulator continues to define the media in India today, state media in India is one arm of the mediascape in globalising India. Graham Murdock's (2004: 29) observations on the nature of participation in this new economy are pertinent. He makes the following points: that in 'marketised economies...access to communicative resources is increasingly mediated through the price system', that 'command over disposable income' has become 'more or less important in regulating choice' and that 'economic location remains the prime determinant of access to the range of social and cultural resources required for chosen self-use'.

India's many and varied cultural industries, while part of an ever-expanding domestic market, are also intricately tied into global cultural industries. While this relationship has led to an exponential growth in export revenues earned through outsourcing, animation and software, one can argue that the price for such integration is the country's capitulation to terms such as in intellectual property set by media governance institutions and global cultural industries. Will these terms hinder or progress India's cultural and informational futures? In the context of an unfolding global recession, will the logic of placing all eggs in one basket—India's primarily US-focussed software export business—have to be reassessed? Will 'differentiated cultural consumption across social sectors constrict access to common experience and thus thwart the shared interrogation of cultural symbols which is at the core of a social and political order' (Golding 2000: 180)? Will a robust software industry become a reality or will patent and copyright restrictions and unequal relationships restrict the potential of this sector? Will the Indian software economy become known for its innovation and creativity or will it be merely recognised for its role in back-end operations such as in Business Process Outsourcing (BPO)? It is clear that there are both winners and losers in globalising India. Will the many small scale media ventures such as the *Musalman* in Chennai survive changing circumstances and big media? And will a level media playing field be forced by the hands of people involved in the 'million mutinies' in India? Will there be attempts by the government, in the light of the scandal at Satyam computers, to scrutinise relationships between the media and real estate? And will community radio be given its rightful space in twenty-first century India? And what role will civil society play in creating genuine spaces for diverse media, varied content and multiple spaces for celebrating another India?

Notes

1. Liang, L. 'The Other Information City'. Available at http://www.t0.or.at/wio/downloads/india/liang.pdf (Accessed on 12 November 2008).
2. http://www.mib.nic.in/writereaddata%5Chtml_en_files%5Cfm/CityWiselist.pdf (Accessed on 14 April 2010).
3. Mergers and Acquisitions (M&A) in Indian Telecom Industry: A Study (1–15), *The Chartered Accountant*, December 2006. Available at http://icai.org/resource_file/9846927-941.pdf (Accessed on 4 November 2008).
4. Liang, L., A. Sethi and P. Iyengar. Briefing note on the impact of software patents on the software industry in India. Available at http://www.sarai.net/research/knowledge-culture/critical-public-legal-resources/whysoftwarepatentsareharmful.pdf (Accessed on 10 November 2008).
5. India—Schedule of Specific Commitments, General Agreement GATS/SC/42 15 April 1994 on Trade in Services (94–1040). Available at http://docsonline.wto.org/GEN_viewerwindow.asp? (Accessed on 12 May 2008).
6. Nirantar. Available at http://www.nirantar.net/khabar_impact.htm (Accessed on 15 May 2009).
7. Policy Guidelines for Setting up Community Radio Stations in India. Available at http://mib.nic.in/informationb/CODES/CRBGUIDELINES041206.doc (Accessed on 24 May 2009).

References

Anand, S. 2005. 'Covering Caste: Visible Dalit, Invisible Brahmin', in N. Rajan (ed.), *Practicing Journalism: Values, Constraints, Implications*, pp. 172–197. New Delhi, Thousand Oaks, London: Sage.

Anandan, S. 2000. 'A Different Television War', *Outlook*, 23 May: 1–3.

Asia-Pacific Broadcasting (APB). 2006. 'Dismay Greeted New Indian Broadcast Bill'. Available at http://www.apb-news.com/index.php?option=com_magazine&func=show_article&id=34&Itemid=50 (Accessed on 28 October 2008).

Banerjee, A. and R. Somanathan. 2006. 'The Political-Economy of Public Goods: Some Evidence from India'. Available at http://econ-www.mit.edu/files/525 (Accessed on 11 September 2009).

BBC News Online. 2004. 'Outsourcing gets Religion in India'. *BBC News Online*, International Version, 22 June. Available at http://news.bbc.co.uk/2/hi/business/3829161.stm (Accessed on 12 November 2008).

BCCL. 2008. 'Response to the Consultation Paper on Media Ownership, 2008', Bennett, Coleman & Co, Ltd. (BCCL). Available at http://www.trai.gov.in/WriteReadData/trai/upload/ConsultationPapers/155/BCCL.pdf (Accessed on 24 September 2009).

Business Line. 2006a. 'BPO Employees Can Form Unions', *Business Line*, 13 December. Available at http://www.business-standard.com/india/storypage.php?tp=on&autono=18589 (Accessed on 4 November 2008).

Business Line. 2006b. 'Unionise Call Centre Employees', *Hindu Business Line*, 20 October. Available at http://www.thehindubusinessline.com/2006/10/20/stories/2006102002160100.htm (Accessed on 5 November 2008).

Caswell, M. 2006. 'The God Commodity', *Beliefnet*. Available at http://www.beliefnet.com/story/8/story_892_1.html (Accessed on 23 June 2008).

Chintala, M. 2008. 'Cross Media Companies are on the Rise'. Available at http://www.indianmba.com/Faculty_Column/FC711/fc711.html (Accessed on 4 November 2008).

Chowdhury, A. R. 2008. 'The Future of Copyright in India', *Journal of Intellectual Property Law and Practice*, 3(2), Consultation Paper on the Proposed Draft of Broadcasting Services Regulation Bill, 102–114. Available at http://mib.nic.in/informationb/policy/ConsultationPapeRegulation%20Bill.htm (Accessed on 29 October 2008).

Dalrymple, W. 2006. 'India: Introduction' in 'A New Sort of Superpower', *New Statesman*, Blackfriars, London, 30 January, p. 20.

Dasgupta, B. 2005. *Globalisation: India's Adjustment Experience*. New Delhi, Thousand Oaks, London: Sage.

Davis, R.H. 1996. 'The Iconography of Rama's Chariot', in D. Ludden (ed.), *Making India Hindu: Religion, Community and the Politics of Democracy in India*, pp. 27–54. New Delhi: Oxford University Press.

D'Costa, A. P. 2005. *The Long March to Capitalism: Embourgeoisement, Internationalisation and Industrial Transformation in India*. Basingstoke, New York: Palgrave Macmillan.

D'Souza, P. R. and E. Sridharan (eds). 2006. *India's Political Parties: Readings in Indian Government and Politics*. New Delhi: Sage.

Fish, A. 2006. 'The Commodification and Exchange of Knowledge in the case of Transnational Commercial Yoga', *International Journal of Cultural Property*, 13(2): 189–206.

George, V. K. 2008. 'Red Alert', *Hindustan Times*, 3 November, p. 11.

Golding, P. 2000. 'Forthcoming Features: Information and Communication Technologies and the Sociology of the Future', *Sociology*, 34 (1): 165–184.

Government of India. 2000. Ministry of Commerce and Industry Department of Commerce, Public Notice No. 64 /1997-2002, New Delhi: 29th January, 2002. Available at http://dgftcom.nic.in/exim/2000/pn/pn01/pn6401.htm (Accessed on 27 March 2008).

Gulf Times. 2008. 'Star TV to take Over Asianet's Entertainment Channels', *Gulf Times*, 14 October. Available at http://www.gulf-times.com/site/topics/article.asp?cu_no=2&item_no=247899&version=1&template_id=40&parent_id=22 (Accessed on 10 November 2008).

Gupta, C. and M. Sharma. 1996. 'Communal Constructions: Media Reality vs Real Reality', *Race and Class*, 38(1): 1–20.

International Intellectual Property Alliance. 'IIPA 2003 Special 301 Report India', Special Report 301. Available online at www.iipa.com (Accessed on 11 May 2008).

Jain, R. S. 2001. 'Spectrum Auctions in India: Lessons from Experience', *Telecommunications Policy*, 25(10): 671–688.

Joseph, A. 2006. 'The Broadcast Bill and the Public Interest', *The Hindu Online*, 31 July. Available at http://www.hinduonnet.com/2006/07/31/stories/2006073100401000.htm (Accessed on 29 October 2008).

Khare, H. 2000. 'Wanted, Sensitivity', *The Hindu*, Chennai, 18 May.

Kohli, V. 2002. 'A Cable and Ink Show', *Businessworld*, 22 July: 38–39.

Krishnamachari, S. 2007. 'Newspaper Nurtures Art', *The Hindu Online*, 2 November. Available at http://www.hinduonnet.com/thehindu/fr/2007/11/02/stories/2007110250930700.htm (Accessed on 10 November 2008).

Leahy, J. 2007. 'India: Crunch Time for Cablewallahs after India TV Shake-up', 16 August, Economist Intelligence Unit. Available at http://globaltechforum.eiu.com/index.asp?layout=rich_story&doc_id=11226&title=India%3A+Crunch+time+for+cable+wallahs+after+India+TV+shake-up&channelid=4&categoryid=30 (Accessed on 10 November 2008).

Loynd, M. 2008. 'Politics Without Television: The Bahujan Samaj Party and the Dalit Counter—Public Sphere', in N. Mehta (ed.), *Television in India: Satellites, Politics and Cultural Change*, pp. 62–86. Abingdon/New York: Routledge.

McDowell, S. D. and J. Lee. 2003. 'India's Experiments in Mobile Licensing', *Telecommunications Policy*, 27(5): 371–382.

Mehta, S. 2006. 'Modi and the Camera: The Politics of Television in the 2002 Gujarat Riots', *South Asia: Journal of South Asian Studies*, 29(3): 395–414.

Mehta, N. 2008. *India on Television: How Satellite News Channels Have Changed the Way We Think and Act.* New Delhi: HarperCollins Publishers India/India Today Group.

Mehta, A. K. and A. Shepard (eds). 2006. *Chronic Poverty and Development Policy in India.* New Delhi, Thousand Oaks, London: Sage.

Menon, P. 2000. 'Drought and Delayed Relief', *Frontline*, 26 May: 130–133.

Menon P., A. Krishnakumar, V. Sridhar, R. Sharma and L. Bavadam. 1997. 'Kidneys for Sale', *Frontline*, 14(25). Available at http://www.thehindu.com/fline/fl1425/14250640.htm (Accessed on 23 June 2008).

Menon, S. 2005. 'The Role of Diverse Institutional Agendas in the Importation of Convergence Policy into the Indian Communications Sector', *Info*, 7(4): 30–46.

———. 2006. 'Localisation of Indian Broadcasting', *Seminar*, 561, May: 44–47.

Miller, Toby, Nitin Govil, John McMurria and Richard Maxwell. 2005. *Global Hollywood 2*. London: BFI Publishing, BFI.

Mohan, A. and A. Kumar. 2008. Response to TRAI Consultation Paper on Media Ownership, Consultation Paper No. 13/2008, Zee Network. Available at http://www.trai.gov.in/WriteReadData/trai/upload/ConsultationPapers/155/ZeeNetwork.pdf (Accessed on 24 September 2009).

Mosco, V. 2006. 'Knowledge and Media Workers in the Global Economy: Antimonies of Outsourcing', *Social Identities*, 12(6): 771–790.

Muralidharan, S. 2007. 'The Shackling of Community Radio', *Himal SouthAsia*, 20(3). Available at http://www.himalmag.com/2007/march/report1.htm (Accessed on 11 September 2009).

Murdock, G. 2004. 'Past the Posts: Rethinking Change, Retrieving Critique', *European Journal of Communication*, 19(1): 19–38.

Naipaul, V. S. 1992. *India: A Million Mutinies Now.* London: Penguin.

Nanda, M. 2006. 'How Modern are We? Cultural Contradictions of India's Modernity', *Economic and Political Weekly*, XLI (6): 491–496.

Nandy, A., S. Trivedy, S. Mayaram and Achyut Yagnik. 1995. *The Ramjanmabhoomi Movement and Fear of the Self.* New Delhi: Oxford University Press.

Naqvi, F. 2008. *Waves in the Hinterland: The Journey of a Newspaper*. New Delhi: Nirantar/Zubaan.

NASSCOM. 2008. 'NASSCOM Presents Animation and Gaming India 2008'. Available at http://www.nasscom.in/Nasscom/templates/NormalPage.aspx?id=55119 (Accessed on 10 November 2008).

Ninan, S. 2006. 'The New Moghuls', *The Hindu Online*, 8 October. Available at http://www.hindu.com/mag/2006/10/08/stories/2006100800070300.htm (Accessed on 23 May 2008).

Ninan, S. 2007. 'Battles Ahead', *The Hindu Online*. Available at http://www.hinduonnet.com/thehindu/mag/2007/01/07/stories/2007010700140300.htm (Accessed on 4 November 2008).

———. 2008. 'Response from Sevanti Ninan', Available at http://www.trai.gov.in/WriteReadData/trai/upload/ConsultationPapers/155/Sevanti.pdf (Accessed on 24 September 2009).

Office of the United States Trade Representative (USTR). 1996. '1996 National Trade estimate India'. Available at http://ustraderep.gov/Document_Library/Reports_Publications/1996/1996_National_Trade_Estimate/1996_National_Trade_Estimate-India.html (Accessed on 23 May 2008).

Patnaik, P. 2000. 'The Performance of the Indian Economy in the 1990's', *South Asia: Journal of South Asian Studies*, 23(1): 193–205.

Pendakur, M. 2003. *Indian Popular Cinema: Industry, Ideology and Consciousness*. Cresskill, New Jersey: Hampton Press Inc.

Policy on Expansion of FM Radio Broadcasting Services through Private Agencies (Phase II). 2005. Available at http://www.mib.nic.in/writereaddata%5Chtml_en_files%5Cfm/FM-PH-II-13072005.htm (Accessed on 24 May 2009).

Prasad, R. and V. Sridhar. 2008. 'A Critique of Spectrum Management in India', *Economic and Political Weekly*, 20 September: 13–17.

Rajagopal, A. 2001. *Politics After Television: Hindu Nationalism and the Reshaping of the Public in India*. Cambridge: Cambridge University Press.

Raman, A. 2005. 'Station Sonia'. *Outlook*, 14 November: 20–22.

Ravindran, G. 2009. 'The Politics of Tamil Television: The Bane of Cross Media Ownership', Edit Room: Wide Screen Journal Editor's Blog. Available at http://blogs.widescreenjournal.org/?p=1557 (Accessed on 24 September 2009).

Roy, A. 1999. *The Greater Common Good*. Bombay: India Book Distributors (Bombay) Limited.

Special Correspondent. 2006. 'Drop Dayanidhi Maran, Demands Jayalalitha'. *The Hindu Online*. 28 April. Available at http://www.hinduonnet.com/thehindu/2006/04/28/stories/2006042808900100.htm (Accessed on 10 November 2008).

Sachdeva, S. D. 2006. 'BPO Employees Fight for Rights, on the Net: 'E-Unions' to Communicate Directly with Stakeholders', *Times of India*, Bangalore, 7 July: 10.

Sainath, P. 1996. 'Poverty, Development & the Press', in *Everybody Loves a Good Drought: Stories from India's Poorest Districts*, pp. 421–437. New Delhi: Penguin Books.

———. 2000. 'Reporting Poverty', in *Communication and the Globalisation of Poverty*, pp. 19–29. London: WACC.

Sainsbury, M. 2008. 'Obama to make call on ICANN', *The Australian*, 11 November: 27–28.

Sanjay, B. P. 2007. 'Media Barons and Press Freedoms', *India Together*, 7 March.

Sen, S. 1998. 'Hurry Up, Maran is Tying up the South', *Buisnessworld*, 7–21 September: 70–71.

Sharma, K. 2008. 'A Trailblazer by Dalit Women Scribes', *OneWorldSouthAsia*. Available at http://southasia.oneworld.net/Article/a-trail-blazer-by-dalit-women-scribes (Accessed on 1 May 2009).

Shaw, P. 2008. 'Media and Politics: Democracy of Lumpenocracy', (pp. 1–21). Paper presented at the Political Economy section of the International Association for Media and Communication Research (IAMCR) conference, 'Media and Global Divides', 20–25 July, Stockholm, Sweden.

Shukla, A. 2009. 'Doordarshan, Half a Century Later', Indian Express.com. Available at http://www.indianexpress.com/news/doordarshan-half-a-century-later/519177/0 (Accessed on 29 October 2009).

Singh, G. 2008. 'India's Next Media Powerhouse', *Businessworld*, 14 March. Available at http://www.businessworld.in/index.php/Media-Entertainment/Indias-Next-Media-Powerhouse.html (Accessed on 23 May 2009).

Srinivasaraju, S. 2005. 'Is it All for Land', *Outlook*, 7 November: 50–53.

Televisionpoint.com. 2007. 'Religious Channels have Great Bhakti and Shakti'. Televisionpoint.Com, 16 April. Available at http://www.televisionpoint.com/news2007/newsfullstory.php?id=1177604273 (Accessed on 10 November 2008).

The Economist. 2008. 'Business: Calling the Shots: Indian Media', *The Economist*, 3 May, 387 (8578).

The Economic Times. 2007. 'Reliance Entertainment to Rock the Regional Film Circuit', *The Economic Times*, 31 December. Available at http://economictimes.indiatimes.com/News/News_By_Industry/Media__Entertainment_/Entertainment/Reliance_Entertainment_to_rock_the_regional_film_circuit/rssarticleshow/2663338.cms (Accessed on 4 November 2008).

Thomas, P.N. 2003. 'GATS and Trade in Audio-Visuals: Culture, Politics and Empire', *Economic and Political Weekly*, 16 August: 3485–3493.

———. 2009. 'Selling God/Saving Souls: Religious Commodities, Spiritual Markets and the Media', *Global Media and Communication*, 5(1): 57–76.

———. 2010. 'Traditions of Public Journalism in India', in A. Romano and S. Mwangi (eds), *Journalism and Democracy: Civic Engagement Models from Around the World*. London: Routledge.

Thussu, D. 2007. 'The "Murdochisation" of News? The Case of Star TV in India', *Media, Culture and Society*, 29(4): 593–611.

TRAI. 2008. 'Consultation Paper on Media Ownership', 23 September. Telecom Regulatory Authority of India, New Delhi. Available at http://www.trai.gov.in/WriteReadData/trai/upload/ConsultationPapers/154/cpaper23sep08no13.pdf (Accessed on 28 September 2009).

Tumbasek. 2007. 'The Stability of Multi-party Democracy in India', India Democracy. Available at http://www.indiademocracy.org/index.php/article/viewArticle/id/662 (Accessed on 10 February 2010).

Venkateshwarlu, K. 2009. 'Maytas Twins', *Frontline*, 26(3) 31 January–13 February. Available at http://www.frontlineonnet.com/stories/20090213260301000.htm (Accessed on 23 April 2009).

Wyatt, A. 2005. '(Re) Imagining the Indian (Inter) National Economy', *New Political Economy*, 10(2): 163–179.

Section 2
Processes and Means

This section, consisting of five chapters, deals with a number of issues that are critical to an understanding of the political economy of communications. These include Chapter 5 that deals with issues related to copyright and the politics and policies supportive of media enclosures and the role of global media governance institutions and business lobbies in advocating the harmonisation of India's IP laws with global standards. Copyright is the means used to fix and profit from ideas as property; thus, contributing to knowledge divides. Chapter 6 explores the processes related to audio-visual trade focussing in particular on the paradoxical position that India is in at the moment, as both an importer and exporter of media content. It explores the concept of 'cultural exception' and the ever-tightening links between trade, IP and the media. Chapter 7 offers observations on the informationalisation of life and life processes and the need for political economy to deal with the ever-expanding hegemony of the digital. The consequences of the major marriages that have taken place between IT and a variety of new technologies—biotechnology, nanotechnology, artificial intelligence, etc.—are yet to become a major focus for research. Political economists, for far too long, have dealt with the digital in the context of the media and information technologies when the digital has become a common language across all productive sectors. This is followed by Chapter 8 on the political economy of Christian broadcasting in India and the processes, means and politics of transnational and national Christian broadcasting in India. It deals with the intermeshings of conservative Christian politics and the media in India today. This section concludes with Chapter 9 that deals with issues related to poverty and the media that are frequently ignored by media academics. Poverty is an inescapable reality in India and it also provides the framework for understanding media narratives in India. I argue that apart from dealing with the representation of poverty, there are other entry points such as exploring the relationship between communication and debt that offers fruitful insights into understanding poverty.

5

The Indian Copyright Conundrum

Some of the more provocative writings on copyright and intellectual property in general in India have been generated by civil society organisations such as the Bengaluru-based Alternative Law Forum and the Delhi-based Sarai network. Work by Lawrence Liang (2005), Ravi Sundaram (2004) and others have explored the micropolitics of knowledge enclosures, the politics of access and the redemptive nature of the 'copy' against the background of India's many 'porous legalities' and its seemingly headlong capitulation to the dictates of the international IP regime. These have been complemented with exciting practical projects such as the establishment by the Bengaluru-based Centre for Internet and Society of a four terabyte pirate archive of material especially for the print and visually challenged students. These contributions, taken in their entirety, are important precisely because they contest the notion that the extension of property rights around knowledge is reasonable in what is visibly an 'unreasonable' context and that corporate control over knowledge is our manifest destiny. In the context of the emerging knowledge economy, such contrary positions are immensely important, for access to and use of knowledge has already begun to define one's quality of life. Enclosures over knowledge restrict access and limit creativity and innovation. Such enclosures also limit culture in the public domain that is a heritage of all humankind. This is why it is necessary for critical media scholars to deal with the politics of the cultural and informational commons. However, contestory voices from civil society are few and far between and these voices rarely rise above the clamour from business and government to extend rather than limit the scope of IP in India.

It would seem to be the case that the Indian government, like the Chinese, is involved in dancing an elaborate routine related to IP. While it recognises the fact that 'soft' IP protection is required to strengthen local creativity especially in sectors such as software, it is under great pressure to extend 'hard' IP protection and to integrate the IP regime in India, as closely as possible, with the international copyright regime. In other words, while piracy in the information and entertainment sectors is rife and public in most Indian cities, despite public pronouncements, the state's response remains episodic rather than consistent. For all the many attempts to corporatise India's IP infrastructure and operations, there remains a disconnect between the state's public IP 'persona' and its private face. This disconnect would seem to suggest that while the extension of property value to intangible products based on 'information' makes economic sense, it is not a practical solution because of the intrinsic nature of the digital itself that is fundamentally 'viral' and infinite.

As Lawrence Lessig (1999), Robert Boyle (1996) and others have pointed out, information is a non-rivalrous resource. Your consumption and mine, of the same resource, does not devalue, corrupt or lessen its value unlike rivalrous resources such as a piece of cake or a biscuit that are finite commodities. If this then is the nature of the digital, how best can we create an infrastructure for the digital that both values and rewards creativity but also maximises the distribution of the digital as a common good. Unfortunately, that is not how the global IP regime deals with the digital. To them, the digital is real estate to be enclosed and only made available for a fee. One can argue that piracy thrives in this context, precisely because a large number of people are priced out of the market. One can also argue that piracy democratises access, precisely through giving opportunities to people who otherwise would not have become computer and digital literate. Lawrence Liang at a workshop held in Trivandrum in December 2008 organised by the international network CopySouth, expressed the need for an 'index on cultural gains' as a result of piracy. While the media is replete with stories of digital piracy, there is little or no information on the pricing of CDs and software that have grown exponentially over the years.

International Pressures and the Emerging Copyright Regime in India

Until very recently, IP was not considered a priority in India. Basheer (2005: 313) describes the findings of the Ayyangar Committee report on patents submitted in 1959 to the Indian government: 'This committee found that foreigners held 80–90 percent of Indian patents and that more than 90 per cent of these patents were not even worked in India.' While these ratios have changed, it is interesting that in the *Annual Report 2005–2006* from the Office of the Controller General of Patents, Designs, Trade marks and Registrar of Geographical Indications reveals that out of the 15,467 external filings for patents, the US led with 5,874 filings in that same year. 4,521 filings originated from India (p. 10). India has made numerous amendments to its Copyright Act (1958) during the last two decades namely in 1983, 1984, 1992, 1994 and 1999. It is presently involved in exploring another amendment that would make the copyright regime compliant with WIPO's 'Copyright Treaty' and 'Performances and Phonograms Treaty'. The range of policy changes that have recently been administered to India's intellectual property (IP) regime are a clear indication of the extent to which a global 'proprietory' agenda has become a significant aspect of India's social and economic futures. The pace of accommodation with the TRIPS treaty has accelerated during the last decade. India had become a signatory to the Paris Convention and the Patent Co-operation Treaty on 7 December 1998 and had earlier become a signatory to the Berne Convention and the Universal Copyright Convention. Recent legislative changes that will have a direct impact on IPR in India include the following—the Patent (Amendments) Act (1999) (also amended in 2002 and 2005), the Geographical Indications of Goods (Registration and Protection) Act and the Designs Act (2000) that is in compliance with TRIPS agreements on Industrial Designs and the Protection of Plant Varieties and Farmer's Rights Act (2001), The Indian Plant Act in line with the International Convention for the Protection of New Plant Varieties (International Union for the Protection of New Varieties of Plants (UPOV) Convention) and the Biological Diversity Act (2002). Other bills that recently have been or are yet to be debated in parliament include the Information Technology Bill (2000), the Semiconductor Integrated Circuits Layout-Design Act (2000), the Patents (Second Amendment) Bill that has been pending since 2003, the Convergence Bill that has been pending since August 2001 and that addresses regulatory issues related to the convergence of communication, IT and broadcasting and the National Innovation Act (2008) (Cullet 2000; Lal 1998; Rangnekar 2000; *Hindu* 2001).

These attempts at harmonising domestic IP legislations with international TRIPS, WIPO and other related legislations have been complemented with major investments in strengthening and modernising the infrastructure of IP and institutional mechanisms to aid coordination, monitoring, training, sensitisation and enforcement. These include the establishment of the Copyright Enforcement Advisory Council (CEAC) under the Ministry of Human Resource Development and the setting up of special copyright enforcement cells in:

> ...23 States and Union Territories, i.e. Andhra Pradesh, Assam, Andaman & Nicobar Islands, Chandigarh, Dadra & Nagar Haveli, Daman & Diu, Delhi, Goa, Gujarat, Haryana, Himachal Pradesh, Jammu & Kashmir, Karnataka, Kerala, Madhya Pradesh, Meghalaya, Orissa, Pondicherry, Punjab, Sikkim, Tamil Nadu, Tripura and West Bengal. States have also been advised to designate a nodal officer for copyright enforcement to facilitate easy interaction by copyright industry organizations and copyright owners.[1]

It also includes joint enforcement activities with international trade bodies such as the Business Software Alliance and the Motion Pictures Association—bodies that represent, in the main, US-based organisations inclusive of Microsoft and Disney—with local trade bodies such as the Society for Copyright Regulations of Indian Producers for Films and Television (SCRIPT), Indian Performing Rights Society Limited (IPRS) and the Phonographic Performance Limited (PPL). The collective administration of copyrights in the popular cultural sector in India is currently enforced by three societies—the Society for Copyright Regulations of Indian Producers of Films and Television (SCRIPT) for cinema, Indian Performing Rights Society Limited (IPRS) for musical works and the Phonographic Performance Limited (PPL) for sound recordings. These societies represent larger industry interests. For instance, the PPL has been constituted by the Indian Music Industry (IMI),[2] an organisation that represents 75 per cent of national and regional music labels.

Apart from multilateral cooperation on IP, the government has signed eight bilateral cooperation Memorandum of Understandings (MOUs) on IP with Australia, Germany, Switzerland, Japan, France, the UK, the European Patent Office and the US. The Annual Action Plans that are included in the MOUs relate to the exchange of best practices, training and enforcement.[3] In Tamil Nadu, video pirates were 'brought under the purview of the Tamil Nadu Prevention of Dangerous Activities of Bootleggers, Drug-offenders, Forest offenders, Goondas, Immoral Traffic offenders and Slum Grabbers Act, 1982' (*Hindu Online* 2004). The Act was used to both prosecute copyright violators as well as close down video parlours that featured pirated videos.

The pressure to align copyright frameworks in India with the emerging global copyright regime stems from a number of sources without—namely multilateral institutions, such as the World Trade Organisation and its Trade-Related Aspects of Intellectual Property Rights (TRIPS)[4] mandate, global governance organisations such as the World Intellectual Property Organisation (WIPO), the EU and most persistently from the US—and from within, namely the transnational and national service industry, trade organisations such as NASSCOM[5,6] and from governments that either have in the past or are currently presiding over globalising India. For the US in particular, copyright is all about expanding and protecting the competitive advantage enjoyed by their cultural industries and services sector that earn the country billions of dollars in revenues. Using the doctrine of the 'free flow of information', the US government backed by its multinational corporations relentlessly communicated a global narrative in which the cultural and services industries were primarily seen in the context of global trade and in which copyright provided one layer of a larger IP framework for trade. As Comor (1998: 225–226) describes it:

> The services as trade issue equation placed United States Trade Representative (USTR) officials in the unexpected role of America's central foreign communication policy agents. Recognising that other countries would need to be pulled towards the reconceptualisation of communication and information issues as trade issues (rather than being pushed into it), the Reagan White House, with congressional support, instructed the USTR to pursue bilateral service and intellectual property agreements.

While IP harmonisation is a key policy plank that is explored through multilateral and bilateral means, global monitoring and enforcement of anti-piracy measures and trade sanctions against offenders is carried out on the basis of annual reports such as the annual Special 301 Reports by the Office of the USTR. As the 2008 Special 301 Report emphatically notes:

> India will remain on the Priority Watch List in 2008. The United States remains concerned about inadequate IPR protection and enforcement in India. The United States continues to urge India to improve its IPR regime by providing stronger protection for copyrights, trademarks, and patents…The United States encourages India to implement the WIPO Internet Treaties by strengthening its copyright laws and to improve its IPR enforcement system by enacting and implementing an effective optical disc licensing scheme to combat optical disc piracy… (p. 35)

In the post-9/11 era, there were strenuous efforts by trade lobbyists in the US to link piracy with terrorism—a discourse that has become an essential aspect of dominant mediations of IP.

Hollywood, Section 301 and India

India's negotiations at the Uruguay Round of General Agreement on Tariffs and Trade (GATT) negotiations had included a commitment to the progressive liberalisation of trade in the audio-visual sector. Hollywood had lobbied hard to reverse the 20 year-old quota policy that restricted the annual import (100 films) and distribution of Hollywood films in India. It had urged the US government to enforce Section 301-based trade sanctions against India for content piracy. The US-based International Intellectual Property Alliance had in 1995 estimated trade losses to the US service industry as a result of piracy in India alone in the region of USD 119 million, out of which USD 58 million was incurred in film, USD 10 million in recorded music, USD 26 million in entertainment software and USD 26 million in the book trade (quoted in Mansell and Wehn 1998: 212). In the year 2000 alone, estimated global piracy-related revenue losses to US motion picture companies was estimated to be in the region of USD 2.5 billion. The issue of piracy was turned into the means by which the Motion Picture Association of America (MPAA), representing the seven major film and television producers in the US inclusive of Walt Disney Company, Sony Pictures Entertainment Inc., Metro-Goldwyn-Mayer Inc., Paramount Pictures Corporation, Twentieth Century Fox Film Corp., Universal Studios Inc. and Warner Bros., made a determined effort to enter the Indian market. With a potential audience of 200 million that includes cable and satellite television viewers, and box office returns of USD 6 million for the Hindi version of *Jurassic Park*, USD 12.5 million for *Titanic* and a similar amount for local blockbusters such as the Hindi-language *Dil To Pagal Hai*, the Indian film market was perceived as a potential source of revenue for Hollywood. In fact as Sidhva (1996: vi) has noted, Hollywood planned to carve 10 per cent of the Indian film market by 2000, through the consolidation of a production, distribution and exhibition strategy, the latter aided by the establishment of multiplexes in Mumbai.

The tightening and strengthening of copyright enforcement with respect to domestic cultural products, film in particular, has also become part of MPAA's New Delhi-based India-wide operations. It would seem that such a prioritising will in the long run also ensure the protection of Hollywood films in India. The reason for MPAA's involvement in copyright protection of local film products becomes clearer when seen against the investments made by one of its members, Sony Entertainment TV, which was launched in October 1995 in the Indian subcontinent and has bought rights to 300 Hindi films and secured exclusive rights for cultural and sporting events in India. Sony also hosts top-rated show *Aahat,* currently has access to and owns 1500 hours of exclusive programming, has invested millions of dollars in dubbing Hollywood films into Hindi and in the making of local feature films and is also involved in making profits from its Sony music label. Similarly, another member of MPAA, Twentieth Century Fox, part of News Corporation, is also poised to break into the film market with 20 productions per year. With such investments at stake, India can look forward to the active involvement of the MPAA in the matter of copyright enforcement. There has also been a similar scramble for film rights by local firms. The Mumbai-based Eros Network, for instance, owns rights to over a 1,000 films; Sippy films, producers of the Bollywood blockbuster *Sholay*, have major plans to brand the film and license its merchandising, and companies like B4U and Star TV have invested vast sums of money into the ownership of film rights. There is, of course, a major commercial reason for copyright enforcement and that has to do with the global cross-sectoral marketing of products. These developments and the emergence of strong contenders in the domestic software and entertainments business, along with the entry of global players and North-South alliances supportive of copyright protection, have led to the emergence of a new culture of IP in India consonant with the global IP regime. The prospects for merchandising have also been explored by international branded satellite channels such as MTV India and Cartoon Network.

The entry of Hollywood into the Indian market led to renewed attempts to highlight the issue of copyright violations and strengthened domestic concerns and initiatives linked to creating an environment favourable to TRIPS and IPR. Market entry was created in a number of ways, both fortuitous and planned. The haphazard entry of satellite and cable television in the early 1990s provided the right opportunity for the global cultural industry to gauge potential revenues in the Indian cultural market. Within the space of five years, 1990–1995, News Corporation's Star TV Network, Time Warner's CNN and Cartoon Network, Viacom's MTV, Sony Entertainment and Disney among numerous others had become established players in Indian broadcasting. However, the relationship between the satellite broadcasters and the local cable fraternity, which is in excess of 70,000 today, was strained from the very beginning because of a conflict of interests and objectives, perceived loopholes in the existing Copyright Act and lax enforcement that resulted in large scale violation of copyright by cable companies. Cable operations in India, for the most part, remain small and it is very much a cottage industry, inspite of the attempts to consolidate 'content and carriage' shares by large groups like

Star TV's Siticable and the Raheja group-owned Hathway Cable, and Datacom, in which the Star TV network has a 26 per cent stake. In 1999, nine Hollywood studios including all those represented by the MPAA filed suits against two of India's largest cable television networks for the infringement of copyright. The Delhi High Court's ruling favoured these studios and led to the enforcement of penalties against these cable firms. The local film industry too has initiated a number of civil cases against copyright pirates—cable pirates, Video Cassette Recorder (VCR) and VCD pirates. However, given the nexus between the film world, the cable networks and organised crime, it has been difficult to enforce copyright regulations nationally or to restrain cable releases of international and domestic films prior to their official release in theatres. The extent of the problem is particularly visible in India's film and finance capital, Mumbai, in which the cable business in the most lucrative parts of the city is run by family members associated with the right-wing head of the Shiv Sena, Bal Thackeray (Anandan 2000; Raval and Aiyer 2001). While the government, along with the film industry, has recently been involved in trying to clean up the industry and give it a new image, the links are institutionalised and involve local and national politicians.

One of the ironies of Bollywood's current attempts at protecting its IP is the fact that in any given year, a large number of films produced are imitations of well-known Hollywood films. As Husain (2007) has observed:

> Part of the way that Bollywood is able to keep making movies that gross lots of money is to take successful films from Hollywood and remake them into Bollywood blockbusters. Movies such as *Entrapment* and *ET* have been made into Bollywood productions by changing the story to make it more akin to a musical than straight theatre and making the characters more identifiable to Indian culture. Almost eighty percent of all Bollywood films have been 'inspired' by a Hollywood film.

A recent case was the lawsuit filed by Warner Brothers against the makers of the Bollywood film *Hari Puttar* in 2008 for its likeness to the Harry Potter series. There are, in any given year, a number of lawsuits filed within Bollywood for infringements of one sort or another. These include script-lifting and the copying of music and lyrics. In the words of Reddy (2008) from the website 'Spicy IP':

> Once again Bollywood music directors are being accused of copyright infringement. Sheela Narayanan & Chang May Choon of The Electric New Paper Show...were the first and so far only media outlet to report that Sony BMG has initiated legal proceedings against Tips on the grounds that Pritam's 'Zara Zara

> Touch me...' song...from this year's Bollywood blockbuster <u>Race</u> has been ripped off from a tune composed by Wang Lee Hom, the rights of which are owned by Sony BMG. According to The Electric New Paper Show, Sony is suing Tips for copying the tune, adding lyrics to it, incorporating it into a movie, playing it on radio stations and TV channels and commercially selling it.

It is also ironic that the T Series, a music company that established itself through flouting copyright in the 1980s, is now involved in issuing notices against Yahoo, MySpace, Guruji.com and other sites for providing platforms for users to download music from the T Series catalogue (Menon 2008).

The Changing Scope of Copyright Law in India

All copyright laws have a dual function—to protect the claims of authorship expressed through a variety of media and to prevent piracy, the unlawful copying of copyrighted products. The Indian Copyright Act (1957) is itself an amended version of the Indian Copyright Act of 1914 which was modelled on the UK Copyright Act of 1911. The 1957 Act conformed to the Berne Convention and to the Universal Copyright Convention. This Act was amended in 1983 in compliance with the revised Berne and UC Conventions effected in 1971 (Paris). The 1957 Copyright Act provided protection for 'original' works of a literary, dramatic, musical and artistic kind, inclusive of architecture, art, cinema and sound recording. The Act was amended on a number of occasions to enable a correspondence between domestic and international laws on copyright. With the advent of new technologies of copying—audio-cassettes, video-cassettes and recently digital media—the incidence and scale of copyright piracy has increased, in certain instances, quite dramatically. The music industry in India has estimated that in 1997, 175 million out of the 580 million cassettes sold were unauthorised duplications (www.indianmi.org). In response to these developments, the Copyright Act (1958) was amended in 1984, 1992 and 1994. The 1984 Amendment, for instance, specified that video films be treated on a par with cinematography for the purpose of copyright. The 1992 and 1994 Amendments have progressively included copyright matters related to cable television and computer software. The amendment effected in 1984 recognised the reality of audio-visual piracy and offered provisions to control piracy. The amendment in 1994 has enabled compatibility between domestic laws on copyright with TRIPS requirements, in particular the extension of the notion of 'literary works' to cover computer programmes, along with an increase to the protection period from 50 to 60 years. The 1994 amendment also vested copyright societies and the Copyright Board in India with powers to handle copyright infringements. It also mandated the establishment of expert benches in the High Court on IP and enforcement cells at the state level. Furthermore, it established conditions of 'reciprocity', meaning the granting of copyright protection for foreign authors (corporations) on a par with that granted to nationals.

At first glance, the Indian Copyright Act seems to have balanced private and public interests in the area of IP. For instance, Section 52 explains legitimate infringements of copyright law—in the context of private study and research, performances organised in the course of study at an educational institution, in front of a limited audience and in a not-for-profit situation. While such provisions do provide the space for non-commercial uses of copyrighted material, it is impossible to predict with any accuracy if these provisions will survive the emerging versions and visions of international proprietorial law or whether such provisions will fall between the cracks, as attempts are consistently made to harmonise global copyright law with domestic laws. The standardisation of trade-related practices—for instance, the extension of 'Most Favoured Nation' status—requires all WTO signatories to treat non-domestic service suppliers on a par with domestic players, offer them the same level of tax breaks, preferential treatment, etc. Point 4b, Article 6 entitled 'Domestic Regulation' in Part II, General Obligations and Disciplines, Trade in Services[7] is the infamous 'not more burdensome than necessary to ensure the quality of the service' clause, which can be invoked by IP holders in the developed world, or for that matter in India, to restrict public, limited uses of cultural material in the interest of commerce.

Interestingly enough, Section 63b of the Indian Copyright Act (1994) reserves the strictest of penalties for those involved in using pirated software—penalties not reserved for any other form of copyright infringement covered in the Act:

> Any person who knowingly makes use of on a computer of an infringing copy of a computer programme shall be punishable with imprisonment for a term which shall not be less than seven days but which may extend to three years and with a fine which shall not be less than fifty thousand rupees but which may extend to two lakhs rupees....(The Indian Copyright Act 1957)

The amended Indian Copyright Law assumes that copyright law related to software exists solely to be of benefit to the business community and no other sector. N. S. Gopalakrishnan, from the National Law School, Bengaluru, suggests that since the benefits of software are bound to accrue primarily to business communities that we must:

> [C]onsider keeping computer programmes outside the domain of the private property monopoly rights regime. It appears that the jurisprudence of considering intellectual property as 'common property' is going to pay better dividends to the average Indian computer developer, researcher and user in the days to come, when compared to the short term benefits of a few million dollars investment and export (earnings) by big companies in India in return for the heavy price that we (will) have to pay in terms of private property rights. (Gopalakrishnan 1993: 6)

Copyright in an Era of the Counterfeit

Ravi Sundaram (2004) in an article in the *Economic and Political Weekly*, describes the many-tentacled copy market in Delhi that is part of the life of that city:

> Delhi is now the centre of a complex coordinate of media markets, small software and hardware factories, and local shops that interact with customers. Production sites in Haryana and Rajasthan supply just in time media to the copy network, in turn linked to factories and routes in Pakistan and Malaysia. Media markets play an important role in distributing to local shops: Nehru Place for computer software and hardware, Palika Bazaar for film music and Lajpat Rai market for low costs hardware and music. Markets typically combine legal and copy nodes, frustrating efforts by the enforcement regime to spatially 'fix' copy culture. Nehru Place is thus one of Asia's biggest computer markets, Lajpat Rai is a distribution centre for music companies along with grey audio hardware, while Palika Bazar sells clothes and craft along with media.

Similar markets are found in all the major and minor cities in India, in Bengaluru on SP Road and the National market whereas in Tamil Nadu, the copy hubs are Chennai (Burma Bazar and Richie Street), Puducherry and Madurai. It comes as little surprise then that the scale of the 'copy' market in India is large although it is dwarfed by the scale of the copy market in China, which has consistently remained on the top of the USTR's Section 301 priority list for a number of years. Nevertheless, a report published in March 2008 by the US-India Business Council (USIBC) and the Federation of Indian Chambers of Commerce and Industry (FICCI) Bollywood-Hollywood Initiative claims that out of the USD 11 billion media and entertainments market in India, USD 4 billion is lost to piracy with the loss of 820,000 jobs, although another report released by the FICCI in 2007 places annual losses to the much lesser amount of USD 186 million in 2005, out of which 92 per cent was suffered by the film industry (Shedde 2007). Piracy in the Indian music market is Rs 650 crores a year which roughly translates into 40–48 per cent of the industry. It is in the context of such large-scale imagined and real losses to piracy that moves have been made by the government to amend the Indian Copyright Act (1957) to make it compliant with Digital Rights Management that would involve the application of a set of technical and legal mechanisms—Technology Protection Measure (TPM) and Rights Management Information (RMI) to protect access, distribution and use of digital content.

Piracy, although an issue of concern for both international and domestic players, needs to be seen in perspective. To use a term that continues to be used to describe violent appropriations of property as, for instance, the capture of ships by Somalian pirates, to copying of material for individual use is problematic, to say the least. The typical software pirate does not carry an AK-47 nor does he/she sport a patch over his right eye. However, this term does have global currency and in the emerging environment of IP, the issue of piracy has the highest priority. Other equally pressing concerns, such as the predatory pricing of cultural products, barriers to cultural appropriation of products conceived in the public domain, the protection of collective authorship, among other issues of concern to ordinary consumers, are rarely, if ever, debated or treated with the importance that it deserves. As Parthasarthy (2001: 13) has observed, the international furore over the case of Napster and piracy has deflected attention from the ways in which the international music business has used that pretext to charge higher prices for their products. The big four in India—Bertelsmann Music Group (BMG), Electric & Musical Industries Ltd. (EMI), Sony and Universal, protected by the umbrella body, the Recording Industry Association of America (RIAA), have increased the price of their products. 'In India, the international foursome has, almost in unison, doubled the price of Western music cassettes in the last three years from around Rs 75 to Rs 125–Rs 150 and CDs can cost over Rs 500 a piece for 8–10 songs.' The fact that over the last 2–3 years, there has been a belated recognition of the need for lower pricing of AV products by the industry is welcome although it can be argued that it still does not provide an answer to the availability of pirated AV products that, in terms of quality, are indistinguishable from the original.

Current Contestations: The Ethics of Copyright

At the heart of the current debate on copyrights are three issues:

1. An economic one, related to the fact that IPR related value amounts to billions of dollars to the trade balance of the US and other developed countries—'The economic value associated with intellectual property rights accounted for $327 billion and 5.5 million jobs in the United States in 1991' (Monberg 1999).
2. A technological issue related to the translatability of information across and between technologies—copyright in a digital world.
3. The contentious maze of moral issues related to differing interpretations of IPR in general and copyright and patents in particular, held by governments, corporations and trade bodies on the one hand and public-domain activists and indigenous groups on the other. From a social perspective, issues related to the ethics of IPR reveal the vast gap that exists between what are largely 'proprietorial', private understandings of intellectual value and those that are firmly linked to the public domain and promote the social value of IPR over its economic value.

The Politics of Authorship

One of the contentious and yet to be resolved issues in the area of copyright, for instance, is the issue of 'authorship', a concept that was developed from Enlightenment scholars such as John Locke in his treatise on the 'natural rights of man' and given legal status through the Copyright Act of April 1710, enacted in the UK and that gave protection to individual authors against print piracy. The original understanding of authorship, meaning reward for an individual's creative labour that evolved during a period when trade was conducted within limited boundaries, is vastly different from its contemporary interpretation. Today 'authorship' accrues neither to the individual nor to the collective authors of traditional texts, software and other cultural products, but to their corporate employers. The migration of rights originally invested in individuals to corporations, and the attempts to legalise such translations, have been primary strategic means employed by corporations in their bids to take control over the knowledge economy. This migration is best illustrated through the relationship between employers, employees and copyright in the section 'Copyright of Software: Frequently Asked Questions' in the NASSCOM website, where it is explained in the following manner—'In the case of a programme made in the course of an author's employment under a contract of service or apprenticeship, the employer shall, in the absence of any agreement to the contrary, be the first owner of the Copyright.' Since 'agreements to the contrary' are invariably the exception rather than the rule, the ownership of copyright is bound to remain with corporations rather than with any group.

In fact, every lingering trace of this original understanding of authorship has been removed from the TRIPS agreement of 1 January 1995, which remains the most comprehensive multilateral agreement on IPR to date. While tightening and consolidating the global IP regime on the one hand, the TRIPS agreement has, on the other hand, dispensed with the 'moral' obligations of IPR. The TRIPS agreement states categorically that:

> Members do not have right or obligations under the TRIPS agreement in respect of the rights conferred under Article 6*bis* of that [Berne] Convention, i.e. the moral rights (the right to claim authorship and to object to any derogatory action in relation to a work, which would be prejudicial to the author's honour or reputation), or of the rights derived therefrom.[8]

When placed against Article 6*bis* of the 'Berne Convention for the Protection of Literary and Artistic Works (Paris Text 1971)', the clause reveals the extent to which IPR has become an extension of corporate rights. Article 6*bis* had affirmed that:

> Independently of the author's economic rights, and even after the transfer of the said rights, the author shall have the right to claim authorship of the work and to object to any distortion, mutilation or other modification of, or other derogatory action in relation to, the said work, which would be prejudicial to his honour or reputation. (Berne Convention 1999)

One of the consequences of the current interpretation is the negation of the social, public value of IP, a value that exceeded its value as private property. Miller (1996: 360) reminds us of that tradition:

> It is central to the legal history of both copyright and patents that although each of them creates a property interest owned by the holder, their primary purpose is the promotion of the public interest by encouraging the creation and widespread availability of socially useful information.

'Authorship', however, continues to be a problematic concept, particularly so in the context of the new, digital technologies of reproduction. Digital technologies have unfixed the singular location, fixed materiality and objectivity associated with products related to the previous generation of technologies. The appropriation and transformation of digitally manipulated material, access to 'sampling' technologies, inter-textual mixing and matching and net-based peer-to-peer sharing of popular culture has further complicated the notion of authorship. The issue of 'illegal appropriation' is, of course, the reason for the current attempts by the Recording Industry in the US to silence the net-based, peer-to-peer music site, Napster. Given the depth and breath of the current intellectual land grab and the corporate appropriation of knowledge—by way of gene banks, code banks and restrictive copyright and patent laws, ordinary people cannot be expected to know when and why they are in breach of IP laws or, for that matter, their own rights to IP. The cultural theorist, Rosemary Coombe (1998), in her book, *The Cultural Life of Intellectual Properties: Authorship, Appropriation, and the Law*, has an answer to that particular quandary. She supports transgressions against the dominant IP regime through 'appropriations' of popular culture. The logic that she uses to support her position is founded on a public domain perspective that affirms that human beings, as heirs and creatures of culture, are indebted to ideas and meanings that circulate in the public sphere—ideas and meanings that antecede any subsequent 'expression' of the idea or meaning for which authorship and originality is claimed. In support of her position that 'cultural distinction is socially produced' (p. 61), she argues that trademarks, for instance, that have their origins in a particular context, are open to the play of meaning available in that context and cultural environment, and thus susceptible to legitimate appropriation. As she explains:

> Increasingly, investment in a mark's signalling function is recognised to create an entitlement to control and appropriate surplus expressive value. The underlying argument is that trademark owners created this value through their investments and should garner any and all available rewards...This, of course, is...the Lockean assertion that one should have the benefit of one's own efforts. [However,] the choice for assigning the benefits of surplus signifying value should at least consider public economic and expressive interests. One could argue that if the public creates meaning for *Barbie* in excess of the signifier's capacity to signal Mattel's toy, they have done the sowing, and thus they should do the reaping: in short, authorship of such meanings might be seen to reside in the public sphere. (Coombe 1998: 67)

Coombe's perspective on IP and appropriation is similar to the view expressed by Henry Jenkins III (1992) in his account of 'textual poaching' of popular culture in the US.

Coombe's cultural studies perspective on copyright and her advocacy of 'direct action' and counter-hegemonic strategies relate to, but are sufficiently different from, the political-economy perspective on copyright, particularly that of Ronald Bettig's (1996), *Copyrighting Culture: The Political Economy of Intellectual Property*. Bettig takes the view that current IPR and copyright laws are intrinsically linked to the 'expansionary logic of capital' (p. 195) and that the seamless incorporation and extension of every new technology and its products within this logic merely results in the reinforcement of the dominance of the intellectual property regime. Bettig illustrates the manner in which the cultural industries in the US, through their inter-sectoral ownership of the media, their connections to the political elite in the US and their global lobbying power, have invested in and control global understandings of IPR. His comments on the manner in which Hollywood has extended its control over IP raises parallels with the current situation in India, where the appropriation of film rights has been complemented by attempts by large media players to establish themselves in every conceivable media sector through which these rights can be exploited. As Bettig has observed:

> The control of intellectual primary material, in particular copyrights in television programme and motion pictures, facilitated Hollywood's capture of new cable and video technology. Rather than undermining the oligopolistic structure of filmed entertainment distribution, these technologies have become means for perpetuating concentrated ownership and control of communications and information industries and for heightening barriers to these sectors. (Bettig 1996)

Bettig's pessimism, although understandable, does not provide a platform for another understanding of IPR, a platform which is explored by James Boyle (1997b) and defined in *A Politics of Intellectual Property: Environmentalism for the Net* (Boyle 1997a: 14). Calling for a political economy of intellectual property, the author explores the means for a politics of IP and a strategy of bringing IP into the 'public domain', rather like what the environmental movement has achieved. He notes that the:

> [P]ublic domain is disappearing, both conceptually and literally, in an IP system built around the interests of the current stakeholders and the notion of the original author, around an over-deterministic practice of economic analysis and around a 'free speech' community that is under sensitized to the dangers

> of private censorship. In one very real sense, the environmental movement invented the environment so that farmers, consumers, hunters and birdwatchers could all discover themselves as environmentalists. Perhaps we need to invent the public domain in order to call into being the coalition that might protect it. (Boyle 1997a)

Boyle's analysis suggests that together with the 'appropriations' of popular culture, there have to be organised, inter-sectoral attempts to legitimise such appropriations and the validity of other IP orders.

Copyright as Rent-seeking

The wave of recent global media mergers and acquisitions has been spurred on by the need for companies to maintain their strategic advantage in a new media environment to invest in 'content and carriage', in futures that guarantee economies of scale, by the desire to create near complete monopolies controlling every aspect of a media product—from production and transmission to its distribution and marketing—to take advantage of the knowledge capital that is the basis for rights to intellectual property and to exploit the many opportunities for marketing these rights through the ownership of a range of media channels. Every Disney-based film is more than just a film for it is conceived as an opportunity to synergistically market a commodity. So a film like the *Lion King* is marketed through numerous media channels—film viewings, theatre performances, videos, DVDs, CD-ROMs, websites, computer games, posters and cassettes and is further marketed through the sale of branded toys, sponsorship of activities in primary schools, kids' meals at fast food chains, clothes and other accessories. In other words, copyrights and patents have become the basis for the exploitation of content over many media and non-media sectors. In this context, Coombe's remarks on the intellectual commodification of 'celebrity' in the context of Hollywood reminds of another potential revenue source in India, a country in which the cult of celebrity, and revenues from celebrities, are already a source of huge revenues for MNCs and local businesses:

> It (IP protection) is no longer limited to the name or likeness of an individual, but now extends to a person's nickname, signature, physical pose, characterisations, 'singing style', vocal characterisations, body parts, frequently used phrases, car, performance style, and mannerisms and gestures, provided that these are distinctive and publicly identified with the person claiming this right. (Coombe 1998: 90)

The assertion of one's 'personality rights' remains a novelty in India although there is the infamous case of the Tamil film star Rajnikanth who:

> [I]ssued a legal notice just before the release of his latest film, 'Baba', prohibiting anyone from imitating his screen persona or using the character of 'Baba' for commercial gain, including by way of advertisements and imitation by mimics on television. Published in a number of leading Tamil and English dailies the legal notice also declared that no attempt should be made to use Rajnikanth's photos or sketches, or attire in the film, such as head-scarves, pendants, etc., for the purpose of endorsing products. (Liang 2003)

It would seem that controversies over the copyright of computer programmes are bound to remain since programme makers use source codes and mathematical algorithms that have, in some cases, been patented, notably in the US. In the context of the anti-trust rulings against Microsoft, the question—would the Windows platform, with its many derivative features including the graphical system of windows, menus, etc., have got to its position of global dominance if copyright laws had been strictly enforced at the time these programmes were developed?—reminds us of the collective origins of much that exists in global culture today. Anne Branscomb (1994: 176) rues the fact that usability has been compromised because of competing standards:

> By encouraging differential user interfaces, the law impedes the adoption of widely shared conventions, frustrating users, unnecessarily requiring programmes to reinvent the wheel, pushing up development costs, and inhibiting the compatibility that encourages a competitive marketplace. The challenge is to devise a legal system that encourages standardised user interfaces while rewarding human labour that leads to innovation and progress.

In Conclusion

I am not for a moment suggesting that intellectual protection is a bad thing per se. But perhaps there is a case to review the concept and worth of intellectual property in an era of the digital. Copyright, in its infancy, might have been a stimulus to invention and innovation and protected the interests of creative artists. But unlike two hundred years ago, when inventors still had property rights to their inventions, the contemporary software programmer who is employed to write codes for Microsoft, does not have any proprietary rights over the codes. So it is with writers and musicians, whose copyrights are owned by companies. Meanwhile, the trade-off that ensured that products would revert back to the public domain has been rather ruthlessly diluted through the most ludicrous extensions given to copyright, leading to a situation characterised by copyright in perpetuity. In other words, the original meaning of IPR as a 'Limited Intellectual Monopoly' has been lost. The 11 copyright extensions (1978–2001) given in the US is the most notorious example of this tendency. Ronald Bettig in an article in the WACC Journal *Media Development*, has commented on the manner in which copyright has been extended just at the moment when works were scheduled to return to the public domain:

> In 1998, Congress offered a quick fix by passing the Sony Bono Copyright Extension Act, often referred to as the 'Mickey Mouse Extension Act' because of heavy lobbying by the Walt Disney Company to protect the mouse whose term was set to expire in 2003. The act extended copyright for an additional 20 years for cultural works, protecting them for a total of 70 years after the death of an individual author or 95 years from publication in the case of works created by or for corporations. (Bettig 2003: 6)

Such extensions, one can argue, have led to the impoverishment of the public domain. There are a number of contemporary examples of attempts being made to extend property rights over knowledge. The informationalisation and digitalisation of all life processes has accentuated the pressure to create enclosures around all knowledge available in digitised form—from the content of an email to the source code of a software programme, to the digitised codes of a cell line and a microorganism. Even the exact number of clicks used to buy products over the online service Amazon.com (one click buy) has been the subject of a patent. Girl Guides have been sued for royalties because they sang songs around campfires for which they had not taken prior permission and the Finnish Composer's Copyright Society have decided to levy royalties for music played in cabs and for recorded Christmas music played in church. The list is endless and, frankly, rather absurd. Given the lack of regulation of enclosures around culture—every aspect of culture has become fair game for cultural entrepreneurs. If prior knowledge is not going to be freely available—the possibilities for creativity and innovation are bound to be severely impaired. When prior knowledge becomes digitised and people are denied access to the source code or to possibilities for reverse engineering—it becomes difficult to build on existing content, improve upon it, learn from its structure and design, make appropriate content and interoperable products. The Digital Millennium Copyright Act (DMCA), echoing the WIPO Copyright Treaty, explicitly prevents the circumvention of technological protection measures, thus, outlawing reverse engineering. What is of real concern is the manner in which the IP edifice is being built right under our noses, without our even noticing it, until recorded Christmas music played in church becomes an object for royalties. The fact remains that most people are unaware of the privatisation of knowledge, in the private as well as public spheres.

Information and the Limitations of the Old Paradigm

However, there is a far more profound question and that has to do with whether the conditions for production today, based on the manipulation of information, requires another framework for IPR, another philosophy, another toolkit. Production in the age of industry and manufacturing was based on the exploitation of finite resources. But the raw material for digital technologies is information which is essentially a non-rivalrous resource—your consumption and mine of the same text does not deplete it or degrade it in any way. In other words, digitised information and knowledge does have the potential to be made available to everyone who has access to a terminal. One must not forget the essentially cooperative basis for the development of version one of the Internet—inventors and programmers freely contributing their time to the development of its backbone. This history is precisely why we need to rethink IPR in a digital age, so that access to knowledge becomes a human right rather than a proprietorial privilege. After all, if we are serious about bridging the digital divide and ushering in the information society, we have to enable knowledge to be free so that the maximum number of people take advantage of the information revolution and contribute to its development—its architecture, governance and policy—through an approach based on participating, sharing and learning.

Just as people in an earlier era freely perfected, through trial and error, an earlier technology to develop optimum agricultural practices—seed, cropping, appropriate technological interventions (also under threat)—one can argue that in the age of information, there is similarly the need for people to craft software to their needs, to culturally appropriate software, since it is fast becoming the basis for all productive processes. In other words, there is a need for open access to 'code', to the creation of open standards and for policies that will allow for the new literacy that is required, if we are serious about moving from a system characterised by knowledge enclosures (the old paradigm) to a system based on open learning platforms (the new paradigm).

Notes

1. Intellectual Property in India, Embassy of India, Policy Statements. Available at http://www.indianembassy.org/policy/ipr/ipr_2000.htm (Accessed on 11 November 2008).
2. The Indian Music Industry. Available at http://www.indianmi.org/ (Accessed on 23 June 2008).
3. IPR Bilateral Cooperation. Available at http://www.patentoffice.nic.in/ (Accessed on 11 November 2008).
4. Overview: The TRIPS Agreement, WTO. Available at http://www.wto.org/english/tratop_e/trips_e/intel2_e.htm (Accessed on 21 March 2008).
5. 'Indian IT Software and Services Industry', pp. 1–7. Available at http://www.nasscom.org (Accessed on 11 January 2003).
6. Intellectual Property Rights (pp. 1–13). Available at http://www.nasscom.org (Accessed on 21 May 2004).
7. Part II: General Obligations and Disciplines, Article II. Available at http://www.wto.org/wto/services (Accessed on 21 May 2005).
8. NASSCOM, Software Copyright FAQs. Available at http://www.nasscom.in/Nasscom/templates/normalPage.aspx?id=6240 (Accessed on 9 May 2008).

References

Anandan, S. 2000. 'A Different Television War' (pp. 1–3). *Outlook,* 22 May. Available at http://www.outlookindia.com (Accessed on 21 May 2004).

Basheer, S. 2005. 'Policy Style Reasoning at the Indian Patent Office'. *Intellectual Property Quarterly*, 3: 309–323.

Berne Convention. 1999. Berne Convention for the Protection of Literary and Artistic Works (Paris Text 1971), pp. 1. Available at http://www.law.cornell.edu/treaties (Accessed on 2 August 2005).

Bettig, R.V. 2003. 'Copyright and the Commodification of Culture', *Media Development*, 1: 3–9.

Bettig, R. 1996. *Copyrighting Culture: The Political Economy of Intellectual Property*. Colorado/Oxford: Westview Press.

Boyle, J. 1997a. 'A Politics of Intellectual Property: Environmentalism for the Net?', pp. 1–23. Available at http://www.wcl.american.edu/pub/faculty (Accessed on 14 May 2006).

———. 1997b. *Shamans, Software and Spleens: Law and the Construction of the Information Society*. Massachusetts, London, England: Harvard University Press, Cambridge.

Branscomb, A.W. 1994. *Who Owns Information: From Privacy to Public Access*. New York: Basic Books.

Coombe, R. 1998. *The Cultural Life of Intellectual Properties: Authorship, Appropriation, and the Law*. Durham/London: Duke University Press.

Comor, E. A. 1998. 'Governance and the "Commoditisation" of Information', *Global Governance*, 4: 217–233.

Cullet, P. 2000. 'Farmer's Rights in Peril', *Frontline*, 17 (7): 1–5, 1–14 April. Available at http://www.frontlineonline.com (Accessed on 11 October 2003).

Gopalakrishnan, N.S. 1993. 'Computer Software Protection, the Dunkel Draft Text and the Indian Copyright Law', pp. 1–8. Available at http://www.iprlawindia.org (Accessed on 20 August 2007) originally published in *The Academy Law Review*, XVII: 1–2.

Husain, S. A. 2007. 'Art Imitates Art: Bollywood Finds Inspiration in Hollywood Films', *The Illinois Business Law Journal*, 9 November. Available at http://iblsjournal.typepad.com/Illinois_business_law_soc/2007/11/art-imitates-ar.html (Accessed on 13 November 2008).

Hindu. 2001. 'India Prepares to Meet TRIPS Obligations', *The Hindu*, International Edition, 24 February, p. 10.

Hindu Online. 2004. 'Tough Action against Video Piracy Coming'. 2004. *The Hindu Online*, 28 September, Available at http://www.hinduonnet.com/2004/09/28/stories/2004092809150100.htm (Accessed on 12 November 2008).

Jenkins III, Henry. 1992. *Textual Poachers: Television Fans and Participatory Culture*. New York: Routledge, Chapman and Hall.

Lal, C.M. 1998. 'The Indian Film Industry and Copyright Laws', (pp. 1–6). Available at http://www.indiaip.com/main.articles (Accessed on 12 June 2001).

Lessig, L. 1999. *Code: And other Laws of Cyberspace*. New York: Basic Books.

Liang, L. 2003. 'Conceptualising Law and Culture: Rajnikanth and the Sign of our Times', Alternative Law Forum. Available at http://www.altlawforum.org/PUBLICATIONS/document.2004-12-18.4121766710 (Accessed on 13 November 2008).

———. 2005. 'Porous Legalities and Avenues of Participation', *Sarai Reader: Bare Acts*, 5: 6–17.

Mansell, R. and U. Wehn. 1998. 'Institutional Innovations for the Governance of Information Services: Enforcing Intellectual Property Rights and Protecting Security and Privacy', in R. Mansell and U. Wehn (eds), *Knowledge Societies: Information Technology for Sustainable Development*, pp. 203–224. Oxford: Oxford University Press.

Menon, N. 2008. 'T-Series Notice to Websites for Copyright Violation', *The Economic Times*, 17 July. Available at http://economictimes.indiatimes.com/News/News_By_Industry/T-Series_notice_to_websites_for_copyright_violation/articleshow/3242429.cms (Accessed on 13 November 2008).

Miller, S.E. 1996. *Civilizing Cyberspace: Policy, Power and the Information Superhighway*. New York: ACM Press and Massachusetts: Addison-Wesley Publishing Company, Reading.

Monberg, J. 1999. 'Identities, Commodities and Information Flows: Intellectual Property Rights and the Construction of Emergent Electronic Social Spaces', in S. J. Drucker and G. Gumpert (eds), *Real Law @ Virtual Space: Regulation in Cyberspace*, pp. 267–286. Cresskill, New Jersey: Hampton Press Inc.

Office of the Controller of Patents, Designs, Trade Marks and Registrar of Geographical Indications. *Annual Report 2005–2006*, Gandhinagar.

Office of the United States Trade Representative. 2008. *2008 Special 301 Report*, pp. 1–51, Office of the United States Trade Representative, Washington. Available at http://www.ustr.gov/assets/Document_Library/Reports_Publications/2008/2008_Special_301_Report/asset_upload_file553_14869.pdf (Accessed on 12 November 2008).

Parthasarthy, A. 2001. 'Napster Case is no Music to Indian Ears', *The Hindu*, Int. Ed., 25 February, pp. 13.

Rangnekar, D. 2000. 'To Balance Regulation and Compliance', *Frontline*, 17(25), December 9–22: 1–6. Available at http://www.frontlineonline.com (Accessed on 25 June 2005).

Raval S. and S. Aiyer. 2001. 'Return of the Dons', *India Today*, 1 January: 1–5. Available at http://www.india-today.com (Accessed on 21 May 2004).

Reddy, P. 2008. 'Bollywood Abound with Suits for Copyright Infringement', *Spicy IP*. Available at http://spicyipindia.blogspot.com/search/label/Bollywood (Accessed on 13 November 2008).

Shedde, M. 2007. 'FICCI Meet Throws Light on Anti-piracy Measures', *Daily News and Analysis*, 27 March. Available at http://www.dnaindia.com/report.asp?NewsID=1087452 (Accessed on 12 November 2008).

Sidhva, S. 1996. 'A Target for Hollywood' (pp. vi), *Financial Times*, 11 July.

Story, A. 2002. Study Paper 5, *Study on Intellectual Property Rights, the Internet, and Copyright* (pp. 1–104), UK Commission on Intellectual Property Rights.

Sundaram, R. 2004. 'Uncanny Networks: Pirate, Urban and New Globalisation', *Economic & Political Weekly*, 3 January, 39(1): 64–72.

The Indian Copyright Act. 1957. Available at http://www.scatindia.com (Accessed on 23 June 2006).

6

The Political Economy of Audio-visual Trade

While the politics of audio-visual (AV) trade has merited some attention (Acheson and Maule 1999; Braithwaite and Drahos 2000; Grantham 2000), it has not received sustained academic attention among critical political economists. There could be a good reason for this lack of attention. Audio-visual trade has not quite figured at the centre of multi-lateral trade negotiations. While the General Agreement on Trade in Services (GATS) under the WTO has come tantalisingly close to opening up this sector, there have been strong counter currents against moves by some countries, the US in particular, to liberalise the AV sector. However, given the US government's contemporary pursuit of bilateral trade negotiations related to 'digital trade', it is more than likely that this avenue will become an important means for the further exploration of 'trade in culture' by net entertainment product exporters such as the US.

I take the view that a critical political economy of communication must take audio-visual trade seriously not least because the opening up of this sector can lead to the further integration of the world with global cultural markets and emerging intellectual property regimes. Trade and intellectual property regimes are two sides of the same coin and the ascendance of both regimes are closely interrelated. The successful opening up of global telecommunications to trade related reform and liberalisation in the 1980s under the aegis of the Uruguay round of trade talks was the first attempt to open up this sector. Today, it would seem that telecommunications reform is being used as a proxy to prise open the AV sector, given convergence and the fact that the internet has become a key conduit for the distribution of AV products. The digital trade umbrella is becoming the basis for a renewed attempt at opening up the global AV sector. Furthermore, with the slowing down of global multilateral trade post-Doha and the global financial and economic crisis, the US government has already signalled its intent to continue pursuing bilateral trade treaties, an easier avenue for negotiating trade in audio-visuals. In fact, by April 2007, the US had entered nine bilateral and two regional free trade agreements on cross border services including telecommunications.

Another reason for the need for critical input related to AV trade relates to the fact that the language of the digital has become the common language across multiple sectors. Any special consideration for 'digital trade', in other words, can have larger consequences and can impact on such areas as trade in genetic products/data. There was a time when AV products were considered 'goods' rather than 'service', a distinction that is disappearing in the context of convergence and the common language of the digital. Wheeler (2000: 35) describes this challenge:

> [T]echnological convergence raises new questions in the audiovisual field, which translate into different measures, policies and frameworks. There will be significant challenges to the concept of audiovisual services as the major media and multimedia players have already begun to absorb their definition of audiovisual within new concepts such as electronic commerce, information and entertainment services, and on-line trading.

In the post-Doha environment and in the context of the deadlock over multilateral trade, the US has pursued bilateral agreements, particularly with a view to prevent the emergence of trade barriers in the context of digital trade. Digital trade includes trade in IT goods, audio-visual and telecommunication and computer services, e commerce supported by strong IP provisions. Sacha Wunsch-Vincent (2003: 9), describes the economic basis for this agenda:

> This ambitious digital trade agenda originates from the fact that within the last couple of years a powerful alliance of American business associations that represent high-tech forms (e.g. Information Technology Industry Council) and associations that represent classical content producing firms (e.g. Motion Picture Association of America) has joined forces to voice its interests in avoiding the rise of new digital trade barriers. Apart from lucrative and bipartisan campaign contributions from these industries, the reasons for their congressional support are their past contribution to American growth and employment, and the strong comparative advantage of the U.S. in the trade of service in general and IT (especially software), entertainment products and activities related to royalties and licence fees in particular.

What is significantly different today, as opposed to two decades ago, is the fact that along with the US and UK, there have emerged significant new players in the global AV market including Brazil, Egypt, China and India. The growth of smaller, secondary export markets such as for Bollywood films from India does indicate that contestations related to AV trade no longer pit a handful of predominantly Western countries against the rest but also includes contestations over emerging export intensive entertainment hubs such as India and Brazil. While these emerging language markets have potential for growth, there is no denying the fact that the entertainment industries that are predominantly based in the US and the UK continue to enjoy a major share of the world's cultural export revenues and consequentially have the greatest incentives to push for a further liberalisation of the global AV sector. US cross-border trade in motion pictures and video services were worth USD 10.4 billion in 2005. UK television exports in 2007 earned GBP 633 million, a jump of 23 per cent from revenues earned in 2006. These revenues also included incomes for the licensing of formats such as Pop Idol and the Property Ladder (Conlan 2008).

The US, AV Trade and India

However, in order to understand AV trade, one has to go beyond discourses related to AV exports and cross border supplies and must deal with aspects such as the synergistic relationship between trade and IP and issues such as the lifting of trade barriers and increase in Foreign Direct Investment in Bollywood that has led to the increasing commercial presence of Hollywood in Bollywood. Inspite of significant new international players, the influence of the US as a global leader in content generation, along with exhibition and distribution of AV matter and as significantly the country with the most political capital and the required influence to pressure greater economic liberalisation places it at a distinct advantage when compared to India or for that matter Brazil. Or to put it in another way, the fact that Anil Ambani owns more than 200 screens in the US, although significant in the scheme of things, is less significant when compared to Hollywood's investments in film production in India, its investments in multiplexes throughout India, its use of Section 301 and the support of the USTR to pressure the Indian government to give it Most Favoured Nation (MFN) status and significant tax breaks. Contemporary efforts by the US entertainment industries to capture foreign markets is also the consequence of falling domestic ticket sales and DVD revenues and rising costs associated with local productions.

The political power of the US is expressed in this categorical statement by Bonnie Richardson, Vice President, Trade and Federal Affairs, MPAA (2002):

> The United States has reserved the right to supplement its initial standstill requests in AV services with targeted requests. We will be seeking to liberalise specific barriers that we feel have a particularly trade distortive effect on our exports...The US film, television and home video entertainment industry looks forward to all countries making commitments in audiovisual services.

Similarly, the ex-US Trade Representative (USTR) Robert Zoellick's (USEU 2002) overall vision was to build on the Doha Development Agenda and to liberalise services, in the light of the overall goal of the progressive liberalisation of the global AV sector:

> The United States request on audiovisual services is designed to contribute to the growth of the audiovisual sector of all WTO members by fostering a transparent, open and predictable environment for trade in audiovisual services...With this in mind, the United States requests countries to schedule commitments that reflect current levels of market access in areas such as motion picture and home video entertainment production and distribution services, radio and television production services, and sound recording services.

The US position on the liberalising of services is of course to be expected, given that services account for '80 percent of US employment', contributes '63 percent to the US Gross Domestic Product (GDP)' and that the US, as the world's largest exporter of services, doubled its exports worth '$137 billion in 1990 to $279 billion in 2000'.

Even as recent as two decades ago, AV imports into India were protected. However, the opening up of this sector to exports involved significant trade-related pressure mainly from the US. In the 1990s, Section 301 was used by the USTR against India, ostensibly in retaliation against India's inability to curb video piracy. There were, however, larger trade and security motives, including economic liberalisation, the lowering of perceived high tariffs in industrial imports, the opening up of the banking and insurance sector to foreign investment, along with the immediate motive of positioning Hollywood in the Indian film market. While piracy is a reality in India—the IIPA has estimated the 2002 trade losses to the US copyrights industry incurred in India in the region of USD 468.1 million covering book, cable, video, music, business software, internet, retail and entertainment software piracies.[1] The infinitely larger prospect of earnings from a potential audience for Hollywood in the region of 200 million, plans to carve out 10 per cent of the Indian film market by the year 2000 and open up the Indian film market, were part of the larger game plan. An immediate goal was to get the Indian government to lift restrictions on annual Hollywood imports that were restricted to an annual quota of 100 films. While the Schedule of Commitments agreed to by the Indian government on trade in services dated 15 April 1994 under 2D Audio-visual Services, rather blandly states that 'ii) Import of titles restricted to 100 per year',[2] it did, in less than a year in 1995, decide to increase this quota from 100 to 200 films a year to the delight of the Motion Picture Association of America (MPAA). The MPAA incidentally represents the interests of seven Hollywood majors inclusive of Walt Disney Company, Sony Pictures Entertainment, Metro-Goldwyn-Mayer, Paramount Pictures Corporation, Twentieth Century Fox Film Corporation, Universal Studios and Warner Brothers. On 29 January 2002, the Government of India Ministry of Commerce and Industry, Department of Commerce issued a Public Notice No. 64/1997–2002, that announced the end of the quota system—'(i) Import of cinematograph feature films and other films (including film on video tape, compact video disc, laser video disc or digital video disc) shall be allowed without a licence.'[3]

The USTR has also imposed sanctions on occasion, 'In April 1992, the President suspended duty-free privileges under the Generalised System of Preferences (GSP) for $60 million in trade from India...Benefits on certain chemicals...were withheld from India, increasing the trade for which GSP is suspended to approximately $80 million.' The USTR's actions are not only directed towards increasing film quotas, but to systematically opening this sector along with a variety of other trade-related sectors to US investments. It monitors the progress of IPR and AV related domestic legislations, exerts pressure on the government to lift restrictions, monitors anti-free trade activities, and follows through its intent to use bilateral and multilateral means to open this sector to US capital. In the case of motion pictures, the USTR is currently involved in negotiating the lifting of domestic barriers to trade including pre-censorship certification of films, the fees involved, entertainment taxes, the import of film/video publicity material and the ceiling of USD 6 million for remittances by foreign film producers for balance of payment reasons. The USTR report, *India: Foreign Trade Barriers*,[4] in the section on motion pictures, includes a veiled threat of the use of Section 301 sanctions if the issue related to entertainment tax on film admittance tickets is not satisfactorily concluded— 'High taxes not only constitute a significant disincentive to much needed construction of cinemas and theatres in India, but impede free and open trade' (p. 64).

In 2001, India imported around 248 films, predominantly from Hollywood. More significantly, the Indian entertainment industry is now open to foreign direct investment in most, if not all, sectors including 100 per cent FDI in film production, exhibition and distribution and 100 per cent in the music industry. However, there are still some barriers including the fact that there are restrictions on the import of film-related publicity material.

It is interesting to note that the entertainments business in the US is increasingly referred to in trade circles and official parlance as 'copyright industries'. In other words, the IP characteristic of a product now signifies its real worth. The report prepared for the International Intellectual Property Alliance (IIPA), *Copyright Industries in the US Economy: The 2002 Report* (Siwek 2002), indicates that the total copyright industries in the US including the 'core' copyright industries, namely the motion pictures industry, the recording industry, music publishing industry, book, newspaper, journal industry, computer software industry along with others contributed USD 531.1 billion or 5.24 per cent of the US Gross Domestic Product (GDP). The IIPA represents the interests of six associations, Association of American Publishers, AFMA, Business Software Alliance, Interactive Digital Software Association, Motion Picture Association of America, Recording. This report also indicates 2001 foreign sales and exports of these products in the region of USD 88.97 billion and core copyright employment in the same year in the region of 4.7 million workers. It is not at all surprising therefore that the US has invested in strengthening its IP writ in the rest of the world, both unilaterally through support for state and civil enforcement initiatives against IP violators and multilaterally through TRIPS and WIPO enforcement provisions.

Trade and IP are common objectives pursued by a range of US-based free trade groups including the Motion Picture Association (MPA), the Business Software Alliance (BSA), International Intellectual Property Alliance (IIPA) and government bodies such as the USTR. The 2007 Special 301 Report (48–50) on India, brought out by the IIPA (2007), recommends the following changes to the local IP environment that would be of benefit to the AV industry in India, foreign and domestic. These include the establishment of special IP courts, the creation of an anti-piracy task force, resourcing IP cells within the state police, increasing raids, passing optical disc regulations, enacting amendments to India's copyright laws that are consistent with the WIPO Internet Treaties, empowering customs to destroy pirate goods and removal of market access restrictions. The intent to liberalise the motion pictures sector in India and provide MFN status to all firms including Hollywood majors is clearly visible in the following recommendation to remove market access restrictions:

> Market access restrictions in Tamil Nadu by way of discriminatory taxes on non-Tamil and dubbed films have only been exacerbated in 2006 by a further reduction in taxes on local films. A number of measures were also taken in 2006 in Andhra Pradesh to discriminate against non-Telugu films. These market access restrictions need to be removed. (International Intellectual Property Alliance 2007 Special 301 Report: India)

The tightening and strengthening of copyright enforcement with respect to domestic cultural products, films in particular, has also become part of the Motion Picture Association's (MPA) New Delhi-based India-wide operations. Such a prioritising will, in the long run, also ensure the protection of returns to the Hollywood industry in India. The reason for MPA's involvement in copyright protection of local film products becomes clearer when seen against the investments made by one of its members, Sony Pictures' Indian wing, Columbia TriStar India. It was the first Hollywood company to cross the Rs 100 crore mark at the Indian box office and India now ranks among the 15 top film markets for Sony. The company earned 30 per cent of its income from the production of Indian English films and 70 percent from film distribution. Hollywood share in the Indian film market is around 10 per cent and this needs to be seen against the Rs 300 crore loss suffered by Bollywood in 2003 (Gumaste 2003). As I have noted in Chapter 5, Sony Entertainment TV has bought rights to 300 Hindi films, and secured exclusive rights for cultural and sporting events in India. Sony also hosts top-rated show *Aahat, Indian Idol* and has also launched new programmes including *Bhasker Bharti* and *Ladies Special*. The company also owns one of the largest film archives in India currently in the region of 1300 films. Similarly, another member of MPA, Twentieth Century Fox, a subsidiary of News Corporation, is also poised to break into the film market with 20 productions per year (Sidhva 1996). With such investments at stake, India can look forward to the active involvement of the MPA in the matter of copyright enforcement. There is, of course, a major commercial reason for copyright enforcement and that has to do with the opening up of AV trade to facilitate the global cross-sectoral marketing of products. Most, if not all, the major US motion picture firms including Warner Brothers, Twentieth Century Fox, Buena

Vista (Disney), United International Pictures, Universal, Paramount, Dreamworks Pictures along with the Japanese firms Sony Pictures and Columbia TriStar have a presence in India through co-productions and involvement in film distribution and exhibition. 'Sony Pictures' decision to unveil *Quantum of Solace*, the latest edition of James Bond's escapades, in India before premiering it in the US is a testimonial to how the business of global entertainment has undergone fundamental changes in the past year' (Indo-Asian News Service 2008).

A Short History of GATS and Trade in AV Services

The overriding aim of economic liberalisation under the WTO is trade in *all goods and services* and this general objective is recognised in GATS Part IV: Progressive Liberalisation, Article XIX: Negotiation of Specific Commitments:

> In pursuance of the objectives of this Agreement, Members shall enter into successive rounds of negotiations, beginning not later than five years from the date of entry into force of the WTO Agreement and periodically thereafter, with a view to achieving a progressively higher level of liberalisation. (Uruguay Round Agreement; see Endnote 10)

The AV sector in GATS includes the production and distribution of audio-visual (AV) content inclusive of motion pictures, television and radio programmes and new digital services that are a consequence of convergent technologies. The Services Sectoral Classification List defines audio-visuals as sub-sector D under Section 2—Communication Services. It lists six sub-categories:

a) Motion picture and video tape production and distribution services.
b) Motion picture projection services.
c) Radio and television services.
d) Radio and television transmission services.
e) Sound recording.
f) Other, that could cover areas such as multimedia services.

The General Agreement on Trade in Services (GATS) negotiated during the Uruguay Round of the General Agreement on Tariffs and Trade (GATT) talks, the forerunner of the WTO, included, among its 130 schedules of commitments, proposals related to a sectoral concern, 'Audiovisual and Related Services'. As Grantham has pointed out, Article IV of GATT did allow members to place quotas on the import of cinema although this was mainly directed towards curbing US AV exports:

> Despite the fact that the principle victim of Article IV was Hollywood, the United States remained largely quiet over screen quotas. However, in the early 1960s, the US raised for the first time the issue of quotas against television programs, claiming that these violated Article III: 4 of the GATT (on discrimination against imports). Others, notably France, argued that television programs represented a service not a good, and were thus not covered by GATT. (Grantham 2000: 92)

However, few countries made extensive commitments to liberalising their AV sector. In fact, towards the end of the Uruguay round in 1993, Jack Lang, the French cultural minister was involved in a public exchange with the US government related to the case in favour of 'cultural exception' (See Riding 1993). While the US did attempt to contest the quota provisions contained within the European Directive 'Television without Frontiers', by the end of the Uruguay round of trade talks, the EU had made minimum commitments to opening up their AV sectors to trade. It is with the negotiation of GATS within the purview of the WTO that we see greater pressures related to the expansion of AV trade. Each member of the WTO was expected to submit commitments in specific sectors covering market access, national treatment, the lifting of quantitative restrictions and the removal of caps on foreign equity holdings. One of the major negotiations decided at the Marrakesh Ministerial at the closing of the Uruguay Round in 1994, was the liberalisation of basic telecom services (See Hendersen et al. 2005). This negotiation was concluded in February 1997 and led a number of countries in the developed and developing world to offer greater levels of market access in basic telecommunications. Tathill (1997: 5) recounts some of the commitments that have been made:

> [C]ommitments cover not only cross border telecommunications services but also their provision through foreign ownership or operation of domestic network infrastructure. Examples of the services under negotiation were voice telephony, data transmission, telex, facsimile, leased circuit services (i.e. the sale or lease of transmission capacity), fixed and mobile satellite systems and services, cellular telephony, mobile data services, paging and personal communication systems.

A new round of GATS negotiations was launched in 2000 with the Doha round and was expected to be concluded by 1 January 2005 although it was suspended following the WTO Ministerial Conference that was held in Hong Kong in 2006. Twelve service sectors were slated for negotiations including communications services covering telecommunication and audio-visuals.

While the liberalisation of other listed communications services, including telecommunications and e-commerce became a priority focus at GATS negotiations, AV services neither become the target for substantive multi-lateral negotiations, nor resulted in commitments. In fact only 17 countries committed to the sub-category (a) Motion picture and videotape production and distribution services, and 10 to sub-category (b) Motion picture projection services (Acheson and Maule 1999). In the late 1990s, there were 33 exemptions covering audio-visual services and eight general MFN exemptions related to AV services under the GATS schedule on communications.[5] A number of key WTO members including Canada, the EU and Australia did not make any commitments in this sector. The only countries that made commitments in all six sectors were the US and the Central African Republic. In the 2000 round of GATS, only three countries, namely Brazil, Switzerland and the US offered further liberalisation of their AV sectors.

One of the problems faced by countries that are keen to restrict AV trade, such as Canada and France, is that unlike less than a decade ago, many countries both within the EU and outside, have more or less gravitated towards a pro-trade position on AV.[6] The UK, for instance, supports AV trade given its strengths in television production. Others, such as Switzerland, want to act as a bridge between the EU and the US, on AV liberalisation at GATS and Brazil and India seem to be open to liberalising some areas under AV. Today, unlike a decade ago, more countries have agreed to GATS Commitments in AV—Printing and Publishing (38), Motion Picture Production and Distribution (23), Motion Picture Exhibition (24), Radio and Television Services (10), Sound Recording (11), Entertainment Services (49), News Agency Services (34), Libraries, Archives and Museums (18).[7]

Culture as Trade versus Cultural Exception

One of the major stumbling blocks for supporters of AV trade is the growing belief in inter-governmental circles such as UNESCO, at the EU and countries such as Canada, France and Spain that 'cultural policy', inasmuch as it is affected by AV services, ought to be governed by instruments not limited to the trade remit. Whether or not this concern will become global in scope is anybody's guess. Nevertheless, issues around 'cultural exception' continue to be discussed at a global level and recent initiatives include UNESCO's Universal Declaration on Cultural Diversity (UNESCO 2001), the inter-governmental International Network on Cultural Policy and their calls for a Convention on Cultural Diversity and initiatives made by national forums such as the Canada-based Cultural Industries Sectoral Advisory Group on International Trade (SAGIT). These initiatives are explicitly against the further liberalisation of AV trade and the commercialisation of culture. In fact, the introductory text accompanying UNESCO's Convention on Cultural Diversity highlights the hope that it will eventually achieve the moral force currently enjoyed by the Universal Declaration of Human Rights (UDHR). Articles 8 and 11 of the UNESCO Convention provide emphatic support for this position.

While Article 8 states the following:

> In the face of present-day economic and technological change, opening up vast prospects for creation and innovation, particular attention must be paid to the diversity of the supply of creative work, to due recognition of the rights of authors and artists and to the specificity of cultural goods and services which, as vectors of identity, values and meaning, must not be treated as mere commodities or consumer services. (UNESCO 2001)

Article 11 states, 'Market forces alone cannot guarantee the preservation and promotion of cultural diversity, which is the key to sustainable human development. From this perspective, the pre-eminence of public policy, in partnership with the private sector and civil society, must be reaffirmed.'

The Canadian Minister for International Trade convened a cultural industries Sectoral Advisory Group on International Trade (SAGIT) in 1999 towards developing a New International Instrument on Cultural Diversity, as a means of achieving global consensus and leverage in the matter of culture as trade. Canada has had one or two bruising encounters with the US on matters related to cultural trade, most recently a run-in over a 'split-run' magazine policy. A split-run is a common technique used in the media industry to combine common editorial content with advertising tailored to particular markets (Acheson and Maule 1999). Canada levied excise tax on *Sports Illustrated* for its adoption of a split-run policy citing local media losses. Time Warner, the parent company took the case to the WTO in 1996 and the WTO ruling went against Canada. The five objectives of the report are as follows:

- recognise the importance of cultural diversity;
- acknowledge that cultural products and services are significantly different from other products;
- acknowledge that domestic measures and policies intended to ensure access to a variety of indigenous cultural products are significantly different from other policies;
- set out rules on the kind of domestic regulatory and other measures that countries can and cannot use to enhance cultural and linguistic diversity; and
- establish how trade disciplines would apply or not apply to cultural measures that meet the agreed upon rules. (Goldsmith 2002)[8]

The Canadian government has used the International Network on Cultural Policy (INCP) forum to pursue these goals. This network met most recently in Seville, Spain in 2007. The Canadian Ambassador to the World Trade Organisation, Sergio Marchi, in an address given to the Canadian Association of Broadcasters at the Banff Television Festival on 10 June 2002, spelt out this position. Speaking on the SAGIT initiative, he made a strong case for a celebration of cultural diversity rather than its enclosure within a trade paradigm:

> [SAGIT is not] a protectionist tool. It is a legitimate expression of Canada's aspirations as a country—an assertion that our cultural experiences are uniquely woven into our very lives and communities in a way that defines and sustains us as a nation and as a people…And beyond our borders, the Instrument offers a means to help ensure that distinctive stories and storytellers from around the world can find space for themselves in the global information society…in short, the working proposition is that cultural diversity is a rich and dynamic part of our global heritage, and we should strive to keep it that way. (Marchi 2002: 6)

While France and Canada have identified audio-visual products as vectors of culture, holders and markers of national identity, as channels for the dissemination of root values and have argued the case for a 'cultural exception clause' and for trade in culture to be dealt with separately from trade in other goods and services, the US simply views culture as just another item for trade, no different from other commercial goods and services. This difference in opinion between the EU and the US does not equally apply to all sectors related to AV in GATS but to only those AV services that signify, celebrate, reflect the 'essence' of a nation and national identity, namely publicly funded motion pictures, television and radio services. The position taken by the EU recognises the fact that, in a cultural environment dominated by Hollywood, the survival of domestic cultural industries, especially film production, is dependent as much on subsidies as on import restrictions.

The US stance reflects its pre-eminent position as the world leader in the production and exporter of audio-visual services—including film, television, recorded music along with multi-media products and the fact that culture in the US has traditionally been equated with commercial entertainment available to anyone for a fee, with little or no claim on values. This difference of opinion continues to be in evidence despite the fact that the position of some countries in the EU and Australia on AV trade has shifted considerably during the last five years. However, strong differences still exist, as illustrated in this recent submission to GATS by Canada, 'Audiovisual and other culturally relevant services' that categorically states that 'Canada will…not make any commitment that restricts our ability to achieve our cultural policy objectives until a new international instrument, designed specifically to safeguard the right of countries to promote and preserve their cultural diversity, can be established'.[9]

The position adopted by Canada is not even remotely alluded to in GATS Articles I-XXVI. In fact, Article XIV: General Exceptions (a) that states that countries can take measures 'necessary to protect public morals or maintain public order' and Article XIX that states that 'The process of liberalisation shall take place with due respect for national policy objectives…',[10] are the closest that GATS gets to dealing with anything resembling 'cultural exception'. However, and in spite of all the efforts that have gone into strengthening the case for cultural diversity, there is a need for us to recognise that 'cultural exception' is a notion and that, as such, it has no legal status and exists as a tacit understanding between like-minded nations of the moral worth of cultural diversity.

AV Trade and the Developing World: The Case of India

From a country that had been a net importer of Hollywood albeit limited to 100 titles a year and with a very limited television sector two decades ago, India today is emerging as a hub for the regional production of entertainment goods and services with projected export revenues running into millions of dollars. Traditionally, Indian cinema did have currency among its diaspora in the UK, US, Middle East and in specific markets in South East Asia, East and West Africa although it is in the post-cable and satellite era, India's opening up of its entertainment sector to foreign direct investment, co-productions, Hollywood dubs in Indian languages and growth in the animation, television and film industries that has led to the globalisation of Indian entertainment products. As the 2007 Annual Report on US Services ('Recent Trends in U.S. Services Trade' 2007: 47) states:

> India, the world's leader in movie production by volume (1,041 feature films in 2005), has begun to expand movie distribution beyond its domestic market to attract box office receipts from its large diaspora population. Indian films are exported around 95 countries...Recent improvements in equipment and facilities have been made in production centres such as Ramoji Film City (RFC) in Hyderabad, whose studios are on the same scale as some of those in Hollywood. Further, in an effort to harness Indian technical expertise and reduce production costs, advanced post-production and visual effects companies such as SIBAR media and Entertainment Ltd. (India) have set up studios in India with the goal of becoming a central post-production outsourcing hub for major film producers.

Export revenue projected for the entertainment industry in India, while not in the same league as the US, is nevertheless substantial. It is expected to reach Rs 18 billion in 2013 from Rs 10 billion in 2008 (see 2009 FICCI-PricewaterhouseCooper report on the Indian entertainment industry). In rupee terms film exports have grown from Rs 2 billion in 1998 (198 titles), Rs 4.5 billion in 2000, (412 titles), Rs 5.25 billion in 2001 (450+ titles) to 12 billion (USD 275.4) in 2003 (*FICCI Arthur Andersen Report* 2002). Animation, too, is slated to become a major future revenue earner. There are currently a clutch of animation houses, many among which are involved in outsourcing for Hollywood. Top companies include Crest Communications, UTV Toons, Sri Adhikari Bros, Films Division, Silverline, Colour Chips, Heart Animation, Sriven Multitech, Digital Studio, Pentamedia, DSQ (TIL) and Visual Vistas.[11] While the Indian film industry will benefit from liberalisation, the larger question that needs to be posed is whether limited access to foreign markets will need to be reciprocated by the total opening up of Indian markets and to the liberalisation of market access that might outweigh any potential benefits. India may not have much of a choice in this regard.

Reverse Cultural Imperialism? Bollywood in Pakistan

Given Bollywood's size, cross-border affinities and shared identities between India and the rest of South Asia, transborder data flows—beginning with Bollywood—flows via commercial stations belonging to the All India Radio network—Vividh Bharathi—followed by satellite television in the

1990s, led to what some South Asians have termed the Bollywoodisation of their worlds. Indian popular culture does exert a predominant influence over other local cultures in Nepal, Bhutan, Bangladesh and Pakistan. This influence is resented especially across the border in Pakistan. In what remains the most accessible introduction to the new television environment in South Asia, David Page and William Crawley (2001: 223) have observed that the threat posed by Bollywood imperialism is especially felt among elites in countries that share a common border with India:

> [T]he popularity of Hindi language entertainment channels has given rise to apprehensions that the culture of Bollywood is swamping other national cultures and even destroying the ideological boundaries of the nation state. Such ideological worries have been most intensely felt in Pakistan; less so in Bangladesh or Nepal, though the popularity of satellite channels has presented a challenge to state broadcasters in those countries as well. In all three countries, those speaking for national cultures see Hindi satellite channels as carriers of an Indian culture which threatens to break down the sense of difference which the state and state broadcasters have been trying to reinforce.

Given deep and abiding political rivalries between Pakistan and India, it is not surprising that Pakistan has banned the import of Bollywood films, although that ban has not been strictly enforced and Bollywood films are freely available in a thriving local pirate film market. As Formentini and Iapadre (2006: 11–12) have observed:

> Since 1965, Pakistan has imposed a ban on Indian films. Besides political tensions, the ban obeys [sic] to industrial concerns as well, as the majority of Pakistan's film industry...continues to claim that the removal of the ban would result in a 'complete Bollywood-isation of Pakistan', and in the definitive end of film production activities in the country...Pakistani government has already shown an overall tough position versus Indian exports, refusing to grant MFN status to India.

India has been trying to explore audio-visual exports within the ambit of the South Asian Free Trade Arrangement without much success. Pakistan does have a strong television drama sector and there are those who advocate reciprocal entertainment flows (See Noorani 2007).

AV Trade: The Dominant Perspective in India

It is clear that the Indian position of AV trade has changed considerably in the post-liberalisation era. A Working Paper written by Arpita

Mukharjee dated April 2002, 'India's Trade Potential in Audio-visual Services and GATS', suggests a framework that is in tune with official AV Indian interests. After providing a comprehensive overview of AV trade possibilities including domestic and external constraints, GATS and audio-visual services and strategies for current negotiations, the author takes the line that with the exception of public broadcasting, India ought to make commitments in a variety of categories under AV services including motion picture, radio and television content, videotape production and distribution services. Mukherjee takes the position that the market ought to be the final arbiter of culture, via the near-total liberalisation of AV trade. The following two quotes capture this market orientation:

> Indian audio-visual industry caters to a niche audience and hence, does not face any direct competition from the major players such as the US. India's trade in audio-visual and related services is steadily increasing and the Indian industry is exploring new markets and delivery platforms. It is, therefore, in India's interest to push for liberalisation of trade in this sector. In this respect, India may consider the possibilities of allying with major players such as the US to push for increased market forces. (Mukherjee 2002: 64)
>
> [M]any countries of export interest to India such as the EU and Canada have imposed various restrictions on broadcasting such as broadcasting quotas and local content requirements. Since India has not imposed similar restrictions, India should negotiate with these countries for removal of such restrictions. (Mukherjee 2002: 66)

This position is taken further in a working paper from the Indian Council for Research on International Economic Relations—'Indo-US FTA: Prospects for Audiovisual Services' (2007: 61), written by Arpita Mukherjee, Paramita Deb Gupta and Prerna Ahuja—that explores the liberalisation of AV trade between India and US in a future FTA between the two countries. This study argues 'that the trade complementarities between the two countries could be further enhanced through a media cooperation agreement with the United States'. While this study clearly identifies some of the mutual benefits accruing from greater cooperation—cheaper labour for the US, access to technical innovation and access to the US market for India AV products, it has little to say about the impact of further liberalisation of this sector on cultural labour in India. While the 'unorganised' cinema industry in India certainly had its drawbacks, it employed thousands of people in the pre-production, production and post-production stages from poster artists to tea-boys. The Hollywoodisation of the film industry will include greater rationalisation, leading to better quality films, perhaps at the expense of a people-intensive culture of film production.

The swamping of local cultures in South Asia by the culture of Bollywood is bound to be detrimental to a variety of local traditions of cinema given that these industries just do not have the reputation or economic muscle to compete with this behemoth from India. While one can argue that Bollywoodisation can lead to the production of new, hybrid, economically viable goods and services in different contexts in South Asia—such as MTV cross-overs all over the world that seem to have reinvigorated local music traditions, surely countries in South Asia will not be happy with products either derived from or that have been substantially shaped by cultural industries in India. Irrespective of the fact that obituaries for 'cultural imperialism' have been written, the impact of mono-cultures on the cultures of small nations is an issue that cannot be wished away by recourse to putative globalisation's manufacture of level playing fields in the field of culture as in economic development. Even in India, the decline of local cultures has been rapid and rather inexorable in the context of hyper-development.

Conclusion

Issues to do with whether or not India should liberalise AV trade further is not as straightforward as it seems. While there is certainly merit in exploring possibilities for better external market opportunities for commercial entertainment products made in India, as for example, Bollywood films, AV trade involves not just flows of cultural products but also includes FDI and the extension of MFN status for large media conglomerates such as Warner Brothers and Buena Vista. The impact of vertically-integrated companies that enjoy economies of scale on local industries built around a plethora of traditions of film production can be devastating for local communities. While the mantra of greater professionalisation of the media in India certainly has merits, there is a need for a greater critical scrutiny of the texts and agreements related to AV trade and for larger, more nuanced understandings of the benefits and weaknesses of such agreements. A related issue is that of the relationship between trade and IP as a single package. A tight harmonisation of global IP laws with local legislations can only lead to the stifling of local innovation and creativity. Issues around cultural identity tend to be dismissed outright because there are those who connect this discourse with the Americanisation of India. While the globalisation of cultural influences and its local impact cannot be made sense of through an analysis of AV export volumes, there is a sense in which cultural identity relates to the substance of a number of practices that evolve around the field of cultural production and the habits of those involved in cultural production. These dynamic practices, grounded in ways of life that are based on the negotiation of tradition and modernity, are more than just functional aspects of life. One can argue that such practices contribute to making cultural identity real. Srivatsan (1991: 3), in an article on film hoardings (billboards) in India, describes the team of artists involved in creating a hoarding:

> The team consists of a hierarchy of skilled painters who do different parts or rather layers of the painting. At the bottom are the boys who paint the ground for the images, and were paid around Rs. 10/- per area of 100 sq ft in October 1990. At the next level are the people who paint in the shapes and silhouettes of the figures. Another level of skill paints in the coarse details of the bodies and faces. Finally the master painter breathes life into the images by painting in the fine details.

While mechanical reproduction (lithographic, laser ink-jet printed hoardings) is rapidly changing this culture, this micro-culture is bound to disappear entirely in the context of Bollywood's move from entertaining the masses to the middle classes, a reality that will only be hastened by the Hollywoodisation of Bollywood.

Finally, there is the issue to do with digital trade that can become the basis for a much larger, potentially more damaging opening of India's natural and cultural diversity to global trade. Given the spread, influence and embrace of the digital as a common language across all productive sectors, all products across all sectors are potentially part of what we now habitually call the 'service' economy. I have in Chapter 1 dealt with the larger marriages that have taken place between IT and other technologies such as biotechnology and nanotechnology, the continuities between nature and culture and its implications, including new sources of power that arise from the common language of the digital. Will the digital finally lead to the 'Trading of the Nation' or will the country have the nerve and gumption to negotiate wisely in an era characterised by 'digital trade'?

Notes

1. India—Schedule of Specific Commitments, General Agreement GATS/SC/42 15 April 1994 on Trade in Services (94–1040). Available online at http://docsonline.wto.org/GEN_viewerwindow.asp? (Accessed on 11 June 2006).
2. www.iipa.co

3. Government of India, Public Notice to be published in the Gazette of India Extraordinary. Available at http://dgftcom.mic.in/exim/2000/pn/pn01/pn6401.htm (Accessed on 21 May 2001).
4. Foreign Trade Barriers: India. Available at http://www.ustr.com (Accessed on 11 May 2004).
5. WTO Restricted S/C/W/40, Council for Trade in Services, Audiovisual Services: Background Note by Secretariat. Available at http://doconline.wto.org/GEN_viewerwindow.asp? (Accessed on 11 June 2007).
6. http://ec.europa.eu/avpolicy/index_en.htm (Accessed on 28 June 2008).
7. www.ebu.ch
8. http://www.dfait-maeci.gc.ca
9. S/CSS/W/46—14 March 2001 (Initial GATS Sectoral/Modal/Horizontal Negotiating Proposals). Available at http://www.wto.orf/english/info_e/search_e.htm (Accessed on 21 May 2004).
10. Uruguay Round Agreement: General Agreement on Trade in Services (Article I–XXVI), (pp. 1–24). Available at http://www.wto.org/english/docs_e/legal_e/26-gats_01_e.htm (Accessed on 21 May 2007).
11. 'Big Animation Houses Reach Out to Grab Bulk Business', Video Post Production News. Available at http://www.studio-systems.com/hotnews.braodcastnews/julyAug2000/PostNews/9.htm (Accessed on 14 May 2006).

References

Acheson, K. and C. Maule. 1999. *Much Ado About Culture: North American Trade Disputes* Ann Arbor: University of Michigan Press.

Audiovisual services and GATS: EBU comments on US negotiating proposals of December 2000, European Broadcasting Union. See www.ebu.ch for this and other documentation on GATS and AV (Accessed on 4 May 2007).

Braithwaite, John and Peter Drahos. 2000. *Global Business Regulation*. Cambridge: Cambridge University Press.

Conlan, T. 2008. 'British Television Exports Soar', *The Guardian Online* (Accessed on 6 March 2009).

Dutta, S. 2001. 'Real Life, Reel Woes', *Business World*, 15 January: 1–3.

FICCI-Arthur Andersen Report. 2002. 'Indian Entertainment Industry: The Show Must Go On', March 2002 (Accessed on 11 August 2007; The Website is no longer available).

Formentini, S. and L. Iapadre. 2006. 'Cultural Diversity and Regional Trade Arrangements: The Case of Audiovisual Services'. Available at http://www.etsg.org/ETSG2006/papers/Formentini.pdf (Accessed on 21 May 2008).

Goldsmith, B. 2002. 'Cultural Diversity, Cultural Networks and Trade: International Cultural Policy Debate', *Media International Australia*, issue 102, February: 35–53.

Grantham, B. 2000. *'Some Big Bourgeois Brothel': Contexts for France's Culture Wars with Hollywood*. Luton: University of Luton Press.

Gumaste, D. 2003. 'Holiywood Piece of Cake', *Rediff.com*, 5 February. Available at http://rediff.com/movies (Accessed on 11 June 2004).

Henderson, A., I. Gentle and E. Ball. 2005. 'WTO Principles and Telecommunications in Developing Nations: Challenges and Consequences of Accession', *Telecommunications Policy*, 29(2–3): 205–221.

Indo-Asian News Service. 2008. 'Hollywood Sharpens Focus on India', Indo-Asian News Service, 5 October. Available at http://newsx.com/story/30314 (Accessed on 21 May 2009).

International Intellectual Property Alliance (IIPA). 2007. Special 301 Report: India. Available at http://www.iipa.com/rbc/2007/2007SPEC301INDIA.pdf (Accessed on 21 May 2008).

Mukherjee, A. 2002. India's Trade Potential in Audio-Visual Services and the GATS, Working Paper No. 81, April, Indian Council for Research on International Economic Relations, New Delhi. Available at http://www.icrier.res.in/pdf/avpaper.pdf (Accessed on 21 May 2005).

Mukherjee, A., P.D. Gupta and P. Ahuja. 2007. 'Indo-US FTA: Prospects for Audio-Visual Services', (1–75), Working Paper No. 192, Indian Council for Research on International Economic Relations, New Delhi, February.

Marchi, Sergio. 2002. 'The World Trade Organisation: From Doha and Beyond', speaking notes for Ambassador Sergio Marchi at the Canadian Association of Broadcasters Third Annual International Broadcaster's Dialogue, Banff Television Festival, 10 June, pp. 1–7.

Noorani, T. 2007. 'Projecting the Real Image', *Dawn Internet Edition*, 21 June. Available at http://www.dawn.com/weekly/review/archive/070621/review5.htm (Accessed on 22 June 2008).

Page, D. and W. Crawley. 2001. *Satellites over South Asia: Broadcasting, Culture and the Public Interest*. New Delhi, Thousand Oaks, London: Sage Publications.

Recent Trends in U.S. Services Trade, 2007 Annual Report, United States International Trade Commission, Washington D.C. Available at http://hotdocs.usitc.gov/docs/Pubs/332/Pub3925.pdf (Accessed on 23 May 2008).

Richardson, B. J. K. 2002. 'Priorities for the US Audiovisual Sector in the GATS Negotiations', Services 2002: Conference on WTO Negotiations on Services U.S. Department of Commerce (No Date).

Riding, A. 1993. 'The World Trade Agreement: The French Strategy Months of Risk, Moments of Isolation, Now Boasts of Triumph', *New York Times*, 15 December.

Sidhva, S. 1996. 'A Target for Hollywood', *Financial Times Survey, Maharashtra*, 11 July (p. vi).

Siwek, E. S. 2002. '*Copyright Industries in the U.S. Economy: The 2002 Report*'. Prepared for the IIPA. Available at http://www.iipa.com.

Srivatsan, R. 1991. 'Looking at Film Hoardings: Labour, Gender, Subjectivity and Everyday Life in India', *Public Culture*, 4 (1): 1–23.

Tathill, L. 1997. 'Historic Deal Paves the Way to a Global Free Market', *Intermedia*, 25 (3): 4–5.

UNESCO. 2001. 'Universal Declaration of Cultural Diversity'. Available at http://www.cesmap.it/ifrao/unescode.htm (Accessed on 11 May 2005).

USEU. 2002. U.S. Announces Proposals for Liberalising Trade in Services, The United States Mission to the European Union, 1 July 2002. Available at http://www.useu.be/Categories/WTO/July0102TradeServicesWTOProposal.html (Accessed on 20 May 2004).

Wheeler, M. 2000. 'Globalisation of the Communications Marketplace', *Press/Politics*, 5 (3): 27–44.

Wunsch-Vincent, S. 2003. 'The Digital Trade Agenda of the U.S.: Parallel Tracks of Bilateral, Regional and Multilateral Liberalisation' (pp. 7–46). Available at http://www.iie.com/publications/papers/wunsch0303.pdf. (Accessed on 11 September 2006).

7

The Informationalisation of Life Processes: Biotechnology, IT and Life as Code

As the digital becomes a common language in India across multiple sectors and reflected in genetic databanks, biotechnology-related and other applications, there is need for critical insights into some of these applications and in particular its consequences for human life. Biometric data, for instance, is already being used for surveillance purposes and insurance companies routinely use cross-referenced data to screen individual applicants for life and health cover. India's first DNA databank, a joint concern between the Lucknow-based IQRA Biotech Services and the Central and UP state government, raises not only significant concerns related to 'privacy' but also to whether it will be used in eugenics and to root our people with a genetic predisposition to crime and terrorism (Dasgupta 2008: 64–65). The Biotech sector in India is projected to reach revenues of USD 5 billion in 2010. Palnitkar (2005) has observed that in the area of bioinformatics, a number of leading software companies in India, including Infosys Technologies, Wipro Health Sciences, Tata Consultancy Services, Kshema Technologies and Satyam are involved in providing data-based services.

The Informationalisation of Life Processes

When James Watson and Bernard Crick announced the discovery of the DNA double helix in 1953, they used the language of cybernetics to describe their find. The gene was described by molecular biologists as the very secret of life that was based on encoded information that could be decoded, cracked, programmed and re-programmed. More than half a century later, in a post-genomic era, the metaphor of the gene as biological information while still extant, has been superseded by the re-inscribed materiality and commodification of biological information, the accentuated informationalisation of life processes along with the increasing hybridity that is a core characteristic of new-technologies that increasingly are being tied together by the common language of the digital. Eugene Thacker (2005: 2), in a significant reading of these developments has observed that DNA chips, genome databases, gene-target software and other hybrid products signify 'not only the integration of the biological and the technological, but also the integration of a material and an immaterial understanding of biological life'. IT and the language of the digital have contributed to the celebration of technology-based re-enchantments of our human and post-human futures. Donna Haraway (1991), for instance, in her celebrated post-feminist reading, the *Cyborg Manifesto*, posits the reconfiguration of the human in informational terms based on couplings between organism and machine and has explored the possibilities that this offers for gender transgressions (See also Waldby 2000 and Mazlish 1993). While human biologicals such as genes and cell lines certainly are valuable, their translated value today as informational commodities has become a core basis for value generation in the industrial life sciences. It is this fluidity and correspondence between tangible biological material and intangible biological information that distinguishes contemporary genetic engineering from earlier traditions of biotechnology. Bioinformatics, that plays a critical role in the generation of DNA sequence data and the analysis of nucleic acids and protein sequences, is based on fluid synergies between biology, computer science and IT. Bioinformatics signifies the informationalisation of biology, an informationalisation that now includes IT-based convergences with nanotechnology, artificial intelligence and the cognitive sciences, military technologies, robotics and the like.

These changes suggest that, in an era characterised by the informationalisation of society and life processes, the focus of a critical political economy of information and communications should not be limited to an exploration and analysis of the many new structurings of the media in the context of globalisation and technological convergence, the economics of its distribution in a networked world, the local-global nature of commodification–consumption and/or the increasingly important regulatory role played by international media governance institutions, but also include an analysis of the viral nature, scalability, vitality and synergistic consequences of the digital as it embraces and re-fashions almost all, if not most, productive and non-productive sectors in society in its image. We are, as communicative human beings, being drawn steadily into a tryst with informational futures that have begun to define the meaning of the social, the economic, the political and the cultural. This shaping of lives by the digital—for instance, in the area of leisure by a variety of networked technologies, the internet and mobile technologies—also affects consumption (GM Foods) and is complemented by the normalisation of a biopolitics that is based on the systematisation of public and private surveillance, informational categorisations and sortings of individuals, along with the bankings of personal and genetic information that are, in turn, commodified and used by the state and private companies to regulate and control life in all its variety. This expansive understanding of the digital has been under-theorised although Dan Schiller (2007), had in the mid-1980s, signalled the need for critical political economists of communications to theorise information in terms of the big picture and not as discrete technologies. The expansionary nature of digital capitalism and multiple convergences has accentuated commodifications of information across numerous sectors. As Schiller pointed out:

> The transition to information capitalism does not depend on or equate with a narrow section of the media-based products. It is co-extensive with a socio-economic metamorphosis of information across a great (and still undetermined) range. As commodity relations are imposed on previously overlooked spheres of production, new forms of genetic and biochemical information acquire an unanticipated equivalence with other, more familiar, genres. Agribusiness, pharmaceutical giants, energy and chemical corporations, and medical companies—all essentially concerned with diverse genetic and biochemical information streams—are in the midst of a continuing technological transformation of the means of information production that is every bit as relevant to our understanding of the parallel trend 'convergence' between television, computing and telecommunications. (Schiller 2007: 25)

The human body, as much as the space shuttle, is the terrain of the digital. In the space of two decades, most, if not all productive sectors—be it in the life sciences, the media, education, transport—along with other sectors, have been reshaped by the technologies and logic of convergence. The informational logic of cybernetics, characterised by information and feedback and expressed via flows and networks, is the basis for an entire range of productive processes across multiple sectors—biotechnology laboratories, just in time manufacturing, clerical work, classrooms, military strategies, public surveillance, the health industry, agriculture, seed production, national and global governance, investments and financial networks, transport, not to mention the cultural industries. This has vastly increased the scope and power of companies such as IBM and Sun Microsystems that now have more than just a passing interest in the life sciences, given that the building blocks of life itself are implicated in a fluid materiality in which the non-material (information) lends itself to material commodification via intellectual property.

The re-shaping of traditional IT firms into handmaidens for the informationalisation of production across sectors is one area that needs monitoring. The leading software companies in India, in terms of market capitalisation and revenue generation, Wipro, Tata Consultancy Services (TCS) and Satyam are now involved in leveraging information across numerous sectors. Satyam Computers,[1] consistently among the top three software companies in India (USD 1.4 billion revenues in 2006) although recently affected by a revenues scam, until recently offered products, solutions and services to the aerospace, automotive, banking, chemical, education, government, healthcare, insurance, life sciences, media, real-estate, telecom and travel industries. And TCS, a subsidiary of India's largest industrial house, the Tatas[2] (market capitalisation of USD 68 billion in 2007), is positioned to offer a range of information services across multiple sectors both within its parent company and outside of it. Palnitkar (2005: 147) in an article on the growth of biotech companies in India has observed that:

> The early entrants were large industrial/pharmaceutical companies...(Biocon, Wockhardt, Nicholas Piramal); thereafter the pure play biotech start-ups focussed on production of recombinant drugs, bioinformatics and custom services (Shanta Biotech, Bharat Biotech, Strand Genomics, Syngene), Software companies which grafted biology branches onto strong IT stems (Wipro, TCS, Satyam) and more recently industrial conglomerates which have diversified into biotechnology (Reliance Industries).

Such trends are also replicated in other countries where the downstream–upstream environment of biotechnology is dominated by pharmaceutical, biotechnology and information companies such as IBM, along with varying levels of inputs from public sector initiatives such as the US-based National Institutes of Health, the European Molecular Biology Laboratory and others.

While the expansion and vertical and horizontal integration of IT/software companies across non-IT/media sectors and similar expansionary trends in non-IT companies, such as the seed giant Monsanto's involvement in genomics, offers us the opportunity to revisit earlier debates on the politics of concentration, conglomeration and commodification, the informationalisation of society and life processes within contemporary capitalism also presents us with opportunities to think through issues related to new technologies, information and power. Foucault (1984: 262) described contemporary biopolitics as the disciplining of the body and 'its integration into systems of efficient and economic controls' along with the expansion of control over biological processes through the exercise of '*regulatory controls: a biopolitics of the population*...characterised by a power whose highest function was perhaps no longer to kill, but to invest life through and through'. In the contemporary post-genomic world, this 'investment of life through and through' also extends to one's post-life. Genetic data-banks, that house human biologicals and human biological information, routinely license the manipulation and engineering of biological material and information as material taken from people who are no longer living. Given that the informational body can now outlast the physical body, its uses are potentially varied, is and can include the screening of immediate, natal family members for insurance and other eligibilities. The power to control lives across generations invests these new technologies and databanks with extraordinary authority to stratify and divide society. As Thacker comments, genetic databanks in an era characterised by cloning and other techniques offer the potential to develop human informational copies:

> The cadaver of the genetic body does not slip away, to be replaced here by pure simulation or abstract information; rather, the genetic body is accounted for on all of its (molecular) surfaces, through the technical practices of a biological-informational science, and the links between a body and a genetic profile.[3]

This chapter specifically deals with the contemporary role of information in biotechnology, in particular, concentration, commodification, enclosures and issues related to contemporary biopolitics. What, from a political economy perspective, are among the key features that demand an exploration? There are a number of issues including the following—there is a need to:

1. Theorise information, from the perspective of inter-sectoral convergences and the universality of information applications across all productive sectors including the manufacture, trade and ownership of genetic and biological information inclusive of 'human biological information' (Boyle 1996).[4] James Boyle refers to the common language of the digital and the resulting 'homologisation of information' (p. 3)—the fact that it makes

little sense today to distinguish between genetic and electronic information, because both types of information have begun to overlap and face the same problems of regulation. When culture and nature are translated and commodified into digital information, the commercial exploitation and ownership of this information does have the potential to become a source of extraordinary power.

2. Monitor the new sources of global economic and political power in an era of convergence.
3. Explore governance and regulation issues in this new economy, namely the organisations, instruments and regimes of intellectual property that protect digital property.
4. Understand and engage with some of the key public issues arising from the interfaces between technological convergences and society, not least the new dynamics of exclusion, that Scott Lash (2002) refers to as the '...new type(s) of stratification, in which social class depends on relations to intellectual property and rights of access to the lifted-out spaces of technological forms of life'(p. 24).

These new instruments of exclusion are a result of the extension of property values to every conceivable aspect of culture and nature, animate and inanimate, critical to the growth of global capital.

The Metaphor of Information as Code

So how did the metaphor of information as code become a staple in the life sciences? The belief in 'code as a source of life' has long been a staple in molecular biology. This way of conceptualising biology on the basis of principles drawn from cybernetics was first mooted by Norbert Weiner, who had, as early as in 1948, drawn parallels between machines and organisms:

> [B]oth...used on-off switches in their information processing (neural in one case, electromechanical on the other) and both used 'feedback loops'—circular processes beginning in the nervous system, emerging as output through muscular activity, and cycling back into the nervous system through sensory input—to interact with their environments. (Dery 1996: 309)

The physicist Erwin Schrodinger was the first to suggest that the gene was an information carrier and that the physical structure of the gene corresponded to a hereditary code script.[5] This determinist, reductionist, mechanistic view of an information-centred understanding of life and of humans as information processing systems is an all too commonplace descriptor in science and the media. In the words of the socio-biologist and Darwinist, popular science writer, Richard Dawkins, 'If you want to think about life...don't think about vibrant throbbing gels and oozes, think about information technology' (quoted in Bowring 2003).

Metaphors borrowed from computing were used to understand life forms as biochemical machines whose efficiency coefficients could be raised via precise genetic reprogramming. Sheldon Krimsky (1991: 5–6) has described the centrality of cybernetic language to the understanding of modern biology.

> The modern conception of the cell is based on a cybernetic materialism involving information transfer, energy, feedback signals, primary and secondary matter...replication, and reproduction...In the language of the new cybernetic materialism of molecular genetics, genes or DNA are referred to as 'bits of information' or the carriers of the 'code' for the production of proteins...DNA is said to be unzipped...Genomes are spoken of as being mapped, DNA as being read or sequenced. The term 'gene machine' has been introduced to describe devices that synthesize specified stretches of DNA automatically. The frequently used expression 'reprogramming micro-organisms' exploits the language of computers to characterise human-induced changes in the DNA 'code'.

The brain too is today likened to a biocomputer that can be reprogrammed with the right commands leading to all sorts of behavioural changes. Jeremy Rifkin (1998: 181) describes the increasing interfaces between computing and biotechnology that are a result of 'real' correspondences:

> It is not only the computer's rules of engagement that make it a suitable communication tool to manage dynamic living systems. The very 'operational language' of the computer is now being grafted onto biological systems. It is this common language that is creating a seamless web between the information and life sciences and making possible the joining together of computers and genes into a single, powerful, technology revolution.

Computers are however not only used for the storage, analysis and retrieval of data, for purely functional purposes. It has also become the means for modelling, design and simulation, imaging products and processes and reprogramming life itself. The databases related to the Human Genome Project consist of informational translations of physical data that have been identified through powerful computers based on parallel processing. As Fukuyama (2002: 74) has observed:

> The Human Genome Project would not have been possible without parallel advances in the information technology required to record, catalogue, search and analyse the billions of bases making up human DNA. The merger of biology and information technology has led to the emergence of a new field, known as bioinformatics. What will be possible in the future will depend heavily on the ability of computers to interpret the mind-boggling amounts of data generated by genomics and proteomics and to build reliable models of phenomena such as protein folding.

Beyond the Metaphor: Code as Life

Sandra Braman has argued that biotechnology and information technology are examples of meta-technologies that differ from earlier technologies in terms of their complexity, speed, scalability and precision.

> Meta-technologies involve many processing steps and there is greater flexibility in the number of steps and the sequence in which they are undertaken. They can process an ever expanding range of types of inputs and can produce an essentially infinite range of outputs…Meta-technologies are always informational, and the internet is a premier example of a meta-technology used for communication purposes. With recombinant DNA, biotechnology entered the meta-technology realm. The change in human capacity enabled by meta-technologies is both qualitative and quantitative. (Braman 2004: 5)

The complexity of information today is best illustrated by the fact that biotechnologies and, in particular, genomics have translated the metaphor of information as life into material reality. When an intangible 'information' as means and ends becomes the *de facto* 'real' version of a tangible product—animal tissue, genes, cell lines—what really is happening and how should we deal with it? Human biologicals and human biological information, although co-extensive and implicated in a single continuum, lead separate lives. And yet, what is significant is not their separateness, but the fact that the tangible and the non-tangible, the material and information as material have now become mutually constitutive. In other words, genomics is based on informational processes that translate 'wet-ware', the material cell line from which information is derived, into information that is, in turn, fed back in a loop to the laboratory and that becomes the basis for re-combined cell lines and eventually to therapies that are commodified. Rajan (2006: 42) explains this process as follows:

> It is knowledge that is always relating back to the biological material that is the source of the information; but is also knowledge that can only be obtained, in the first place, through extracting information from the biological information. The abstraction of information away from the biological material has a specific function in making therapeutically relevant knowledge.

DNA can be extracted, transferred, encoded, digitised, synthesised, materialised and re-materialised (See Thacker 2005). This abstracted information—information as the material—has a life of its own and is commodified, packaged and marketed.

The Ownership of Global Biological Resources

On the surface, corporate dominance continues to be a reality in every economic sector. While media concentration is a well-known fact, the concentration of ownership is a reality in non-media sectors as well. For instance, in pharmaceuticals, the first three leaders in terms of sales, profits and percentage share of the global market in 2004 were Pfizer, Glaxo/SmithKline and Sanofi-Aventis. In biotechnology, the top three companies in 2004 included the US based Amgen, Monsanto and the top 10 accounted for 72 per cent of revenues (ETC 2005). The first three among the top agrochemical companies in 2000 were Syngenta (Novartis + AstraZeneca), Pharmacia (Monsanto) and Aventis (AgrEvo+Rhone Poulenc) with a combined 45 per cent share of the world market. Among the three top seed companies in 2006 were Monsanto+Delta and Pine Land, Dupont, and Syngenta with control over 39 per cent of the commercial seed market (ETC Group 2007). The top three food and beverages corporation included Nestle, Philip Morris and ConAgra Inc. The top three global grocery retailers included WalMart (US), Carrefour (France) and Metro AG (Germany). The late 1990s saw same major mergers by industries related to agricultural biotechnology. Chaturvedi (2002: 1216) has observed that:

> Monsanto has emerged as the biggest player in the game. In the process it has acquired some of the largest firms in the US commodity markets and holds important patents. For instance DeKalb has 11 per cent of the US commodity market…Similarly, Delta and Pineland is the largest US company for cotton seeds. Monsanto has also acquired the international seed operations of Cargill for $1.4 billion…Ciba and Sandoz have merged their pesticide and seed business

of $5 billion to form...Novartis...the merger of Hoechst and Rhone Poulenc to form Aventis (which has) an R & D budget of $3 billion and annual sales of $20 billion all over the world.

Mergers have also affected the pharmaceutical industries that are now dominated by a handful of mega-companies. These global firms own databanks and control both upstream and downstream research and development and production.

Ownership and Control in the Bioinformatics Sector

It can be argued that the most far-reaching developments today relate to the new synergies being formed between the IT and biotech sectors. The bioinformatics market that is devoted to making sense of the sequence, structure and function of genes and proteins is an industry worth a projected USD 6.9 billion in 2007. The IT market in the life sciences is estimated to be in the region of USD 30 billion in 2004. In fact, a report in the *Financial Times* (Cookson 2001: II) states that the 140 collaborations between the IT and Life Sciences industries that year covered 'bioinformatics, DNA microarrays (gene chips), data analysis and visualisation, chemical and biological library integration, detection of human genetic variation (SNPs), microfluidics and *in silico* research (modelling drug effects in computers)'. There are a range of bioinformatics companies catering to a variety of interests—custom-built software and consulting services and web businesses and tools and services aimed at pharmaceutical and biotechnology companies. Proteomics—the study of the interaction between genes, proteins and disease—is highly computer-dependent, given the vast quantities of data that need to be generated, 'computing power measured in teraflops, or trillions of operations per second' (Kenward 2001: 1). Proteomic alliances include Myriad Genetics Inc. with Hitachi Ltd. and Oracle Corp., IBM and MDS proteomics and Oxford Glycosciences Plc's venture with the telecoms equipment group Marconi Plc. Key players of IT fame involved in the life sciences include Compaq, Hewlett Packard, Motorola, Sun, Fujitsu, Hitachi and the leader IBM. IBM, for instance, has begun to invest heavily in the life sciences through making direct equity investments in companies such as MDS Proteomics (Canada), Devgen (Belgium) and Structural Bioinformatics (US) (Cookson 2001: II). Owning more than half of the world's top 500 super computers, IBM has a head start on companies involved in a race to build a special super computer 'Big Blue' to analyse the protein structure. IBM's Deep Computing Institute has a Bioinformatics and Pattern Discovery Group which uses supercomputing to solve problems in molecular biology. Among IBM's many patented algorithms are Teiresias and MUSCA that are used for gene-pattern discovery and alignment and SPLASH that is used for pattern discovery. Microsoft's Bill Gates and Paul Allen have invested in a leading biotechnology company aptly named Darwin Molecular that is involved in gene sequencing (1994).

Biotechnology and pharmaceutical companies too have integrated bioinformatics capabilities in house. One such example, Lion Bioscience, has built bioinformatics capabilities across all divisions within the pharmaceutical firm Bayer. Many pharmaceutical companies have built strategic alliances with bioinformatics firms, entered into licensing agreements and bought up smaller firms. There is a limited number of public and private genetic databanks. While, in principle, the publicly funded GenBank maintains its databanks in the public interest, as Rajan (2006: 55) has observed, those who make use of it are primarily pharmaceutical companies who prefer to exploit this information in the public domain than deal with private companies who charge for the licensing of material such as tissue and informational biologicals. As Rajan has observed, these pharmaceutical companies use the 'free flow of information' argument to gain access to public databanks and use a 'rhetoric that suggests that information is part of a *gift*, rather than a *commodity*'. The sheer volume of sequences that are being generated today and maintained at GenBank is extraordinary. As the GenBank website notes:

> GenBank® is the NIH genetic sequence database, an annotated collection of all publicly available DNA sequences... There are approximately 65,369,091,950 bases in 61,132,599 sequence records in the traditional GenBank divisions and 80,369,977,826 bases in 17,960,667 sequence records in the WGS division as of August 2006. (NCBI 2007)

Biopolitics, inclusive of opportunities to manipulate information deposited in databanks furthers the inability of individuals to control the ownership and use of personal information (See Gandy 1993). The abstraction and location of information in databanks gives it a life of its own, removes its connectivities to living things and, in this process, makes human beings dispensable.

Biological Exchanges in a Networked World

To a large extent the success of bioinformatics can also be attributed to the global nature of computer networks that have enabled global flows of biological information. In other words, the circulation of biological information and its licensing and sharing in a networked world, is a critical aspect of bioinformatics today. Thacker (2005: 7, emphasis in the original) has defined biological exchange as '*the circulation and distribution of biological information, be it in a material or immaterial instantiation, that is mediated by one or more value systems*. Biological exchange is the ability to render the biological not only as information, but as mobile, distributive, networked information.' The networking logic of convergent technologies has allowed for flexibility, scalability and integration (Castells 2001: 70–71) and to the globalisation of biotechnology. It has enabled the outsourcing of intellectual capital in the bioinformatics industry 'in the form of temporary and long-term, domestic and international, strategic alliances with peers and vendors' (Lloyd 2003: 97). Such circulations have also led to the globalisation of a biopolitics, transfers of biological information across territorial boundaries, the routine screenings of clients carried out by a variety of agencies, inclusive of the police and insurance companies, and the extension of surveillance. It has also led to the reinforcement of divides between the beneficiaries of new therapies and the stratified underclass, who often play a key role in clinical trials carried out in countries like India. More often than not these people are denied its benefits, given that therapies are often accessible to only those who can pay for treatment.

Information Enclosures

Why and how did enclosures around biological information become so universal and dominant within a relatively short space of time? To a large extent, it had to do with economics, the imperatives of trade and the politics of comparative advantage. The global recession in the 1970s and 1980s, the fall in the price of primary commodities and the decline in manufacturing exposed weaknesses in the traditional economy that was based on industrial manufacturing. There was a need for alternative means of value creation. By the early 1980s, computing had emerged as a powerful tool in value creation. The products and processes of digital capitalism were projected as a potential means of reinforcing global economic dominance by US, Western Europe and Japan over the rest of the world. There was a need to extend, maintain and reinforce market share in the trade of new informational products and lay down the terms of protection for trade in the emerging digital economy. Proposals related to Trade Related Intellectual Property Services (TRIPS) were included in the Draft Final Act submitted on 20 December 1991 at the Uruguay round of Multilateral Trade negotiations of the General Agreement on Tariffs and Trade (GATT). This proposal was opposed by the developing world, Brazil and India in particular, who were of the opinion that the UN-related, World Intellectual Property Organisation (WIPO) that had been set up to deal precisely with IP issues, ought to oversee global IP-related concerns. It is interesting to observe that among the 12 US corporations that formed the Intellectual Property Committee and that played a critical role in advocating for the TRIPS initiative, there were key corporations, including IBM, General Electric, Monsanto and Pfizer, who are contemporary leaders in the new synergistic industries—the life sciences, the cultural industries, computing and military technologies.

While the periodisation of the global intellectual property regime can be queried, its actualisation was hastened by the patent regime in the 1980s that recognised human invention in genetically engineered micro-organisms, cell-lines, tissues and other human biologicals followed in the 1990s by the patenting of information-based genetic sequences in the wake of the Human Genome Project and the establishment of a variety of proprietorial data-banks. Two landmark cases—*Diamond versus Chakrabarty* that involved advocacy related to the recognition of the 'invention' of a genetically engineered bacterium used to clear up oil spills and the *Moore versus Regents of University of California* case that involved a patient with hairy cell leukaemia who sued the university and other related companies and lost his appeal for patenting a cell line excised from his spleen because the court felt that the patient no longer exercised a proprietorial right over biological material that had been excised from his body—paved the way for the large-scale patenting of genetically engineered biologicals (Gold 1995; Waldby and Mitchell 2006). In the case of Moore too, the argument put forward by the courts was that the free flow of information is essential for research and that property rights must be given to those who carry out the research and mining because 'property is an essential incentive to research' (Boyle 1996: 101). The idea that the gene was in reality 'informational material' and the informational materialisation of code that can be infinitely manipulated has facilitated enclosures around human biologicals information (Bowring 2003). As Boyd has observed, the rush to create enclosures in the wake of genomic information has been unprecedented.

> [I]ndustry leaders such as Monsanto and DuPont have been pursuing patenting strategies based on expressed sequence tags, or ESTs, ...from the genome of major commercial crops...because the new sequences are essentially computer-generated information, the chemical compound analogy that provided the basis for granting gene patents in the past may no longer be appropriate. (Boyd 2003: 46–47)

As convergence results in applications based on interlocking correspondences between areas that used to previously be autonomous—chemistry, modelling, biotechnology, telecommunications, bio-medical technologies and computing, among other areas—IP issues have become a lot more complex. A single application can be governed by a range of patents which is why it makes sense for the major players in this area to build up a formidable inter-sectoral IP presence. In fact, the patenting of research tools including screening systems, expressed sequence tags (ESTs) and techniques related to DNA sequencing among other tools further strengthens control over the downstream research of companies involved in bioinformatics. IBM's leading edge in computer hardware design and innovation is built on an aggressive patents regime. IBM's extensive IT-based investments in the life sciences, inclusive of research centres, discovery and development, pharmacogenomics, solutions, manufacturing, sales and marketing services, is worth billions of dollars and is founded on their position as the leading MNC involved in building enclosures around knowledge in the US.

> In 2005, *IBM* received 2,974 U.S. patents from the *USPTO*. This is the thirteenth consecutive year that *IBM* has received more US patents than any other company in the world. In addition to delivering these innovations through its products and services, *IBM* maintains an active patent and technology licensing program.[6]

The top 20 academic-based biotechnology patent filers in 2007, while led by the Japan Science and Technology Agency, includes 18 US-based academic institutions, while in the corporate bio-tech sector Genentech Inc. and Millennium Pharmaceuticals, both US-based companies remain market leaders (Williams 2007). It is, in other words, an imperative that we interrogate the source of property power in the knowledge economy—the structures, systems and instruments of intellectual property that have become the means of maintaining corporate dominance in the new economy.

Human Biological Information as a Non-rivalrous Resource

Despite corporate dominance in the biotechnology sector, there have been attempts to free up biological information in the public domain. Organisations such as the Open Bioinformatics Foundation, the Bioinformatics Organisation and the SNP Consortium offer free access to DNA, RNA and protein sequences (Waldby and Mitchell 2006). There is also a thriving open-source movement that is involved in sharing and exchanging bioinformatics code and expertise. Greco (2007: 185) notes that, 'In 2005, the major Open Source Bioinformatics projects were Bioperl, Ensembl, Biojava, Biopython, O/B/F, Omnigene, Bioruby, "Glue" Projects, DAS, bioinformatics.org…, EMBOSS, Biofortran, BioLisp, BioSVG and many other smaller projects.' These projects endorse information as a non-rivalrous resource. We need to remember that there is a difference between human biologicals that are a rivalrous resource, meaning that its distribution and circulation is limited, and human biological information that is a non-rivalrous resource. Your consumption/reading of this paper does not curb, limit or take away from another person's consumption of the very same product. In this sense, it can potentially be read, circulated and accessed by all within the entire online world irrespective of boundaries, status and ability to pay. The only thing that stands in the way of unlimited circulation is the desire for profit, the hoarding of information because of rivalry or a monopoly instinct. An informational product is unlike biscuits and toothpaste that are products of industrial manufacture based on tangible raw materials that either need to be grown in the field or manufactured in a lab or factory. Non-informational goods generally tend to be finite. However, the copy is in the very nature of the digital. This is the reason why, in spite of the best efforts by the Business Software Alliance and the Motion Pictures Association of America to popularise new encryption technologies, the copy is global and an inherently natural way of circumventing the restrictions of code. In other words, the information revolution really has opened up a Pandora's Box full of issues related to information as a product, the ownership of information, the potential and real availability of information as copy. It is this intrinsic quality of the digital that is both potential and threat to the corporate sector. The open-source movement has demonstrated that the free flow of information can be used to construct a vision of society based on non-proprietorial futures.

Notes

1. Satyam Computer Services Ltd. Available at http://www.satyam.com/aboutsatyam/a_factsheet.html (Accessed on 23 March 2009).
2. Tata Group. Available at http://www.tata.com/ (Accessed on 11 July 2006).
3. Thacker, E. 'Database/Body: Bioinformatics, Biopolitics, and Totally Connected Media Systems'. Available at http://switch.sjsu.edu/web/v5n3/E-1.html
4. Boyle, J. 'A Politics of Intellectual Property: Environmentalism for the Net', pp. 1–23. Available at http://www.wcl.american.edu/pub/faculty/boyle (Accessed on 5 June 2007).
5. Reimer, U. and G. Fuellen. 'Biocomputing in a Nutshell', (p. 1). Available at http://merlin.mbcr.bcm.tmc.edu:8001 (Accessed on 13 August 2008).
6. http://www.ibm.com/ibm/licensing/

References

Bowring, F. 2003. *Science, Seeds & Cyborgs: Biotechnology and the Appropriation of Life*. London/New York: Verso.

Boyd, W. 2003. 'Wonderful Potencies: Deep Structure and the Problem of Monopoly in Agricultural Biotechnology', in R. A. Schurman and D. D. K. Kelso (eds), *Engineering Trouble: Biotechnology and its Discontents*, pp. 24–62. Berkley/Los Angeles/London: University of California Press.

Boyle, J. 1996. *Shamans, Software and Spleens: Law and the Construction of the Information Society*. Massachusetts, London, England: Harvard University Press, Cambridge.

Braman, S. 2004. 'The Meta-technologies of Information', in S. Braman (ed.), *Biotechnology and Communication: The Meta-technologies of Information*, pp. 3–36. Mahwah, New Jersey/London: Lawrence Erlbaum Associates.

Castells, M. 2001. *The Rise of the Network Society*. Vol. 1. Malden, MA: Oxford; Carleton, Victoria: Blackwell Publishing.

Chaturvedi, S. 2002. 'Agricultural Biotechnology and New Trends in IPR Regime: Challenges before Developing Countries', *Economic & Political Weekly*, 37(13): 1212–2222.

Cookson, C. 2001. 'Scientific Buzz Surrounds Test Bed of Ideas in Supercomputing' (p. II) and 'Case Study IBM: Breadth of Range is Well-suited to Tackling the Big Problems in Biology' (p. II), *Financial Times Survey, Biotechnology*, 27 November.

Dasgupta, D. 2008. 'India's Biodata', *Outlook*, 1 December: 64–65.

Dery, M. 1996. *Escape Velocity: Cyberculture at the End of the Century*. London: Hodder and Stoughton.

ETC Group. 2005. Oligopoly Incorporated 2005: Concentration in Corporate Power, ETC Group Communique, Issue No. 91. Available at http://www.etcgroup.org/en/materials/publications.html?pub_id=44 (Accessed on 21 November 2007).

———. 2007. 'The World's Top Seed Companies—2006. Available at http://www.etcgroup.org/en/materials/publications.html?pub_id=656 (Accessed on 23 March 2008).

Foucault, M. 1984. 'Right of Death and Power Over Life', excerpt from the *History of Sexuality*, Volume 1, in P. Rabinow (ed.), *The Foucault Reader: An Introduction to Foucault's Thought*, pp. 258–272. London: Penguin Books.

Fukuyama, F. 2002. *Our Posthuman Future: Consequences of the Biotechnology Revolution*. London: Profile Books.

Gandy, O. 1993. 'Towards a Political-Economy of Personal Information', *Critical Studies in Mass Communication*, 10 (1): 70–97.

Gold, R. 1995. 'Owning Our Bodies: An Examination of Property Law and Biotechnology', *San Diego Legal Review*, 32(4): 1167–1247.

Greco, J. F. 2007. 'The Commercialisation of Bioinformatics and the Threat of Open-source Software', *Journal of Commercial Biotechnology*, 13(3): 183–194.

Haraway, D. 1991. 'A Cyborg Manifesto: Science, Technology, and Socialist-Feminism in the Late Twentieth Century', in *Simians, Cyborgs and Women: The Reinvention of Nature*, pp. 149–181. New York: Routledge. Also available at http://www.stanford.edu/dept/HPS/Haraway/CyborgManifesto.html (Accessed on 11 March 2008).

Kenward, M. 2001. 'When the Finest Minds are up for Sale' (p. 12), *Financial Times*, 4 July.

Krimsky, S. 1991. *Biotechnics and Society: The Rise of Industrial Genetics*. Connecticut, London: Praeger, Westport.

Lash, S. 2002. *Critique of Information*. London, Thousand Oaks, New Delhi: Sage Publications.

Lloyd, W. 2003. 'Editorial: A New Era in Networking', *Journal of Commercial Biotechnology*, 9(2): 97–98.

Mazlish, B. 1993. *The Fourth Discontinuity: The Co-Evolution of Humans and Machines*. New Haven/London: Yale University Press.

National Centre for Biotechnology Information (NCBI). 2007. 'What is GenBank?' Available at http://www.ncbi.nlm.nih.gov/Genbank/index.html (Accessed on 3 June 2007).

Palnitkar, U. 2005. 'Growth of Indian Biotech Companies, in the Context of the International Biotechnology Industry', *Journal of Commercial Biotechnology*, 11(2): 146–154.

Rajan, K. S. 2006. *Biocapital: The Constitution of Post-Genomic Life*. Durham/London: Duke University Press.

Rifkin, J. 1998. *The Biotech Century: How Genetic Commerce will Change the World*. London: Phoenix, Orion Books Ltd.

Schiller, D. 2007. *How to Think About Information*. Urbana & Chicago: University of Illinois Press.

Thacker, E. 2005. *The Global Genome: Biotechnology, Politics and Culture*. Massachusetts, London/England: The MIT Press, Cambridge.

Waldby, C. 2000. *The Visible Human Project: Informatic Bodes and PostHuman Medicine*. London/New York: Routledge.

Waldby, C. and R. Mitchell. 2006. *Tissue Economics: Blood, Organs, and Cell Lines in Late Capitalism*. Durham/London: Duke University Press.

Williams, G. 2007. 'A Maturing Industry: Strategic Patenting Trends, US and Academic Dominance, and the Global Biotechnology Landscape', *Journal of Commercial Biotechnology*, 13(3): 163–175.

8

Christian Fundamentalism and the Media: The Case of Christian Broadcasting in India

Christian fundamentalists rank among the world's foremost users of the media. Ever since early forays into tele-evangelism in the US, conservative Christian groups have monopolised Christian broadcasting, not only in the US but throughout the world. India is no exception to this rule. In their way of thinking, every medium of communication is a gift from God and a potential ally in the dissemination of God's unvarying, eternal truth. Instrumentalism, professionalism and pragmatism are typical attitudes underlying media use by religious fundamentalists.

Writings on religious fundamentalism in India focus more or less exclusively on the ideologies, and the cultural and political strategies used by organisations associated with Hindutva (the term used to describe the group of fraternal organisations linked to the project of Hindu nationalism) and on issues related to religious nationalism and the media (Basu et al. 1993; Das 1990; Hansen and Jaffrelot 2001; Juergensmeyer 1993; Ludden 1996; Nandy, et al. 1997; Rajagopal 2001). Other expressions of religious fundamentalism in India, including Christian, have generally not merited sufficient academic attention. One can, of course, argue that Christians being a minority group, currently consisting of 2.4 per cent of the population, pose little or no threat to the Indian nation. When compared to Hindutva's many tentacles and the traditions of Islamic fundamentalism, the Christian right-wing hardly feature in the media or in the Indian imaginary. In fact, Christians are almost always the victims of right-wing Hindu groups. Be that as it may, I think that it is important to point out that no religion has a monopoly over fundamentalism and that all religions have their share of fundamentalists. In other words, Christian fundamentalists do exist in India and are involved in Christianising the nation through fair means and foul. While there are a handful of academic writings on Christian fundamentalism in India (Bayly 1994; Caplan 1987) with the most recent book on the subject by the journalist Edna Fernandes (2006), *Holy Warriors: A Journey into the Heart of Indian Fundamentalism*, these writings offer, at best, only a partial view of Christian fundamentalisms in India. Although the book by Fernandes includes chapters on the history of the Inquisition in Goa and Christian mission and separatism in Nagaland, a state located in North East India that has been involved in a struggle for independence for more than half a century, it does not offer a comprehensive perspective on the issue. The separatists in Nagaland are mainly Baptist Christians. Christian groups investigated in this chapter belong mainly to the Pentecostal and neo-Pentecostal traditions that are present throughout India and who form the bulk of new Indian Christians.

The violence against Christians in Orissa and Karnataka is once again an illustration of the impunity with which organisations belonging to the Sangh Parivar operate in India and the protection that they receive, particularly in BJP-ruled states. While that violence cannot be condoned, one can argue that 'low-intensity' forms of Christian mission contribute to raising the ante and that there is a need for some introspection on the part of the church in India on the meaning and vision of Christian mission in India in the twenty-first century. The churchscape in India today is very different from what it was three decades ago when the so-called historical and 'colonial' churches were the dominant entities. Today, there are any number of independent, Pentecostal and neo-Pentecostal churches, para-church organisations and ministries found throughout India who do not necessarily believe in the social agendas of the historical and 'colonial' churches but whose primary goal is Christianising India.

This chapter argues that there is a need to assess Christian fundamentalism in India and, in particular, the role played by the media, broadcasting in particular, in the expansion of narrow forms of Christian mission in India. It explores the political economy of international and national Christian broadcasting along with its cultures of mediation. Based on the Sage volume *Strong Religion, Zealous Media: Christian Fundamentalism and Communication in India* (2008), it argues that it is necessary to understand religion as a field and, in particular, the use of broadcasting as a tool and 'instrument of salvation' in the context of contemporary struggles within Indian Christianity and religion in India.

Jeremy Stolow (2005: 125), in a review of writings on religion and media, makes a case for less instrumentalist approaches to the study of the media and religion and more studies that deal with negotiations over meaning and explorations of 'how media and mediation constitute inherently unstable and ambiguous conditions of possibility for religious signifying practices…'. While there certainly is merit in exploring the complexities of mediation, I argue that in the context of global religious revivalism, the globalisation of the religious market, the transnationalisation of religious broadcasting and jockeyings for position and power within religion as a field, there is need for economic as well as cultural analysis for an exploration of structures as well as practices. I take the position that there is a need to study Christian fundamentalism in the South precisely because this area has been under-theorised and under-studied. There is also a concurrent need to study the structures and forms of Christian broadcasting in the South.

Defining Christian Fundamentalism

Nancy Ammerman (1991: 4–8) has described North American Protestant Fundamentalism as based on:

a) 'Evangelism'— 'aimed at convincing the unconvinced that eternity in heaven is better than the eternal damnation in hell that surely awaits the unsaved'.
b) 'Inerrancy'— 'a faith in Jesus Christ grounded in unwavering faith in an inerrant Bible'. They 'are confident that everything in Scripture is true' and that 'true Christians must believe the whole Bible'.
c) 'Premillennialism'—'They... expect to find in Scripture clues to the future destiny of this world, what will happen in the End Times… the idea of the Rapture' of what will happen 'when the Son of Man comes …lends both urgency to the evangelistic task and comfort to persecuted believers.' Along with the need to be prophetic 'Believers are not content to know that Jesus is coming for them; they want to know when and what will happen next'.
d) 'Separatism'—'Fundamentalists insist on uniformity of belief within the ranks and separation from others whose beliefs and lives are suspect.'

To reiterate, Christian fundamentalists abide by a handful of Bible-inspired core tenets—evangelism and the salvation of souls, belief in the inerrancy of Scripture, belief in 'premillennialism' (Bible-based knowledge of the end times) including a belief in prophecy and the 'Rapture' (Mathew 24: 37–41: 'Then shall two be in the field; the one shall be taken, and the other left'; 1 Thessalonians 4: 15–18: 'caught up together with them in the clouds, to meet the Lord in the air') and separatism. I argue that in addition to believing in such fundamentals, militant Christian fundamentalists are actively involved in either using an explicit politics to legitimise their national and global projects related to a religion-inspired social change and/or are involved in covert acts of mission, that contribute to the goal of Christianising the world.

Christian Fundamentalism in India

While the project of making India Hindu continues to fracture secular India and compromise its fragile democracy, one can argue that muscular forms of Christian mission in India have contributed to the heightening of inter-faith tensions in the country. Christian fundamentalism in India rarely makes the headlines in the media in India, although the investigative news agency *Tehelka* (Shashikumar 2004) did carry an exposé of Christian mission in India.

The project of Christian fundamentalism in India is based on a number of strategies:

1. Christian separatism based on armed struggle against the state.
2. Christian involvement in domestic politics.
3. Spiritual warfare.
4. Spatial strategies including the embrace of cityscapes and public arenas.
5. Aggressive mission strategies.
6. Christian broadcasting.

These projects do not amount to a composite strategy. Different groups adopt one or more of these projects. It is this multi-faceted strategy that makes the study of Christian fundamentalism in India a fascinating project in its own right (see Thomas 2008). What is clear is that each of these options is based on a literal understanding of the 'Great Commission' (the Biblical injunction to spread the Word) and on a clear perception of the nature of the adversary. In the case of military strategies, the adversary is the state, that in the recent past has aided and abetted the project of Hindu nationalism and attempted to subvert 'indigenous' identities. Armed struggles against the Indian state have been carried out by Baptist Christians in the northeastern state of Nagaland. With respect to politics, it is the perceived need to counter mainstream exercises of power through Christian representation and involvement in local and national politics. Spiritual warfare is directed towards defeating the principalities and powers that exist in the Hindu spirit world and claiming India for Christ. The embrace of city-space through the acquisition of real estate, the organisation of worship in malls, the use of advertising, icons, mega-events such as crusades and rallies are the means to imprint the city symbolically as well as economically. The focus of global evangelical mission on what they refer to as the '10/40 window', lands that have not as yet heard the Gospel, include the 'unreached' tribes of Central and North India who live in a territory that is also the heartland of contemporary nationalist Hindu revivalism in India. Gospel for Asia (GFA), for example, a transnational Dallas-based Christian mission organisation, operated by an Indian missionary K. P. Yohanan, has featured consistently among the top three highest foreign income earners in India and focuses explicitly on church-planting, the establishment of Bible schools and conversion in North India. Para-church organisations such as the GFA have embraced both new and old media for outreach purposes.

Unto the Ends of the World: The Christian Broadcasting Network

Christian fundamentalists use a variety of media to fulfil their mission. However, broadcasting—both radio and television—remain their favourite media. Christian broadcasting is a multi-million dollar industry. While there are significant variations within this industry from radio and television owned and operated by the mainstream churches to broadcasting that is specifically oriented towards fulfilling the Great Commission—taking the Word of God to the four corners of the earth—there is also a Christian broadcasting characterised by close correspondences with politics and political agendas. A well known example of such correspondences is found on the US evangelist Pat Robertson's flagship programme, the 700 Club, on his Christian Broadcasting Network. This programme has regularly featured US politicians who have openly sought the electoral favour of the Christian Right and who have, in turn, supported conservative social agendas flagged by these groups—for example, on issues such as gun control, gay marriage, stem cell research, the war on terror, Iraq and the conflict between Israel and Palestine. Guests on this programme have included Tom DeLay, US Majority Whip, Oliver North, Al Liberman, Al Gore, Jimmy Carter, Ronald Reagan, Mel Gibson, Charlton Heston, among others. George Bush Jr has often featured on a weekly radio programme. Using a format that includes interviews, special reports, commentary and news, this syndicated programme is carried across the world on ABC Family Channel, the Trinity Broadcasting Network, FamilyNet and numerous other television stations in the US and elsewhere. The news coverage on *700 Club* deals with:

> International news coverage on the persecution of Christians around the world including Sudan, Pakistan, Cambodia, Bangladesh, Egypt, China, Burma and Indonesia; Israeli election; and the nuclear proliferation in Iraq, Iran, and North Korea were covered. Extensive political coverage of the 2000 election and post-election legal battle. Breaking news coverage of the September 2001 terrorist attacks against America. As well as up-to-date facts and forecasts on the stock market and the economy.[1]

Their webpage Inside Israel,[2] provides fascinating insights into Christian Zionism and the extent to which the Christian Right have invested in Israel as a bulwark against the Islamic tide. This page has links to key Israeli news sources inclusive of *Ha'aretz* and the *Jerusalem Post* and to three sites devoted to media reporting of the conflict in this region, establishing 'accuracy' and the representation of stories in favour of the policies and military solutions advocated by the Israeli government Palestinian Media Watch, Committee for Accuracy in Middle East Reporting in America (CAMERA) and the Middle East Media Research Institute. These sites are devoted to the contestation of meanings on the conflict and use liberal sub-texts to convey conservative ideas. A story on the CAMERA website dated 7 November 2006 headlined 'Guardian Conceals Facts about Gaza Casualties' begins with this opening paragraph—'In a newspaper prone to extreme anti-Israel coverage, readers now find shoddy reporting on casualty numbers that, not surprisingly, tilt against Israel.'[3] Pat Robertson's combination of prosperity theology with an intense materialism has led to his lobbying on behalf of a number of extremely conservative politicians with notorious human rights records—from Mobutu to Charles Taylor, in exchange for gold and diamond mining contracts (See Marley 2007: 189–193). His public critique of Hindus and Hinduism on his syndicated programmes has, in turn, contributed to a generalised Christian baiting by any number of Hindu nationalists. Indian Christian evangelists such as the late G. S. Dhinakaran of Jesus Calls were frequent guests at the CBN.

While the most aggressive expressions of Christian fundamentalism are represented by globally networked Christian television stations such as the Christian Broadcasting Network (CBN), the Trinity Broadcasting Network (TBN) and God TV, there are also local/indigenous expressions of Christian fundamentalist media that are bound by language, region and nation. Writing on mediated Christianity in Ghana, DeWitte (2003: 177) has observed that the 'Church's extensive use of mass media has generated a religious, charismatic Pentecostally oriented public sphere... which is characterised by the intertwining of religion with both national and global politics and the field of commerce and entertainment.' Local Christian TV supported by local entrepreneurs also plays a role in reinforcing a conservative politics and interpretation of Scripture at local, regional or national levels. While Asamoah-Gyadu (2005) does point to the influence of US-based tele-evangelists such as Oral Roberts and Benny Hinn on local expressions of tele-evangelism in Ghana, he is of the opinion that despite such correspondences, 'the media ministries of Ghana's CMs (Christian ministries) reflect modern African ingenuity in the appropriation of neo-Pentecostal techniques, style and strategy in organisation and expression' (p. 21). While it is certainly important that we treat indigenous expressions of mediated Christianity in context, I believe that it is also critical for such studies to explore the extent to which correspondences between the global and the local have contributed to the normalisation of a global Christian politics and belief in a handful of unvarying doctrinal essentials.

Selling God

The mainstreaming of fundamentalist Christianity, which is an on-going process, has been achieved through global marketing strategies. The marketing of Paradise is big business today. God sells. There is a battle on for the souls of the global community as much as for its purse in a context teeming with a variety of communication options—video and audio, terrestrial, cable and satellite broadcasting, the internet along with print and older forms of communication. Anne Borden (2007: 68) has observed that the Christian books and products market is a USD 4.2 billion dollar industry. And as is to be expected, big media houses are involved in Christian media. Rupert Murdoch's News Corporation, for instance, owns Zondervan, one of the largest evangelical book publishers in the world and it also has rights to the New International Version of the Bible that is an evangelical favourite (See Clarke 2007: 25–26).

Pat Robertson, for example, has used new technologies and his own entrepreneurial business skills to transform the Christian Broadcasting Network into a multi-media conglomerate that sells everything from pharmaceutical products to products that enhance healthy living. Frankl (1998), in a perceptive essay on Pat Robertson's transformation of his media business into a business empire, reveals the vertically integrated nature of the business that is based on the acquisition of lucrative companies and the ownership of the complete production chain from production to delivery systems.

> Pat Robertson exemplifies this strategy, both producing *The 700 Club* and owning the cable network to carry it. From the cable network, the Family Channel and a variety of other enterprises developed: CBN television productions; CBN University (now Regent University, comprising graduate schools in business, communication, law and public policy); CBN Publishing offering a 'Superbook Audio Cassette and Colouring Book' for children ages four to eleven; 'Sing, Spell, read and Write', an instructional system for children in primary grades; and Video Tracts 'designed to be used by the individual or as a key element in a church's or organisation's overall evangelistic outreach'. CBN Travel and Operation Blessing became separate endeavours, as did his company American benefits Plus. (Frankl 1998: 166)

A number of these networks are no longer owned by Christian interests. Today Pat Robertson's Christian Broadcasting Network (CBN) empire is connected through inter-locking directorships to a variety of secular institutions that are broadly supportive of his ultra-conservative views. In 1997, CBS sold International Family Entertainment Inc. (IFE) to Rupert Murdoch and Murdoch subsequently merged Fox Kids Worldwide with IFE. Pat Robertson remains co-chairman of the board. Similarly, the Brazilian neo-Pentecostalist, Edir Macedo, who runs the mega-church, the Universal Church of the Reign of God, is a major player in commercial broadcasting in the region. He purchased a commercial TV network consisting of 30 stations and Rede Record in 1989 for USD 45 million and controls 400 temples, numerous radio stations, newspapers and a bank (see Smith and Campos 2005).

Methodology

I had as part of field work related to a larger project on Christian fundamentalism and the media in India carried out interviews in Chennai, India during December–January 2005–2006 with evangelists, Christian broadcasters and theologians, attended Christian rallies and Pentecostal church services, collected secondary data through archival research, accessed relevant websites and watched a number of hours of Christian television. The primary purpose of this exercise was to gather data on the political economy of Christian fundamentalism and broadcasting in Chennai. Concepts borrowed from Bourdieu—'field', 'habitus', 'distinction', the politics of misrecognition, his attempts to overcome key dualisms in the social science—between structure and agency, the material and the cultural and his emphasis on a reflexive sociology—contributed to a framework that I used to make sense of a discourse that was not by any stretch of the imagination straightforward. The relationship between religion as a field in India and the habitus of its citizens is extraordinarily complex. Religion plays a significant role in the lives of its citizenry and is a primary consciousness. As Martin Marty and Scott Appleby (1993) have pointed out in their volume *Fundamentalisms Comprehended*, religious fundamentalisms share, at best, family resemblances. As I was to find out in my research, in a globalised world in which entanglements between religion and the market have become deeply textured, key purveyors of religious fundamentalism in India, despite publically stated antipathies for the Other, do share and exchange the same currency and platform.

Locating the Study

Arvind Rajagopal's (2001) study on the central role played by the state broadcaster Doordarshan's telecasts of Hindu mythologicals and its contributions to the electoral fortunes of the Hindu right-wing is among the better known writings on the relationships between Hindu fundamentalism, politics and the media in India. There are, however, other writings on this phenomenon including Peter Manuel's (1993, 1996) studies of popular cassette culture and the role of music in reinforcing communal divides in North India, Hindu video discourses and mission (Little 1995), the press and communalism (Gupta and Sharma 1990; Varadarajan 1999), the mediation of televised Hindu 'soaps' (Lipner

2001; Malinar 1995), Hindu nationalism and Bollywood (Dwyer 2006), radical Hinduism online (Brosius 2004; Chopra 2006; Thomas 1999), the mediation of a market-based Hindu religious nationalism (Dasgupta 2006) and cultural activism against religious fundamentalism in India (Bharucha 1998) among other writings. There is a conspicuous absence of texts on other traditions of mediated religious fundamentalism in India.

The resurgence of Hindu nationalism and the globalisation of new forms of Christianity have been undergirded by diaspora nationalisms and the globalisation of the market for religious and 'spiritual' products offline and online. Big media interest in religious television is also evident in India. For instance, Zee Telefilms, one of India's largest broadcast networks entered the 'spiritual' media sector in 2004 with its channel Zee Jagran that features programmes related to popular Hinduism and programmes on astrology, Hindu serials and devotional music.[4] Transnational Christian cable and satellite channels available in India including the Christian Broadcasting Network, Daystar, God TV, Miraclenet, the Eternal Word Television Network and national channels including Angel TV, Blessing TV and Shalom TV among numerous others are, for the most part, exclusively owned by Christians who align themselves to Pentecostal and neo-Pentecostal traditions.

Pentecostal Christianity and Politics in South India

While the relationship between Christian leaders and an overt politics is absent at a national level, at a state-level, in the majority Christian, so-called 'tribal' states in North East India and some of the states in southern India, this relationship is visible and, at times, explicit. While the presence of the church in Chennai and in Tamil Nadu has traditionally been strong and Bishops belonging to the mainstream Church of South India (CSI) have previously been courted by politicians, it is clear that the new churches, their leaders and the vote banks they represent have been actively courted by Tamil political parties, in particular those aligned to Dravidian politics. The descriptor Dravidian refers to a distinctive language-based South Indian identity that stands in contrast to the more dominant North Indian Aryan-based language identity, although it has also been used to describe a racial identity that is distinct from that of the North Indian Aryans. Factions within the Pentecostal movement and neo-Pentecostal movements in Tamil Nadu are aligned to the two key Dravidian parties—the Dravida

Munnetra Kazhagam (DMK) and the All India Anna Dravida Munnetra Kazhagam (AIADMK). Bishop Ezra Sargunam, who heads the Evangelical Church of India and who has served as the Chairperson on the state's apex Minority Commission, is a supporter of the incumbent DMK party. When the rival AIADMK has been in power, Bishop M. Prakash, who heads the Synod of Independent Churches, has acted as Chairperson of the Minority Commission, most recently between 2004–2005. These two church representatives from the Pentecostal/Independent traditions have been recognised by rival politicians for the vote banks that they represent. Bishop Prakash was involved in administering the Annandham poor feeding scheme linked to the populist politics of the ex-Chief minister Jayalalitha. He has been connected with the Trinity Broadcasting Network and his programme Blessed Time is available weekly on three local channels—Raj TV, Tamilian TV and SS Music. While both leaders stand for 'family values' and express socially conservative Christian ideals, they are not politically strong enough to press forward this agenda at a national level. They have, however, used their connections and political acumen to smoothen the way for the continuation of uninterrupted mission work in the South through actively, publicly supporting the right to convert, and have taken an instrumental lead in organising Pentecostal-led Christian rallies and conventions and played a key role in manufacturing and communicating globally a specific version of Christian identity in India.

While there is, to date, scant evidence to suggest that these two leaders are actively involved in advocating separatism, their commitment to muscular forms of mission and evangelism and, in particular, to conversion, has taken them on a collision course with Hindu nationalists and secularists. Leaders from the Pentecostal traditions have also, on occasion, acted as *de facto* spokespersons for Indian Christians, featured on Capitol Hill in the US, at the US Commission on International Religious Freedom and cited in the US State Department's annual report on International Religious Freedom. They have played a key role in the consolidation of the independent and Pentecostal churches and have used their political power to get the government of Tamil Nadu to repeal the bill against 'forced conversions' that was promulgated by the previous AIADMK government. They have used their influence to leverage space and support for Christian conventions and rallies that are a platform for conversion. Furthermore, some of these leaders feature regularly on Christian cable and satellite channels where they reinforce their brand of conservative Christianity. Bishop Prakash, the founder of the South India Soul Winner's Association, is the President of the Synod of the Independent Churches of India that number around 1700 and is the national coordinator of the US-based

Trinity Broadcasting Network, the world's largest Christian broadcasting network. Bishop Ezra Sargunam leads the Evangelical Church of India and is a vocal support of conversion. While Bishop Sargunam's stance on Dalits and tribals has taken him on a collision course with the Sangh Parivar, it is arguable as to whether such contestations contribute to substantive human rights over and above the right to convert. The present Chief Minister of Andhra Pradesh (AP), the largest state in South India, Samuel Rajasekhar Reddy is a Seventh Day Adventist who has allegedly provided tacit support for Christian missions, including Christian broadcasting. Incidentally, Hyderabad, the capital of Andhra Pradesh, is the location of the Christian Broadcasting Network's Indian operations.

The Pentecostal and neo-Pentecostal churches in India have played an extremely important role in popularising a global, transnational version of Christianity based on the cultivation of 'distinctions' that include the organisation of the church, preaching styles, modes of worship, pastoral outreach that include Cell Churches, Houses of Prayer and CARE cells. These distinctions that are reinforced through Christian broadcasting have become a powerful draw for youth belonging to the mainstream churches who, in turn, have pushed their own churches to adapt and accommodate new forms of worship modelled on the new churches. In other words, there has been a sharing of distinctions between charismatics from the mainstream church, evangelicals and Pentecostals. While the sharing of these distinctions has led to a renewal in churches that had become bogged down in tradition, it has also led to congregational demands that Christian pastors belonging to the mainstream churches follow styles of worship perfected by Pentecostal preachers. What this points to is the fact that there is a 'war of position' within Christianity as a field in India. Bourdieu (1991: 22–23), in an article entitled Genesis and Structure of the Religious Field, describes this war of position in the following manner:

> Since the position of religious claimants, institutions or individuals, in the structure of the distribution of religious capital dictates all their strategies, the struggle for monopoly over the legitimate exercise of religious power over the laity and over the administration of the goods of salvation is necessarily organised around the opposition between *the church* and *the prophet*… *The prophet* (or the heresiarch) and his sect contest the very existence of the church by their very existence, and more precisely, by their ambition to satisfy their own religious needs without the intermediation and the intercession of the church. They call into question the monopoly over the instruments of salvation… (emphasis in the original)

There is an on-going struggle between traditional expressions of mainstream Christianity including the historical Syrian Orthodox church, the Catholic church and the Protestant church on the one hand and the new expressions of Christianity on the other. While not all these new churches are necessarily fundamentalist in their outlook, these churches have contributed to the creation of an Indian Christian identity around a narrow set of markers.

The relationship of these new churches with mainstream politics is often on public view at key Christian crusades and conventions. At the Every Tongue Every Tribe convention organised by the Indian Pentecostal Church that I attended in January 2006 in Chennai—the first national convention specifically devoted to celebrating the missionising of 'tribal' India—the chief guests included India's present Finance Minister, P. Chidambaram, along with a host of politicians from the Congress government and the then opposition DMK government. That this convention was specifically convened to celebrate the conversion of 'tribals' was not an issue of concern for these politicians. Politicians in India often have a tangible relationship with religion. Politicians are present at all major religious rallies, from crusades organised by the internationally known tele-evangelist Benny Hinn, to conventions organised by Hindu 'God' men and women and can be seen actively seeking spiritual guidance and blessings from religious leaders. Correspondences between religion and politics and disjunctures between public expression and private morality link politicians on the Hindu right with fundamentalist Christian leaders. There is a politics of accomodation based on political expediency and money transfers, which does, at times, lead to the most unlikely of alliances. While interviewing employees at the Chennai-based Jesus Calls, one of the largest evangelical organisations in India, I was told of liaisons and 'understandings' between prominent members of the nationalist Hindu BJP and this organisation. While such relationships may seem far-fetched, the logistics of a Christian crusade by the well-known tele-evangelist, Benny Hinn, simply requires that connectivities be forged, for instance, as was the case in Mumbai, with the Shiv Sena, a right-wing Hindu group that controls the local municipality. In fact, Bal Thackeray, the leader of the Shiv Sena and the scourge of minorities in Mumbai, was a chief guest at this event.

Christian Broadcasting in India

While evangelical Christians in India have always had a presence in off-shore radio broadcasting, the advent of cable and satellite broadcasting, along with the liberalisation and privatisation of broadcasting, led to the availability of a profusion of religious channels including a number of transnational Christian channels, national Christian channels, the availability of syndicated Christian programmes on all major vernacular cable and satellite channels and internet-based television. While government regulations do not restrict religious cable and satellite television channels, there are restrictions on the ownership of commercial religious FM radio, although, rather intriguingly, religious bodies are not barred from owning community radio stations. Government strictures related to religious broadcasting have not been applied rigorously. Inspite of its avowed public role as a secular broadcaster, the state radio network, All India Radio, has consistently provided air-time for explicitly religious majoritarian high culture on the basis of a disingenuous argument that equates Indian national culture and Hindu culture. This attitude is also evident in Doodarshan's support for Hindu high culture inclusive of mythologicals based on the *Ramayana* and the *Mahabharata* that played an important role in the ascent of the Hindu Right in India. Thus, tacit support has reinforced the perception among minority communities that broadcasting in India has favoured majority Hindu fare at the expense of programmes representative of minority religious traditions. This view was echoed a number of times in interviews that I had with Christian broadcasters in Chennai. Such restrictions do not, of course, apply to Christian radio transmissions up-linked from outside India. There are a number of Christian radio stations that currently broadcast into India. K. P. Yohanan's Ontario-based Gospel for Asia radio alone broadcasts in 92 Indian languages including many tribal languages. The Far Eastern Broadcasting Association (FEBA) broadcasts in 24 languages while *Viswavani* is available in 58 languages. Along with the GFA and FEBA, there literally are hundreds of Christian radio broadcasts into India including Radio Veritas Asia, Vatican Radio, FEBA Radio, Sri Lankan Broadcasting Corporation (SLBC) Sri Lanka, Adventist World Radio, Bible Voice Broadcast Network, Christian Vision/Voice, KWHR Hawaii, Trans World Radio, WFYR Family Radio along with numerous others. Trans World Radio (TWR) broadcasts in over 62 Indian languages. TWR's core values reflect one of Ammerman's (see point b under sub-heading 'Defining Christian Fundamentalism', p. 180) descriptors of Christian fundamentalism—the inerrancy of scripture, 'We believe in the verbal and plenary inspiration of the Old and New Testaments; that they are infallible, inerrant in the original writings, and the final authority of faith and life.'[5]

Christian Broadcasting and the Politics of Tele-evangelism

Without a doubt the advent of satellite and cable television in the early 1990s began the renewal of religious broadcasting and, in particular, Christian broadcasting in India. David Page and William Crawley's (2001) classic, *Satellites over South Asia: Broadcasting, Culture and the Public Interest*, remains the most accessible introduction to what continues to be an evolving phenomenon. There are broadly speaking five avenues for Christian television in India:

1. The occasional space on the national broadcaster Doordarshan for Christian programmes.
2. Transnational satellite channels including GOD TV, CBN, TBN, MiracleNet and Daystar TV that are available via cable.
3. Christian programming on a variety of secular cable channels available throughout the country on Raj TV, Zee TV, Vijay TV and others channels.
4. Stand alone indigenous Christian cable channels such as Blessing TV, Angel TV, Shalom TV, Jeevan TV and others.
5. Web-based telecasting, for instance, 'Jesus Calls' on 'Num.TV'. Webcasting remains an evolving reality in India with limited audiences.

So, what are the features of Christian broadcasting in India? These channels backed up Christian organisations and agencies representing a type of muscular Christianity based on a promise of health and wealth for all those who are Christian. At the same time, it offers an uncertain future for those who either do not belong to the Christian faith or are opposed to it. For a Christian audience in Chennai not previously exposed to Biblical justifications for right-wing politics, such programmes, sandwiched between Joyce Meyer's homily on 'familial strife' and Sam Chelladurai's 'prosperity theology', offer justifications for a range of issues from Christian Zionism to easy understandings of the causes and nature of evil in contemporary society. The average Christian in India has a very conservative understanding of politics in the Middle East, and these channels, CBS and God TV in particular, routinely privilege and sanction the right-wing politics of the Israeli government and reinforce stereotypes of Muslims and people of other faiths. The fact that God TV's operations are Jerusalem-based and, thus, 'anointed', is frequently alluded to. The truth of these stories have been revealed to God's anointed and therefore have been blessed by God. In a situation characterised by the mainstream church's distance from interrogations of global and national politics, the primary Christian version of politics on public display is that advocated by tele-evangelists. The de-centring and fragmentation of Christianity in India today provides a perfect opportunity for the project of re-centring Christianity along conservative lines by the global Christian right supported by its foot soldiers in India.

These channels tap into and are sustained by the core message of the prosperity gospel, that the pursuit of wealth and profit-making are premier Christian values. Chennai today, with its call centres, salaried professionals and the rising spending power of its youth, has the space to celebrate the religions of globalisation. Sam Chelladurai's ministry, the Assemblies of God churches, Brother Dhinakaran's ministry, that of PowerHouse, and numerous other ministries celebrate the health and wealth gospel. The MTV style Gospel rock music on God TV with its bland and repetitive lyrics is also on offer at the Powerhouse, Aashriya and Vineyard, where young IT professionals and stock brokers rock to an anodyne version of Christianity. The lyrics may be modern, but they are, in essence, a throwback to the triumphalist hymns of yore that celebrated the primacy of the Christian God.

These channels have reinforced evangelism as a family business proposition. Just as the Dhinakarans and most other evangelists in Chennai including Dr Manickam Prakash's South India Soul Winner's Association (SISWA Trust) involve their entire family in the business, the regional director of God TV, Daystar TV, Christian production houses such as Good News TV are all family concerns. There is Rory and Wendy on God TV, Sarah and Michael Hughes on MiracleTV, Marcus and Joni Lamb of Daystar TV, the Crouches of Trinity Broadcasting Network and, of course, assorted tele-evangelists such as the Copelands, the Dollars and the Robertsons, among very many other family-based missions. Mission initiatives that are not answerable to a board of directors have had a history of problems to do with accountability best exemplified by the history of many infamous tele-evangelists including the contemporary Benny Hinn. Problems related to accountability are legion in the new churches. While the mainstream Church of South India and the Catholic Church in India have had their share of financial scandals, there are checks and balances in place that act as a deterrent to a cleric who has his eye on the parish finances. That system of accountability is just not there in many of these new church circles. As a travel agent in Chennai who books tickets for a stable of evangelists confided, 'There is a lot of fraud and first class travel.'[6]

Conclusion

There are obvious reasons for this lack of focus on minority fundamentalisms in India. Christians are a minority (2.4 per cent) of the overall population and their overall public image has not been dented in the way that that of the Muslims has been in the post-Partition, post-Independence and post 9/11 periods. The Christian vote has been marginal in most of the larger states in India with the exception perhaps of Kerala and the district of Kanyakumari, Tamil Nadu. They are not in direct economic competition with the majority community in most parts of India, with significant exceptions such as in Goa, Kerala and the North Eastern states and Indian Christians are not associated with terrorist acts in the sub-continent. Their association with health and education, service to the nation and as brokers of modernity have, in general, contributed to a positive public image. Moreover, in an era characterised by Hindu nationalism, media reports have represented Christians as the victims of violence by the Rashtriya Swayamsevak Sangh (RSS), Vishwa Hindu Parishad (VHP), Bajrang Dal and other groups associated with Hindutva. Global media reports, certainly after the murder of the Australian missionary Graham Staines and his sons in Orissa in 1999 by a right-wing Hindu and the recent violence in Orissa and Karnataka, have painted Christians as a minority who are persecuted by sections of the Hindu right-wing. This framing has been reinforced by the endless stories of persecution on channels such as the Christian Broadcasting Network and the global Christian crusade specialist and tele-evangelist Benny Hinn. There is, of course, no denying the fact that Christians involved in missionary work have been persecuted. And it is a fact that in BJP-ruled states, the criminal justice system has protected those who have committed crimes against minority communities. While there is a need to acknowledge and actively counter such injustices, it is at the same time necessary to understand the larger landscape of zealous religion in India; in this case, new Christian mission as a discourse, unravel its motivations, its support both domestic and external, its political economy and its outreach strategies that include its embrace and utilisation of broadcasting.

Notes

1. Christian Broadcasting Network. Available at www.cbn.com (Accessed on 18 April 2006).
2. CBN News: Inside Israel, CBN.Com Web page. Available at http://www.cbn.com/cbnnews/world/Israel/index.aspx (Accessed on 18 July 2006).
3. Committee for Accuracy in Middle East Reporting in America. Available at http://www.camera.org/index.asp (Accessed on 21 July 2006).
4. Broadcasting Nirvana: http://www.businessworld.in/index.php/Media-Entertainment/Broadcasting-Nirvana.html.
5. TransWorld Radio India: Core Values. Available at http://www.twr.in/corevalue.htm (Accessed on 21 June 2008).
6. Personal communication, 20 March 2006.

References

Ammerman, N. T. 1991. 'North American Protestant Fundamentalism', in M. Marty and R. S. Appleby (eds), *Fundamentalism Observed*, pp. 1–65. Chicago and London: The University of Chicago Press.

Asamoah-Gyadu, J. K. 2005. 'Anointing through the Screen: Neo-Pentecostalism and Televised Christianity in Ghana', *Studies in World Christianity*, 11(1): 9–28.

Basu, Tapan, Pradip Datta, Sumit Sarkar, Tanika Sarcar and Sambuddha Sen. 1993. *Khaki Shorts Saffron Flags*, Tracts for the Times/1. New Delhi: Orient Longman Ltd.

Bayly, S. 1994. 'Christians and Competing Fundamentalisms in South Indian Society', in M. E. Marty and R. S. Appleby (eds), *Accounting for Fundamentalisms: The Dynamic Character of Movement*, pp. 726–769. Chicago and London: The University of Chicago Press.

Bharucha, R. 1998. *In the Name of the Secular: Contemporary Cultural Activism in India*. Delhi: Oxford University Press.

Borden, A. L. 2007. 'Making Money, Saving Souls. Christian Bookshops and the Commodification of Christianity', in L. S. Clark (ed.), *Religion, Media and the Marketplace*, pp. 67–89. New Brunswick, New Jersey, London: Rutgers University Press.

Bourdieu, P. 1991. 'Genesis and Structure of the Religious Field', *Comparative Social Research*, 13(1): 1–43.

Brosius, C. 2004. 'Of Nasty Pictures and "Nice Guys": The Surreality of Hindutva', (pp. 138–151), *Sarai Reader* 2004—Crisis/Media. Available at http://www.sarai.net/ (Accessed on 18 June 2008).

Caplan, L. 1987. 'Fundamentalism as a Counter-Culture: Protestants in Urban South India', in L. Caplan (ed.) *Studies in Religious Fundamentalism*, pp. 156–176. Basingstoke/London: Macmillan Press.

Chopra, R. 2006. 'Global Primordialities: Virtual Identity Politics on Online Hindutva and Online Dalit Discourse', *New Media and Society*, 8(2): 187–206.

Clarke, L. S. 2007. 'Introduction: Identity, Belonging and Lifestyle Branding: Fashion Bibles, Bhangra Parties and Muslim Pop', in L. S. Clarke (ed.), *Religion, Media and the Marketplace*, pp. 1–33. New Brunswick, NJ, London: Rutgers University Press.

Das, V. (ed.). 1990. *Communities, Riots and Survivors in South Asia*. Delhi: Oxford University Press.

Dasgupta, S. 2006. 'Gods in the Sacred Marketplace: Hindu Nationalism and the Return of the Aura in the Public Sphere', in B. Meyer and A. Moors (eds), *Religion, Media, and the Public Sphere*, pp. 251–272. Bloomington and Indianapolis: Indiana University Press.

De Witte, M. 2003. 'Altar Media's Living Word: Televised Charismatic Christianity in Ghana', *Journal of Religion in Africa*, 33(2): 172–202.

Dwyer, R. 2006. 'The Saffron Screen? Hindu Nationalism and Hindi Film', in B. Meyer and A. Moors (eds), *Religion, Media, and the Public Sphere*, pp. 273–289. Bloomington and Indianapolis: Indiana University Press.

Fernandes, E. 2006. *Holy Warriors: A Journey into the Heart of Indian Fundamentalism*. New Delhi and New York: Viking.

Frankl, R. 1998. 'Transformation of Tele-evangelism: Repackaging Christian Family Values', in L. Kintz and J. Lesage (eds), *Media, Culture and the Religious Right*, pp. 163–189. Minneapolis, London: University of Minnesota Press.

Gupta, C. and M. Sharma. 1990. *Print Media and Communalism*. New Delhi.

Hansen, T. B. and C. Jaffrelot (eds). 2001. *The BJP and the Compulsions of Politics in India*. Delhi: Oxford University Press.

Juergensmeyer, M. 1993. *Religious Nationalism Confronts the Secular State*. Delhi: Oxford University Press.

Lipner, J. 2001. 'A Remaking of Hinduism? or, Taking the Mickey Out of Valmiki', in H. De Vries and S. Weber (eds), *Religion and Media*, pp. 320–338. Stanford, California: Stanford University Press.

Little, J. T. 1995. 'Video Vacana: Swadhyaya and Sacred Tapes', in L. A. Babb and S. S. Wadley(eds), *Media and the Transformation of Religion in South Asia*, pp. 254–283. Philadelphia: University of Pennsylvania Press.

Ludden, D. (ed.). 1996. *Making India Hindu: Religion, Community, and the Politics of Democracy in India*. Delhi: Oxford University Press.

Malinar, A. 1995. 'The Bhagavadgita in the Mahabharata TV Serial: Domestic Drama and Dharmic Solutions', in V. Dalmia and H. von Stietencron (eds), *Representing Hinduism: The Construction of Religious Traditions and National Identity*, pp. 442–467. New Delhi: Sage Publications.

Manuel, P. 1993. *Cassette Culture: Popular Music and Technology in North India*. Chicago: University of Chicago Press.

———. 1996. 'Music, the Media, and Communal Relations in North India, Past and Present', in D. Ludden (ed.), *Making India Hindu: Religion, Community and the Politics of Democracy in India*, pp. 119–139. New Delhi: Oxford University Press.

Marley, D. J. 2007. *Pat Robertson: An American Life*. Lanham and Oxford: Rowman & Littlefield.

Marty, M. and S. R. Appleby (eds). 1993. *Fundamentalisms Comprehended*. Chicago: University of Chicago Press.

Nandy, A., S. Trivedy, S. Mayaram and A. Yagnik. 1997. *The Ramjanmabhumi Movement and Fear of the Self: Creating a Nationality*. Delhi: Oxford University Press.

Page, D. and W. Crawley. 2001. *Satellites over South Asia: Broadcasting, Culture and the Public Interest*. New Delhi, London, Thousand Oaks: Sage Publications.

Rajagopal, A. 2001. *Politics after Television: Hindu Nationalism and the Re-shaping of the Public in India*. Cambridge: Cambridge University Press.

Shashikumar, V. K. 2004. 'Preparing for the Harvest', *Tehelka*, 1(1). Available at http://www.tehelka.com/story_main.asp?filename=ts013004shashi.asp (Accessed on 12 February 2008).

Smith, D. and L. S. Campos. 2005. 'Christianity and Television in Guatemala and Brazil: The Pentecostal Experience', *Studies in World Christianity*, 11(1): 49–64.

Stolow, J. 2005. 'Religion and/as Media', Review Article, *Theory, Culture and Society*, 22 (4): 119–145.

Thomas, P. N. 1999. 'Web-Wars and Inter-Faith Futures in India', *Media Development*, 4: 39–46.

———. 2008. *Strong Religion, Zealous Media: Christian Fundamentalism and Communication in India*. New Delhi, Thousand Oaks, London, Singapore: Sage Publications.

Varadarajan, S. 1999. 'The Ink Link: Media. Communalism and the Evasion of Politics', in K. N. Panikkar (ed.), *The Concerned Indian's Guide to Communalism*, pp. 160–229. New Delhi: Viking Penguin India.

9

Poverty and the Media

A critical political economy of communications explores deficits in the media's relationship with society with a view to exploring reasonable solutions to persistent problems, for example, issues related to representations of poverty. Deficits in the representation of people often are a by-product of habitual ways of representing society but could also be a consequence of deliberate policy decisions that are reflected in contemporary, mediated constructions of reality.

The cultural theorist, Stuart Hall (1977: 346), in an influential essay 'Culture, the Media and the Ideological Effect', notes the way in which the media manufacture consensus:

> What constitutes this, not simply as a field, but as a field which is 'structured in dominance', is the ways its limits operate—to rule certain kinds of interpretation 'in' or 'out', to effect its systematic inclusions...and exclusions (for example those groups, interpretations, positions, aspects of the reality of the system which are regularly 'ruled out of court' as 'extremist', 'irrational', 'meaningless' 'utopian', 'impractical', etc).

One can add to this ideological effect, the media's deliberate silencing of large sections of any given population through ignoring and/or refusing to acknowledge them in the narrative of the nation.

In the context of globalising India, the media have more often than not dealt with chronic poverty or the growing gaps between rich and poor only when starvation or farmer suicides have become a public concern or the subject of a state or national enquiry. This emphasis on the elite was graphically illustrated during the terrorist attacks in Mumbai in late November 2008 when both national and global television networks focussed on the unfolding drama at the Taj and Oberoi hotels but ignored those who were equally affected at the Chatrapathi Shivaji Terminus, another site for this attack. As a Tamil writer from Chennai, Gnani Sankaran, observed in an email:

> It is a matter of great shame that these channels simply did not bother about the other icon that faced the first attack from terrorists—the Chatrapathi Shivaji Terminus (CST) railway station. CST is the true icon of Mumbai. It is through this railway station hundreds of Indians from Uttar Pradesh, Bihar, Rajasthan, West Bengal and Tamilnadu have poured into Mumbai over the years, transforming themselves into Mumbaikars and built the Mumbai of today along with the Marathis and Kolis. But the channels would not recognise this. Nor would they recognise the thirty odd dead bodies strewn all over the platform of CST. No Barkha Dutt went there to tell us who they were. But she was at Taj to show us the damaged furniture and reception lobby braving the guards. And the TV cameras did not go to the government run JJ hospital to find out who those 26 unidentified bodies were. Instead they were again invading the battered Taj to try in vain for a scoop shot of the dead bodies of the page 3 celebrities. In all probability, the unidentified bodies could be those of workers from Bihar and Uttar Pradesh migrating to Mumbai, arriving by train at CST without cell phones and pan cards to identify them. Even after 60 hours after the CST massacre, no channel has bothered to cover in detail what transpired there.[1] (See also Deb 2008)

Bailing out the rich—those representing banks, the automobile industry, accounting firms, the IT industry—a trend that has become world-wide in the context of the economic recession, has not been paralleled with a bailing out of the poor. While some media did critique these bail-out plans, there has been little media emphasis on the need for public investments in projects that would make a difference in the lives of the global poor.

In this chapter, I address issues related to the representation of poverty in India. The coverage of poverty includes not only the media's representation of different categories of the urban and rural poor and those outside of the purview of the market, but also those who are stateless—refugees, migrants and displaced people. The chapter concludes with a section on the IT fix that is increasingly beginning to displace solutions that require real political commitment and the will to change the constancy of feudal India.

While the reporting of poverty in India today is largely episodic, there are a handful of media outlets that consistently deal with issues around poverty including the national daily newspaper *The Hindu* and its magazine *Frontline*. This is altogether rather surprising, given the extent of poverty in India that affects more than 350 million people. The poor who play an extremely important role in building the infrastructure of globalising India and servicing its players hardly feature in the story of globalising India since they only play a marginal role in India's burgeoning consumer economy. Such deficits in reporting reflect the fact that the media in India today resolutely caters to the aspirations and needs of the middle and upper classes, with the result that life in India is seen through a narrow and extremely limited prism. The mainstreaming of citizen journalism in India including sites such as Merinews also reflects the extent to which the middle classes are involved in framing key issues in India.

Given the global financial crisis that made headlines in 2008 and the projected impact on the middle classes, the chances are that issues related to poverty will become an unavoidable aspect of global reporting. For the moment, however, poverty remains an episodic concern that surfaces when there are tragedies such as famine in Ethiopia and farmer suicides in India.

So, why is poverty a non-issue in the media? There are, of course, the usual reasons. The media largely represent the interests of the middle classes and are not interested in content that will not sell or that is not of interest to advertisers. Stock market success stories and other feel good narratives fuel what is a massive consumer media industry in India that involves the English and vernacular press, cable and satellite television, FM radio and the internet. There are occasions when poverty is represented in the most unlikely contexts, such as in the pages of *Vogue India* that published a 16-page photo-shoot of poor, rural Indians modelling high-fashion clothes and accessories in its August 2008 issue. While the issue was critiqued by the media in the West, it was supported by a number of people in India, for whom poverty is an acceptable, day to day, although ignored, reality and for whom its commodification is entirely in keeping with the commodification of life in globalising India. Interestingly enough, there was a strong culturalist, subaltern perspective that seemed to suggest that such representations were perfectly okay since the poor too needed to be represented as 'having a life'. In Anindita Ghose's (2008) words:

> I wonder how much of the outrage stems from a cultural and racial perspective. Is it because the people in these pictures look different or are dressed differently that they elicit more pity than an underage Russian model exploited in the high fashion circuit? Would it have been charming if it used Italian farmers instead? If exploitation of the poor, or the less fortunate is an issue, I don't see how the two are any different.

It would seem that for most media in India, poverty remains a non-issue. Ammu Joseph (2007), in an article on media coverage of poverty, on the 20th International Day for the Eradication of Poverty (17 October), rues the fact that coverage of that day was limited. In her words:

In fact, barring a few editorials, the only substantial and original contributions to raising awareness on poverty and related issues during a week when poverty was supposed to be in the news were by people outside the media, especially in the form of editorial page articles. As a result the International Day for the Eradication of Poverty passed by without making much of a dent on public consciousness here.

Theorising Poverty and the Media

There are a handful of academic writings on poverty and the media and these include Golding and Middleton's classic text, *Images of Welfare: Press and Public Attitudes to Poverty* (1982), along with volumes by Eoin Devereux (1998) and Diana Kendall (2005). Golding and Middleton's work explored the ways in which the press contributed to shaping public opinion in the UK on welfare through creating moral panics around welfare scroungers and the army of undeserving poor who swindle their way through life. Grounded in the context of an economic recession and a changing politics, theirs is a study of the ways in which 'poverty is semiotically constructed' (Hills 2000: 4) against the background of individualism, competition and the discourse of just rewards. As they have observed:

> [M]arket forces have expunged from British national journalism a whole tradition of socialists and social democratic responses...That the contemporary press is predetermined to lack a political commitment to the poorest and weakest in society is an inescapable result of the political economy of the newspaper industry. (Golding and Middleton 2002: 221 222)

Although one can add that in a context characterised by economic globalisation, this commitment to the market runs deep and affects all sectors in society, not just the media. It is anybody's guess as to whether a Keynesian approach to the economy will lead to global investments in welfare.

The London-based Joseph Rowntree Foundation published a sequel to Golding and Middleton's study *The Media, Poverty and Public Opinion in the UK* (2008: 55) in which they conclude that:

> [T]here is a need to redress the discrepancy between the nature of poverty problems in the UK and the poverty that is reported in the media. The dearth of coverage of disabled people experiencing poverty is striking. The greater prevalence of coverage of men (rather than women) and of the working poor (rather than the non-working poor) is perhaps indicative of the concern

> with welfare to working contemporary poverty debates, as opposed to the 'scroungerphobia' of previous times (in which the non-working poor were the primary focus of attention). Both of these reflect the centrality of a work ethic to underlying attitudes towards poverty and welfare in the UK.

The journal *Media Development*[2] devoted an entire issue to dealing with media and poverty although there are surprisingly few journal articles of note on the media and poverty. The London-based international NGO, Panos, did bring out a text called *Making Poverty the Story: Time to Involve the Media in Poverty Reduction* (Panos 2007) although it is a very general study and veers to the prescriptive. While the representation and non-representation of the poor and poverty and the framing of issues needs to be explored, there is additionally also the need for materialist understanding of the media and poverty that deals with structures and systems such as debt and trade that directly and indirectly impact on the nature of poverty in any given country.

Poverty and Plenty: Representing the Poor in India

Over the last decade, a number of new opportunities for the coverage of poverty in India have arisen and not all of these are from within mainstream journalism. The vernacularisation and localisation of journalism have led to the establishment of newspapers such as *Khabar Lahariya* in UP that cover poverty related issues in a consistent manner. Citizen journalism (CJ) offers possibilities although the issue of access remains a significant barrier throughout India. One of the more intriguing sites is the Chhattisgarh People's News Site. The Chhattisgarh People's News Site—CGNet—is primarily devoted to discussing local issues in the northern state of Chhattisgarh that is primarily 'tribal'. The Hindi script is used to express a variety of tribal languages. It has sections on Tribals and Forests, Dalits, Culture, Agriculture, Education, Youth, Employment, Mining and Industry, Media, Naxal Issues, Water, Women and Health. What is interesting about this site is that it offers locals an opportunity to speak up on issues in this state, particularly the plight of local people caught up in the cross fire between Maoists (known as Naxalites) and the state police, as well as the para-military group, the Salwa Judum. Tribals, also known as 'Adivasis' in India, rank among the most marginalised of Indian citizens. While they live in resource rich environments, development has favoured large industries such as mining at their expense. High rates of poverty and illiteracy along with state neglect have led to tribals becoming core members of Maoist movements in India. They have faced the brunt of state-sponsored counter terrorism. CJs related to CGNet, mainly of tribal origin, have played an important role in exposing human rights violations. In this process, CGNet has become a common platform for tribal groups, the space for a variety of discussions on issues related to tribal life in Chhattisgarh. Shubhranshu Choudhary (2009), who co-founded CGNet, writes of the critical role played by CGNet in an environment where there are virtually no journalists of tribal origin. Not only has CGNet trained tribal CJs, 'CGNet has trained some young adivasis in simple tricks of citizen journalism, such as how to record and convey their concerns over mobile phones using the built-in camera. These images are then uploaded on the website and discussed on the forum through email.' CGNet meetings have become the space for stakeholder meetings between representatives of mining agencies and tribal leaders. CGNet also has plans to establish a community radio station. To the locals, CGNet is an online public 'Panchayat' (local village council), a shadow Panchayat that functions as a watch on authority and a space where people's voices can be heard and concerns discussed. An example of such an issue is that of bio-piracy. The Swiss Life Sciences firm, Syngenta, had, in 2006, been implicated in the purloining of the germplasm of 20,000 rice varieties from Chhattisgarh. A local anti bio-piracy movement uses CGNet as the basis for action on another case of bio-piracy, this time related to local varieties of Jatropha, shrubs and plants that are used primarily in the manufacture of bio-fuels. Although the cultivation of Jatropha in Chhattisgarh is controversial, 18 varieties of Jatropha germplasm that have high oil content and are disease resistant were stolen from a farm house in Raipur, leased by the UK-based company D. I. Oils. The report blamed the local Indira Gandhi Agricultural University for failing to act as a custodian of germplasm and instead acting as a conduit for stolen germplasm. The report itself is a call to tribal actions related to bio-piracy.

While poverty related issues are being covered by journalists in India, the best known journalist covering the poverty beat is Sainath. The Indian journalist, Palagummi Sainath, has over the last three decades created a journalistic dossier of the forgotten people and places of India, precisely during a time when reporting poverty had become a non-issue in the media. His best known publication—*Everybody Loves a Good Drought* (1996)—provides a most incisive interpretation of the gaps between principle and practice, policies and their implementation, in the context of globalising India. His various writings in newspapers such as the *Times of India* and more recently in *The Hindu* have explored issues such as farmer suicides, the food crisis and the agrarian crisis in Wayanad District, Kerala. The strength of his writings is his ability to communicate the reality of poverty through human-interest stories that make the link between the global and the local, inequality and political economy. Writing on the demise of the local film theatre in Wayanad—a direct result of the agrarian crisis, he quotes a theatre owner, Raman Kutty:

> Television did cause us problems. But the past three years demolished us. Take the two large plantations near my theatre. Both are in collapse. The number of workers is down. The migrants are down. Wages are down. Pepper, coffee, everything is down. Only debt is up. (Sainath 2004)

Writing in *The Hindu* (2008: 1), Sainath reported that there were 16,632 farmer suicides in India in 2007 with the majority occurring in five states—Maharashtra, Andhra Pradesh, Karnataka, Madhya Pradesh and Chhattisgarh. To put it more graphically, Ajay Uprety writing in *The Week* (2008: 34) has noted that:

> [T]he seven districts of Bundelkhand (in Uttar Pradesh)—Banda, Mahoba, Hamirpur, Jaluan, Jhansi, Lalitpur and Chitrakoot—have witnessed around 2000 unnatural deaths in the last four years...Most victims were impoverished farmers or landless labourers driven to the edge by the fall-out of the five-year drought.

Similarly, another report by Sainath (2001: 45) indicates that the problem is far more serious than what is officially admitted. 'Recent government figures show that in Anantapur, just one district of Andhra, 1,826 people, mainly farmers with very small holdings of two acres or less, committed suicide between 1997 and 2000.' The suicides do not normally make headline news, although it occasionally does, when the issue is debated in parliament. While Sainath is recognised globally and nationally for his writings, there are also less high-profile journalists involved in reporting poverty. The poor, low-caste women involved with the fortnightly rural newspaper *Khabar Lahariya* from Chitrakoot, Uttar Pradesh (See Naqvi 2007) have played an important role in resisting feudalism and uncovering the face of rural poverty in India. Similarly, the Jharkhand and Bihar–based *Prabhat Khabar* has covered a number of issues affecting the indigenous (tribal) people in this area including starvation deaths in the Palamau region (See Harivansh 2005).

There seems to be a pattern to these suicides irrespective of the community. A combination of factors, rising costs of inputs, low returns, landlessness, increase in the prices of essential commodities, food grains in particular, the lack of subsidies, an increase in debt payments, the lack of back-up social services and the dismantling of the welfare economy—seem to be the key factors that have contributed to the suicides.

In direct contrast to this image of pre-colonial penury is the image of the new Andhra Pradesh on the move. It is an image of a technological paradise, of software engineers, of dot com companies, of the stern, laptop carrying ex-Chief Minister, Chandra Babu Naidu, of e-commerce, software parks, Cyberabad—the new name for the capital city Hyderabad—and electronic democracy, of literally thousands of students seeking opportunities in the US but first hoping for a benevolent nod from the Visa-God, the presiding deity of the Chilkur Balaji temple close to Hyderabad, which draws thousands of applicants, especially during the peak December–January season (Pillai 2008).

Along with the two other South Indian states of Karnataka and Tamil Nadu, Andhra Pradesh is in the vanguard of the information revolution in India. The unravelling of the fourth largest software company in India, the Hyderabad-based Satyam Computers in December 2008 as a result of fraud, has exposed the nexus between banks, internal auditors, senior company executives, the state and central governments. This particular fraud has also exposed the extent to which blue chip companies such as Satyam Computers are involved in other sectors such as real estate, often to the disadvantage of marginal and small farmers. Srikanth Srinivas (2009), writing in *Business World*, on one of the founders of Satyam, observes that:

> From information currently available, it appears Raju, who hails from a traditional land-owning clan, became infatuated with the idea of cashing in on India's booming realty market. Using his closeness to two Andhra Pradesh (AP) chief ministers, N. Chandrababu Naidu and the late Y.S. Rajasekhara Reddy, he acquired large tracts of land through his family-owned property firm, Maytas Properties, and the publicly listed Maytas Infrastructure. To raise the cash to pay for the land, Raju used his stake in Satyam as collateral. It is said he also gave some powerful AP politicians stakes in both Maytas companies. Maytas Infrastructure raised eyebrows when it bid for the Hyderabad Metro rail project, and offered to put down cash for the project instead of borrowing as other competing bidders did.

The corporate media's silence over such deals is another illustration of the clear limits of the role of the media in India as a watchdog of corporate propriety. This state's efforts to usher in an IT revolution stands in stark contrast to ground realities that include a thriving Naxalite (Marxist-Leninist) peasant movement that in itself is a consequence of poverty.

An Eloquent Silence: Refugees, Migrants and the Media

Poverty affects both settled and unsettled populations in countries in South Asia. We now recognise the fact that chronic manifestations of poverty are not just about low calorific intake, or access to land, employment, credit, health determine subsistence but are also related to numerous social determinants such as caste, class, gender and conflict. These multiple determinations of poverty affect both settled and unsettled populations. Some of the most deprived populations in India consist of the internally displaced, due to military, civil, development-related and environmental conflict and refugees from neighbouring countries such as Bangladesh. India has traditionally been a haven for refugees from all over South Asia. These include Tibetans, Chakmas and Rohingyas from Bangladesh and Tamils from Sri Lanka along with many other groups who have either fled to India because of political persecution or are economic refugees. The internally displaced include those who have been the victims of state-based mega-development projects such as roads and dams along with those who have had to flee environmental disasters, civil or inter-faith conflicts within the country.

In terms of media representation of refugees in India, Tibetan refugees are probably the one community that have been represented sympathetically in the media, although India's rapprochement with China over the last two decades has resulted in less media sympathy for the Tibetan cause. In terms of displaced people, the plight of the Kashmiri Pandits have evoked more sympathetic media coverage than, say, Muslim communities in Gujarat and Mumbai who have been the victims of anti-Muslim riots. Kashmiri Pandits have been backed by both Congress and the BJP governments for obvious reasons. In stark contrast, Tamil Sri Lankan refugees who have been relocated in camps in Tamil Nadu have scarcely received any positive coverage. In fact, most journalists are ignorant about the existence of such camps and rarely if ever visit these camps or bothered to write about the plight of these refugees. In fact, following the assassination of Rajiv Gandhi, there has been a noticeable decline in the coverage of Tamil refugees and increased negativity when they have been covered, a situation that has continued in the context of the exacerbation of and post-conflict situation in Sri Lanka today. The issue of why some of the more progressive newspapers in India have opted to only tangentially cover the plight of the Tamils remains a significant blind spot.

An organisation that has carried out important work on the media coverage of refugees in India is the Mahanirban Calcutta Research Group.

In a volume entitled *Media and Displacement II: Three Case Studies, Media Coverage of Forced Displacement in Contemporary India*, the situation with regard to media coverage of displacement is explored in Jammu and Kashmir (J and K), West Bengal and Assam. These studies clearly reveal that both the English speaking and vernacular media fall short of adequately covering displaced people. Anuradha Bhasin Jamwal, in the case study of media coverage of displacement in J and K, has observed that media reportage has been selective, lacking in analysis, frequently based on frameworks that are jingoistic and nationalistic and rarely if ever deal with rape and violence committed by the Indian armed forces on displaced people.

> In the insurgency-hit areas of Jammu and Kashmir, the media has not only remained engaged in the pursuit of selective reporting to project the image that the armed struggle is communal by nature by invoking words like *Jehad* and 'Islamic Fundamentalism' but has in turn largely vitiated the atmosphere by communalising the situation… Even in the displacements from the borders, … vested interests and politicians preaching hate-soaked anti-Pakistan ideology have been provided more space than the displaced lot, in an obvious bid to shift focus from mundane issues as well as to justify war or troops buildup. There is a clear design to use media to 'manufacture consent'…in the name of 'national interest'. If the traumas of the displaced and their issues are highlighted, they are seen as isolated from the content, from the 'wisdom' behind wars, which the media feels must not be questioned. (Jamwal 2004: 48)

We would do well to encourage representations of refugees that are sympathetic rather than hostile. Since the media plays a key role in the making of public opinion, in the creation of strangers and friends, in mediating a sense of national identity, in the setting of agendas, drawing the boundaries of discourse on refugees and creating a national consensus on issues such as citizenship, immigration, resettlement and repatriation among other issues, it is necessary that we periodically interrogate the media practices and routines that media professionals employ in their coverage of refugees. This is easier said than done, since the reporting of refugee related issues and concerns tend to be connected to, even over-determined by regional conflicts, local politics and the perceived impact of refugee flows on local economies. We would, of course, like all journalists to be objective, independent, even sympathetic in the manner in which they report issues to do with refugees—but the stark reality is that media professionals work in value-laden environments and reflect a variety of interests. Given competing claims and concerns and the fact that the refugee beat is not exactly a glamorous or, for that matter, lucrative one, chances are that it would be difficult to find a critical mass of journalists in any given country who are committed to covering refugee related issues. It would be more likely than not that there could be one or two journalists per country who are committed to providing regular space for refugee related issues. The fact that there are such journalists indicates that all is not lost, despite the fact that journalism is going the way of Rupert Murdoch rather than that of a Robert Fiske or John Pilger. As long as there is one journalist of the calibre of Peter Mares at ABC in Australia, Gary Younge with the Guardian in the UK, Irene Fernandez, Steven Gan of the net-based news service Malaysiakini in Malaysia, along with Sainath, Max Martin and other journalists in India, there is hope.

The Information Technology Fix

While the debate about the usefulness of technology or otherwise, especially IT in development, is an on-going one, it would seem that this debate does have a central blind-spot. The focus on the usefulness or otherwise of technology is, I believe, the wrong end of the stick. Satellite technology can be used to track hurricanes and map land areas belonging to indigenous populations but it can also be used for military purposes. What is important and often neglected are the need for policies supportive of the sustainable uses of IT in development based on the logic of cost-effectiveness and efficiency.

Take, for instance, the use of IT in education—through distance learning and in the context of local learning initiatives. The logic that is frequently used to favour distance learning over conventional education is ease of delivery, universality and cost-effectiveness. Although this logic is impeccable in the context of remote areas and difficult terrains, in less difficult geographical contexts, policy decisions in favour of IT in education usually impact on the recruitment, training and prioritising of teachers in rural education. In most cases, while not openly acknowledged, IT becomes a substitute for teachers and part of a self-fulfilling circle—where the lack of teachers is weighed against the cost-effectiveness and availability of IT, leading to the edging out of the teaching fraternity. While in contexts characterised by wide employment opportunities, re-skilling and employment are a real possibility, such scenarios do not hold true for rural contexts in the South, where employment opportunities relate to a fixed number of professions. In other words, cost-effectiveness related to the induction of IT and virtual learning environments can lead to the death of 'expendable' professions, like that of teachers, resulting in poorer learning environments bereft of face to face learning. Such policy initiatives are, in turn, a consequence of the many pressures to centre IT at the heart of development efforts. There are hidden strings attached to such efforts as IT-based applications are a significant part of the mantra of globalisation. Current IT inductions in development fit perfectly in with current policies that are anti-subsidy, anti-welfare and pro-WTO. Such applications often fulfil the free market conditionalities imposed by the World Bank and the IMF on indebted governments.

The IT fix approach is, of course, central to both the central and state government's poverty alleviation programmes. Support for a range of IT-based solutions—from Information & Communication Technology (ICT) kiosks, to e-governance and e-villages—reflect this fixation. While IT-based solutions such as the Bhoomi project in Karnataka that involved the computerisation of land records, has demonstrated the benefits of 'disintermediation'—bypassing the middle-man, who often, as a village accountant or revenue officer, altered, traded and expropriated land from poor peasant farmers—the impact of e-governance projects has been less pronounced. One of the major issues in India is whether the government has the political will to back up IT initiatives with social projects focussed precisely on dismantling the feudal constancy of rural India. In other words, caste, class, gender and other social identities and factors continue to restrict the potential of ICT projects aimed at empowering local communities. Access and use of ICTs are based on the existence of equitable social relations and the absence of caste and gender-based discriminations. Caste-related human rights abuses are commonplace in Central and Eastern India and it is unfeasible to rely on IT-based solutions as the sole basis for changing social relations that have been shaped over many centuries.

Another central issue with respect to ICTs in development is sustainability. Too often, ICT projects are time-bound and dependent on external funding. For ICT projects to make a difference, there also has to be prioritised investments in local training, local language-based software and in the computerisation of related networks, government departments and services. There are also other issues related to the prioritisation of scarce funds in development. Should people-centred investments be made to strengthen the local health and educational infrastructures rather than investments in tele-health and distance education that is reliant on the unimpeded availability of resources such as electricity and bandwidth that can be used to download material in the absence of rural libraries?

In a recent study of tele-centres and e-governance in India (Thomas 2009), I came to the following conclusions. It is clear that governments throughout the world now rely on the private sector to support development and have, as a consequence, backed down from any extensive involvement in development. This, after all, is a global trend in the context of SAPs, economic liberalisation and the new rules of multi-lateral and bi-lateral trade.

The lessons from the Bhoomi project and Gyan Ganga tele-centre suggest the value of multi-stakeholder, participatory approaches in development. While there are ICTs in development projects that are based on multi-stakeholder participation, it is clear that both Bhoomi and the Gyan Ganga projects did not significantly include people's participation at all stages of the project. How to strengthen popular participation is of critical importance given the examples from the right to information (RTI) movement that clearly demonstrates the advantages derived from the involvement of local people in the planning, implementation and evaluation of information projects. The RTI movement offers multiple examples of how information can be transformed into a tool for social change, lessons that can result in ICTs becoming more than just a 'passive' technology but an active, appropriate technology in social change.

Technological determinism has not disappeared. One of the questions that need some exploration is whether communication and development projects are in danger of repeating the very same mistakes that they committed in the 1960s and 1970s—when an older generation of technological interventions were seen as a sufficient input for change, while the context was completely ignored. There have been significant exceptions such as the Kheda Project that was an off-shoot of the larger Satellite Instructional Television Experiment (SITE) project and that did attempt to focus on the structural factors in development. However, its findings were not allowed to contaminate or, for that matter, influence, the larger SITE project.

With a handful of exceptions, ICTs in development projects are not located in an enabling environment that is backed up by economic policies, political will, availability of trained social capital and supported by local culture/s. This is a major drawback given both capital and content needs. If ICTs are made to 'adjust' to existing politics and the status quo, its impact will be strictly limited.

To make a difference, as a network technology, ICTs projects need to be connected to larger ICTs networks. While ICTs can be used for stand-alone projects, for example, data processing and the archiving of Indigenous Knowledge System (IKS), local cultures, its impact on development is conditioned by its functioning within an integrated network. Scalability too is a major issue and it would seem that too many ICTs in development projects remain as silos.

Notes

1. Email message from G. Sankaran, 'Hotel Taj: Icon of Whose India'. 2 December 2008.
2. Communication and the Globalisation of Poverty, *Media Development* 1/2000.

References

Choudhary, S. 2009. 'CGnet and Citizen Journalism in India', 1 June. Available at http://www.america.gov/st/peopleplace-english/2009/June/20090616175845mlenuhret0.1840588.html (Accessed on 1 August 2009).

Deb, S. 2008. 'The Mumbai that didn't Make the News', *The Hindu*, International Edition, 4 December.

Devereux, E. 1998. *Devils and Angels: Television, Ideology and the Coverage of Poverty*. Luton: University of Luton Press/John Libbey media.

Ghose, A. 2008. 'On Vague and Public Taste', Subaltern Media. Available at http://subalternmedia.com/?p=1629 (Accessed on 30 September 2009).

Golding, P. and S. Middleton. 1982. *Images of Welfare: Press and Public Attitudes to Poverty*. Oxford: Martin Robertson.

Hall, S. 1977. 'Culture, the Media and the "Ideological Effect"', in J. Curran, M. Gurevitch and J. Woollacott (eds), *Mass Communication and Society*, pp. 315–348. London: Edward Arnold in association with Open University Press.

Harivansh. 2005, '*Prabhat Khabar*: An Experiment in Journalism', in N. Rajan (ed.), *Practising Journalism: Values, Constraints, Implications*, pp. 46–62. New Delhi, Thousand Oaks, London: Sage Publications.

Hills, M. 2000. 'Conceptualising the Fourth World: Four Approaches to Poverty and Communication', *Media Development*, 1: 3–8.

Jamwal, A. B. 2004. 'Auditing the Mainstream Media: The Case of Jammu & Kashmir', in S. K. Das (ed.), *Media and Displacement II: Three Case Studies Media Coverage of Forced Displacement in Contemporary India*, pp. 10–49. Kolkata: Mahanirban Calcutta Research Group.

Joseph, A. 2007. 'Is the Media Watching Poverty Enough?', India Together. Available at http://www.indiatogether.org/2007/oct/ajo-medpov.htm (Accessed on 1 December 2008).

Kendall, D. 2005. *Framing Class: Media Representations of Wealth and Poverty in America*. Lanham/Boulder/New York/Toronto/Oxford: Rowman and Littlefield Publishers Inc.

McKendrick, John H., Stephen Sinclair, Anthea Irwin, Hugh O'Donnell, Gill Scott and Louise Dobbie. 2008. *The Media, Poverty and Public Opinion in the UK*. Joseph Rowntree Foundation, September, York/London.

Naqvi, F. 2007. *Waves in the Hinterland: The Journey of a Newspaper*. New Delhi: Nirantar/Zubaan.

Panos. 2007. *Making Poverty the Story: Time to Involve the Media in Poverty Reduction.* London: Panos.

Pillai, V. 2008. 'Ink Fresh on their Passport, the Only News Comes Back Home', *Outlook,* 1 December: 76–79.

Sainath, P. 1996. *Everybody Loves a Good Drought: Stories from India's Poorest Districts'*. New Delhi: Penguin Books.

———. 2001. 'None so Blind as those Who will not See', *The UNESCO Courier,* June: pp. 44–46.

———. 2004. 'Hope Dies Slowly in Wayanad', *The Hindu Online*, 18 December. Available at http://www.hinduonnet.com/2004/12/18/stories/2004121806321200.htm (Accessed on 1 December 2008).

———. 2008. '16,632 Farmer Suicides in 2007', *The Hindu*, Bangalore, 12 December.

Srinivas, S. 2009. 'Corporate Fraud: Shocked and Awed', 9 January. Available at http://www.businessworld.in/index.php/Corporate/Shocked-And-Awed.html (Accessed on 12 October 2009).

Thomas, P. 2009. 'Bhoomi, Gyan Ganga, E-governance and the Right to Information: ICTs and Development in India', *Telematics and Informatics*, 26(1): 20–31.

Uprety, A. 2008. 'Empty Plates and Ghost Villages', *The Week*, 17 August: 34–35.

Section 3
RESISTANCE

The final section deals with a central aspect of a critical political of communications—the ways in which ordinary people resist media dominance through public campaigns such as the right to information and community radio movements and build another communications order based on access, justice and freedom. Resistance is the key to social change. Both Chapters 10 and 11 foreground the fact that India has been the location for many traditions of resistance media and that these expressions, at specific times, have invigorated democracy and democratic futures. The case of the right to information (RTI) movement that began in a handful of villages in Rajasthan and became a national movement exemplifies the value of grassroots, need-based solutions. I contrast this movement with the community radio movement that is struggling to establish itself in the face of foot-dragging by the state. The concluding chapter explores an Indian tenor for communication rights. In many ways communication rights ought to be a fundamental human right. In my way of thinking communication rights is the other side of a critical political economy of communication. It is in the context of communication rights that reflections on a critical political economy of communications become translated into projects supportive of meaningful, sustainable, equitable communication futures.

10

Resistance: Community Radio and the Right to Information Movement in India

Studies on the political economy of communication have tended to remain at the level of a critique of existing media structures and processes and only occasionally have become the basis for advocacy. This has consistently been the norm and numerous studies over the years have explored many an intriguing pathway towards an understanding of the new sources of power in the media and illumined the ways in which this power has reinforced traditions of dominance by the state and the private sector over citizens. While this critique of media structures and dominant ideologies have certainly contributed towards an understanding of the complexity and the layered nature of relationships between economics, politics and culture and the ways in which these coalesce to exercise power, this critique is, as theorists such as Herb and Dan Schiller, Peter Golding, Graham Murdock, Robert McChesney and Cees Hamelink have observed in their many writings, the necessary basis for working towards another, just social world and communications order. That commitment to theorising as well as doing is best illustrated in the stance taken by public intellectuals such as McChesney and his involvement in the media reform movement in the US, Peter Golding's involvement in child poverty action and Cees Hamelink's many and varied attempts to advocate communication rights at global and national levels.

Understanding Resistance

A commonly shared reason for resistant media is the perceived need to counter what Habermas has described as the colonisation of the life-world by the system. The life-world is the private sphere that has been steadily encroached by the system that consists of commercial forces and through the extension of governmentality—a term used by Foucault to describe the steady inroads made by order and power that are continuously involved in making us pliant citizens, controlled by the state and beholden to its forces and commercial interests. Foucault used the term to describe the ways in which those who are considered deviant are marginalised, even institutionalised through the endless mill of speech and discourse. This then is the overall environment in which community media emerge.

Media Resistance over the Ages

We would, of course, be wide off the mark if we were to insist that community media is a by-product of modernity. While it is true that the validation of voice, community, agency and subjectivity have assumed heightened importance in the context of Modernity, such struggles have existed from time immemorial. We have ample evidence from around the world of oppressed people using the media to resist, subvert or overthrow an unjust order. Peasant struggles, for instance, in Europe and Asia, the great slave rebellions in Haiti and the US, revolutions such as the one that led to the overthrow of the Bautista regime in Cuba and in more recent times anti-apartheid struggles in Rhodesia and South Africa, included a very definite use of small media—from song and dance, such as the 'chimurenga' gatherings in Rhodesia that has been described in the book by Fredrikse (1982) *None but Ourselves.* The Colombian media scholar Jesus Martin-Barbero (1993) introduced the notion of mediation to describe the many ways in which we are continuously negotiating and being negotiated by the media and by culture. To him, the issue is not community media per se, but mediations; not the text, but how people interpret symbolic products and ascribe meanings. In this sense, it would be wrong to ascribe alterity to the media per se, for instance, community radio.

I am fond of quoting the example of Basavana, a tenth century poet belonging to the medieval Virasaivite movement in South India, who wrote poems intended to subvert the ossified traditions of a caste-based Hinduism and, in its place, offer a Hinduism based on Bhakti (devotion) and a personal relationship with God. Here is a poem entitled, 'The Temple and the Body', translated by A. K. Ramanujan (1973: 88):

The rich
Will make temples for Siva
What shall I
A poor man,
Do?
My legs are pillars,
The body the shrine
The head a cupola
Of gold.
Listen, O Lord of the meeting rivers,
Things standing shall fall,
But the moving ever shall stay.

Indian temples are built on the image of the human body. However, in real life, there is little correspondence between the human body and temple, as temples more often than not, become static and institutionalised. This poem calls for a return to the real temple, which resides in the heart of every human being. The poem makes a distinction between making and being. The rich can build and make a temple hoping that they will get some future merit in doing so. However, what will remain far after the stones crumble and the temple is destroyed by time, is spirit. What will remain immortal is the human body. As the translator of this poem A. K. Ramanujan (1973: 21) points out, 'The Virasaiva movement was a social upheaval by and for the poor, the low-caste and the outcaste against the rich and privileged; it was a rising of the unlettered against the literate pundit, flesh and blood against stone.'

At a different level, James Scott (1990) has written of the many ways in which ordinary people have used artefacts, ruses, songs, attitudes to subvert the order from within—what can best be described as counter-hegemonic means. In his book, *Domination and the Arts of Resistance: Hidden Transcripts*, Scott deals with the ways in which subordinated people use 'rumours, gossip, folk tales, songs, gestures, jokes and theatre of the powerless as vehicles', as everyday resistance that allows for a 'critique of power while hiding beyond anonymity or behind innocuous understandings of power'. Clifford Geertz (1973) in the classic book, *The Interpretation of Cultures*, contrasts the figure of the clown in the Javanese shadow puppet theatre, Wayang, with that of Falstaff in Shakespeare's *Henry the IV*:

> Both figures…provide a reminder that, despite overproud assertions to the contrary by religious fanatics and moral absolutists, no completely adequate and comprehensive human world view is possible, and behind all the pretence to absolute and ultimate knowledge, the sense for the irrationality of human life, for the fact that it is unlimitable, remains.

We also have that wonderful example of Chaucer's *Canterbury Tales,* again from the medieval era in which verse and rhyme and many a bawdy line were employed to prick the pretensions of prince and pauper.

Theorising Alternative Media

As Rodriguez (2001) and Downing and Ford (2000) have pointed out in their writings on citizen's/radical media, there are essentially two broad ways of theorising these forms of media. These two ways fit into ways of theorising social movements—old social movements that are essentially about struggles over resourcing and that link to older forms of class-based organisation and understandings of the nature of power—and the new social movements that are based on a post-Marxian understanding of struggle, power and politics and that validates identity struggles and struggles over meaning. Old theorising of community media linked to Bertolt Brecht (1983), Paulo Freire (1972) and Augusto Boal (1979) see community media as a means of struggle against the establishment. In this way of thinking, popular theatre and community radio are the means to counter dominant power—over both real and symbolic resources through a validation of voice and through the empowerment of local communities. Following what can be termed the Chomskyian model, the exercise of power in contemporary society is hegemonic, be it in Latin America where ruling oligarchs supported by US interests maintained their power over the people through media, or in Israeli-Palestinian relationships where brute force is used to maintain order. Power, in this sense is one-dimensional and is most often described as a battle between binaries—good and bad, right and wrong, poor and rich, proletariat and bourgeoisie.

In contrast to this position, post-structural thinkers including Chantal Mouffe and Ernesto Laclau (2001) introduced the notion of Radical Democracy and Latin American media scholars such as Martin-Barbero (1993) and Canclini (1993) introduced us to issues related to mediation, cultural hybridity and the multiplicity of struggles. The key struggles in Europe in the 1970s were over cultural identity and community media were used as tools to establish the identity of a variety of movements. Class was not the only social marker, but one along with race, gender, sexuality, etc. Struggles were not focussed on the overthrow of capitalism but on the validation of identity and citizen's involvement in making democracy work for them. In other words, as against old struggles to overthrow capitalism, identity based struggles aimed to give capitalism a human face. There was no permanent class struggle. Attention shifted from the macro to the micro, from structural change to micropolitics. In this way of thinking, people do not have a single identity. People use media to fight for the right to have a kaleidoscope of identities. People are not wedded to any single struggle. Struggle itself is impermanent and the media are adapted to whatever people want to struggle for.

In the words of Clemencia Rodriguez (2001: 20):

> [R]eferring to 'citizen's media' implies first that a collectivity is enacting its citizenship by actively intervening and transforming the established mediascape: second, that these media are contesting social codes, legitimized identities, and institutionalized social relations; and third, that these communication practices are empowering the community involved, to the point where these transformations and changes are possible.

In her way of thinking, community media is a tool that is used to fashion democracy by citizens. It is a moving feast in a post-modern understanding of struggles over identity and meaning.

Whether or not struggles over identity are the only way of conceiving struggles in India in the twenty-first century remains debatable, given that for millions of people, the struggle over basic needs is indeed the most basic, daily struggle. However, the terrain and objectives of struggles have become a lot more complex as different communities at a variety of levels use the media to resist the many traditions of dominance.

Critiquing Resistance Media

Resistance to the dominant media order, however, is not merely limited to the public activities of critical media theorists but has historically been carried out by many generations of activists who have attempted to reform existing media, resist dominant cultural traditions and establish resistance media and a new ethic for communications and culture. India has witnessed numerous subaltern struggles directed towards reclaiming cultural space and voice—from the medieval Bhakti movement and its critique of ossified, corrupt, high-caste religion through its accent on experience rather than ritual; the activities of the Indian Political Theatre Association (IPTA) in the anti-colonialist struggles; the literally thousands of people-based media advocacy initiatives including gender and media,

media education, popular theatre and other types of community media, including recently community radio and, in the recent past, newer movements such as the anti-copyright and free software movements. Taken in their entirety, these traditions of protest are an integral aspect of India then and India today, the land of a 'million mutinies'.

This chapter deals with two movements—the right to information movement and the community radio movements. While both movements are resistance oriented, the politics of resistance differs in each case. While the right to information movement was a wholly indigenous movement that began in a remote part of Rajasthan and that was a response to felt needs, lobbies for the community radio movement have mainly consisted of international and national NGOs, UNDP, UNESCO—in other words, representatives of local and global civil society. While community radio certainly has a role as a third broadcasting sector along with private and state broadcasting services, one of the issues that it faces relates to the setting of its agendas—where does the imperative for community radio come from? Who has been involved in the articulation of this need? Who, in other words, is the interpretive community backing the community radio movement? To what extent are NGOs that are involved in setting up community radio truly participatory and involve local people in the setting of agendas?

I highlight these questions not because I am opposed to this movement. On the contrary, I strongly believe that community radio does have an important role to play in social change in India. Nevertheless, the question related to the articulation of needs cannot be brushed away, primarily because community radio is typically pitched as a resource for change at a grassroots level. While it would be invidious to claim that the internationally-supported NGO movement in India that is a conduit for foreign capital and, thereby, interests, is the face of the new imperium, a view expressed by the established Left in India, it is nevertheless prudent for us to recognise the consequences of dependent development.

In contrast, the right to information movement began as a locally-supported and financed initiative. I am not suggesting that the right to information movement in India today is free of inconsistencies. While its initial phase in Rajasthan was characterised by exercises of substantive democracy, its subsequent iterations have been problematic given that state inaction and foot-dragging have blunted its potential. The issue really is not about the worth of the community radio movement, for that has been established. We are aware that the community radio movement has played a significant role in social change processes in many countries in Latin America, Africa, Europe and more recently in South-East Asia and South Asia. The issue, rather, is one of how it can become representative of felt needs. More importantly, it is also about how the community radio movement can become an important ally in extending the right to information movement in India. Community radio is not an all-sufficient answer to the country's myriad communication problems. Radio can act as a tool and resource to extend the quality and scope of democracy. It can play a vital role, however, in extending 'Voice' and in supporting key civil society initiatives such as the right to information movement. In other words, community radio will make a difference when it is linked into larger initiatives that are directed towards the democratisation of society.

The State and Community Broadcasting in India

India is a late comer to community radio in South Asia. Sri Lanka and Nepal have established community radio networks supported by the state and the NGO community respectively. While community radio has been on the cards for many decades, the World Association for Christian Communication (WACC) supported consultation on community radio held in Bengaluru in 1996, which led to the Bangalore Declaration that was used for lobbying the government and provided a major momentum to free the airwaves. In December 2002, the government released its 'Community Radio Guidelines' that restricted licenses to established educational institutions. The government's response thus far has been to award a limited number of licenses for community broadcasting, with the majority to government-funded educational institutions—Anna University, MOP Vaishnava College (Chennai), Jamia Milia Islamia, the Indian Institute of Mass Communication, along with 10 other FM stations run by educational institutions (Pinglay 2005). Campus radio, however, has very limited potential in becoming a tool for development.

Inspite of the fact that a Supreme Court judgement in 1995 ruled that the airwaves are public property, the Indian State has continued its post-Independence commitment to broadcasting as first and foremost a property of the state. While its watertight hold over broadcasting was breached by the cable and satellite revolution that began in the early 1990s and further diluted by subsequent policies that ushered in the era of deregulation and privatisation of broadcasting services, the state continues to exert an extraordinary influence in the governance and licensing of broadcasting in India. It is clear that key power brokers in government and representatives of successive coalition governments, while benefiting from the vast revenues earned through the sale of FM radio licences and 2G and 3G cellular licences, have, at every given opportunity, attempted to claw back and/or needlessly delay the full and transparent opening up of the broadcasting sector to public use and scrutiny. The ponderous, over-bureaucratised, licensing system linked to the community radio sector is perhaps the most potent illustration of this trend. As has been reported:

> [W]ith its no-news policy and other restrictions, community radio remains one of the Indian media's tightly controlled segments, as against a very large measure of freedom for the print media...Getting access to a licence and understanding the procedures to do so remains another maze for most.

Section 3 Selection Process and Processing of Applications in the document Policy Guidelines for Setting up Community Radio Stations in India[1] lists a complicated, inherently corruptible process of licensing. It is clear that there is an attempt to ghettoise this sector, contain it within a strict definition of community, bureaucratise it and weigh it down with multiple restrictions, for example, on advertising, restrictions that stand in stark contrast to the freedoms given to commercial broadcasters.

The clearest commitment yet to community radio in India is contained in the Telecom Regulatory Authority of India's (TRAI) Recommendations on Licensing Issues Relating to Community Radio Stations, 9 December 2004. This report is divided into seven sections— background, eligibility, licensing process, funding, regulation and monitoring, other alternatives and summary of recommendations. Section 7.3 Funding includes the following recommendations:

- Any organisation engaged in social, cultural development work in any community and getting Government funding/grants for the same will not be disqualified from receiving the Government funding/grants, if it sets up a community radio station.
- Commercial advertising may be permitted on Community Radio.
- The Community radio stations should be permitted to accept grants/funds as per the provisions of FCRA (Foreign Contributions Regulations Act).

While the TRAI Consultation Paper on Licensing Issues Relating to Community Radio Stations released on 25 August 2004 did consider the pros and cons of these recommendations, the scale of the proposed changes took most community radio watchers in India by surprise. Prior to this, the government's position on community radio was lukewarm at best, reflected in the fact that the only community radios licensed to operate were one form or another of campus radio run by educational institutions. In hindsight, this rather cautious approach to community broadcasting is entirely in character with a radio broadcasting structure that has, until of late, revelled in its position as a monopoly broadcaster. As I have observed in an earlier article (Thomas 2003: 25), 'Long years of centralised control is reflected in its over-cautious approach to programming, its extreme sensitivity to criticism, its highly politicised environment and its susceptibility to policies that are influenced by the dictates of political expediency.' While the deregulation of radio and, in particular, the moves to open up commercial FM broadcasting has changed the radio ownership equation, it would seem that the authorities are still cagey about opening up radio to the community sector. Pavrala and Malik's (2007) book *Other Voices: The Struggle for Community Radio in India* offers the most up to date history of this sector.

Inspite of what seems avowedly like moves to free broadcasting space for the community radio sector, TRAI's recommendations have been crafted within a needlessly top-heavy licensing process that is a throwback to an earlier era, that of the 'license Raj', a euphemism for the days of red-tape and excessive bureaucracy. The process of attaining a community radio licence remains convoluted, involves a labyrinthine process and offers the government in power ample opportunities to delay or even reject an application. Section 7.2 Licensing Process (TRAI 2004: 43) states:

> The applications should be filed directly with the Ministry of Information & Broadcasting. The Ministry of Information and Broadcasting should refer the applications received to it to the Ministry of Home Affairs. The Ministry of Home Affairs should examine the applications from the point of view of internal security...the Ministry of Information & Broadcasting to issue licenses after consultation with the WPC wing of the Ministry of Communications,

This process that takes about a year from application to the actual granting of a Wireless Operation Licence. The renewed emphasis on government-based regulation rather than that of an independent broadcast authority does seem unfortunate in the light of the fact that a stated intent of this exercise is to promote the freedom of expression. A matter that is considerably more problematic is the exercise of centralised control by any future government that is not sympathetic to the aims of community radio. By tying in community radio to the dictates of existing broadcast policy, the government has relinquished an opportunity to be involved in exploring another culture for broadcasting in India.

In an article entitled 'Ten Theses on State Politics in India', Yogendra Yadav and Suhas Palshikar (2008) describe the many ways in which state politics has broken away from national politics and has become the arena for autonomy, political choice and identity-formation. They describe the gradual leaching of power from the Centre to many Peripheries and observe:

> The emergence of the states as the central platform of politics might actually weaken the capacity of democratic politics to withstand the pressures of organised economic interests; and may open the doors wider for consolidation of the oligarchic control of dominant social groups, reducing the real political choices available to the citizen. (Yadav and Palshikar 2008: 22)

National politics continues to play an overarching role in key areas such as the economy, national security and, for our purposes, in broadcasting.

While the balance of power now lies with the states, the Centre has resisted the de-centralisation of key areas such as state broadcasting. The late Chief Minister of Karnataka, Ramakrishna Hegde (1986), had, in the mid-1980s, suggested the de-centralisation of All India Radio and for state-based and controlled broadcasting services, a suggestion that had been shelved for more than two decades. Today, there is a resurgent interest in state-based broadcasting and five state governments—Madhya Pradesh, Bihar, Delhi, Karnataka and Punjab—have expressed an interest in establishing their own local radio channels. While the Information and Broadcasting ministry is yet to give its approval for this project, Anuradha Raman, writing in *Outlook*, quotes views expressed by the Watchdog Community Radio Forum who believe that this will merely provide a further opportunity for states to strengthen their propaganda base and clog up broadcast space at the expense of the community radio sector.

> It is an entry through the backdoor by state and local governments into the community radio space...It is a deeply sinister move which will completely undermine the credibility and worth of community radio. Community radio is radio of, by and for the community, and 'state-run community radio' is not only a contradiction in terms, it will be little more than a mouthpiece for the party in power, an instrument for political propaganda. (Raman 2008: 14)

All India Radio and Community Radio

Rather paradoxically, the key player in community radio remains the state broadcaster, All India Radio. This national network includes national, regional, local and community stations. It operates five community radio centres in North East India, two in Nagaland, two in Meghalaya and one centre in Mizoram. It began leasing time slots on its 177 local radio stations to NGOs from the late 1990s onwards. For all practical purposes, this type of broadcasting remains the dominant form of community radio in India. These local radio stations have been part of AIR's network since the 1970s and have, on occasion, dealt with local issues, some times successfully. Research done on the Ooty Radio Station, in South India, suggests that the programmes caters to that region's populations and needs including that of five indigenous communities and the dominant agricultural community, the Badagas. While the state broadcaster's control of community radio output does have obvious drawbacks, there are instances where these programmes have resulted in social change. One of the recent examples is a programme called 'To Be Alive' produced in Western Gujarat that specifically addressed corruption and compensation claims related to earthquake victims. Another programme, 'Pardafash' (Expose) produced by AIR's local Radio Ujjas (Light), has been used to expose corruption in government hospitals. Their programmes have led to numerous exposes of corruption. Radio Ujjas, run by a multi-NGO team—the women's group, Kutch Mahila Vikas Sangathan, the Drishti Media Collective and the Centre of Alternatives in Education, along with the UNDP—have dealt with issues including women's leadership and governance, female foeticide, harassment of women for dowry and maternal mortality. Another local radio located in the 'tribal' region of Jharkhand, in Palamau District, is organised by two local NGOs, the Alternative for India Development and the Manthan Yuva Sangathan, and is financially supported by the National Foundation for India. The Ford Foundation is involved in funding a programme on AIR Darbhanga, and 11 other local radio stations—Panchayat Vani (People's Voice).

Pirate Radio

The landmark judgement by India's Supreme Court in 1995 that recognised that airwaves are public property, the lobbying by the media reform movement in India best reflected in the Bangalore Declaration (1996) and the Pastapur Declaration (2000) and impatience with the government's foot dragging has led to creativity, novelty and innovative uses of radio in development and social change. During 2005–2006, there were reports of at least two 'pirate' community radio initiatives in India. In 2007, *BBC Online* had reported the story of a home-grown FM radio station produced by a village radio mechanic in the state of Bihar. Programmes included public interest messages on HIV and polio, and missing children, along with film-based and devotional music. The costs involved in setting up FM Mansoorpur 1 were minimal. In fact, his kit cost Rs 50, which is little more than 1 US dollar! A month later, *BBC Online* reported that the station had been shut down by the authorities. His case has been taken up by Reporters Without Borders who observed, 'To forcibly close down a community-type radio is a sign of intransigence by the authorities over the emergence of pluralism on the airwaves'(quoted in *BBC Online* report 2006). In 2003, the *Washington Post* had a story on community radio in India including a report that a lobby group for community radio in India, Radiophony, had supplied a low-cost production and transmission kit costing USD 25 to a women's group in Oravakallu village, Kurnool District, Andhra Pradesh (Lakshmi 2003). The station was called Mana Radio (Our Radio), operated between October 2002 and February 2003, before it was closed down by the government (Venkateshwarlu 2002). The Radiophony website carries the following information on the closure of Mana Radio:

> In the Hyderabad based Deccan Herald, a news item on Feb 13, 2003 reported, 'According to the official who seized the transmitter on Tuesday, he received an advisory from the DoT's monitoring agency to seize the transmitter since it had not been licensed by the Wireless Planning Coordination wing as required under the law.' Significantly, the Wireless Planning Coordination wing of the ministry of telecommunications is the last in a long list of agencies whose approval is necessary before broadcasting can be initiated. The WPC issues a licence for broadcasting only after all the others have given their approval.[2]

At the moment, community radio in India includes the following expressions:

1. Hiring time and space on local All India Radio for development broadcasts (Namma Dhwani, Bengaluru; Radio Ujjas, Kutch Mahila Vikas Sangathan, Bhuj; AID-Bihar, Palamau District, Jharkhand.
2. Narrow-casting through cable TV as is the case with the Bengaluru-based Namma Dhwani.
3. Hiring air time on the global satellite digital radio broadcaster Worldspace (Uttaranchal Radio, Dehradun).

4. Pirate Radio.
5. Independent Community Radio stations related to a handful of NGOs and International Non-governmental Organisations (INGOs).
6. Campus Radio.

With the steady decrease in the costs of local radio production and transmission, this is an option that is bound to be explored by a number of organisations and individuals either because they are ignorant of the laws related to licensing or because they are tired of waiting for the government to give them the signal to go ahead. The example of the radio mechanic in Bihar would seem to suggest that there is bound to be demand for local forms of community radio that are flexible in terms of content, production quality and delivery, but what reflects community needs, be it the need for local language broadcasts, local music, awareness or entertainment.

Apart from the issue of licensing that is yet to be sorted out, there are a number of issues that the community radio movement in India needs to address. These include the following:

1. While it is clear that there is a need for local forms of radio, the need of the hour is for diverse expressions of community radio, not only radio owned by the NGO movement but by a range of communities involved in development.
2. Since community radio is a valuable tool in local development, the state must invest in financing the spread of community radio, just as it has been involved in establishing rural phone connectivity throughout India.
3. There is a need for NGOs themselves who have been among the most vocal supporters of community radio to push for a regulatory framework to ensure that standards and objectives are maintained, in particular, the need to maintain inter-subjective, inter-faith and inter-community harmony. While the government's delays can be seen as a case of foot dragging, given the communal tensions that have periodically wrecked India, there is arguably a case for their making sure that a proper regulatory framework for community radio is in place before licensing community radio stations. After all, the examples of Radio Mille Collines in Rwanda and state radio in Serbia remain potent examples of the misuse of radio and its tragic consequences.
4. For the moment, the experiments in community radio tend to be localised, without an all-Indian reference. I would argue that there is a need for the community radio movement to explicitly connect

to the Right to Information Movement in India. The Bengaluru-based Namma Dhwani is involved in creating awareness of the need for public accountability and transparency although one can argue that this ought to become a key objective of the community radio movement. Radio can be used to reinforce accountability, transparency and empower local communities. It can be used to explore the gaps between government principles and institutional performance and to push for another development.

5. There is a need for the community radio movement to establish a pan-Indian organisation that not only operates as a lobby group, but is also involved in providing infrastructural support and advice, gathering information on and supporting local Research and Development (R&D) related to the technology of community radio, involved in framing policy, standards, a code of ethics, financing of the movement and exploring new radio technologies.
6. While the government's intent to open up the community radio sector to advertising is a positive sign, it is important that the movement explores different local funding options rather than rely on funding support from outside that often arrives with strings attached. Sustainability remains a key issue for community radio stations that depend on exogenous financial support in every part of the world.
7. Community radio needs to be seen as a tool for development. It is not an all-sufficient alternate to the needs for mobilisation, education and empowerment. While it can be used to push forward these processes, it must be part of an integrated approach to development.

The Status of Community Radio Today

In 2008, the Information and Broadcasting (I&B) Ministry had received 297 CR (Community Radio) licence applications, out of which 141 were from NGOs. There are currently 38 operational community radio stations in the country, out of which only 2 are run by NGOs. The rest are run by educational institutions.

Continuing issues include the following:

- Only non-profits/NGOs with a three-year track record can apply for a CR licence. The trouble with this position is that it marginalises those who would like to establish a dedicated CR station.

- Licensing is convoluted and involves approvals by five different government ministries. This makes it very difficult to assess the status of an application.
- All prospective CR licensees are required to carry out a survey of community needs available in English. The survey needs to be based on data from at least 1,000 respondents and many have complained that a one-size-fits-all survey is not what is needed.
- Until very recently, the FM transmitter had to be bought from three authorised vendors. The entry of Nomad that sells locally made transmitters in 2008 has led to a fall in costs.
- CR policy prescribes that a station should be owned by an NGO. This is problematic as it does not give space for a diverse governing structure that includes local people.
- Another issue is with the five minutes of advertising per hour allowed. There are significant limitations related to this, given that the financing of CR revenues are a perennial problem for the global CR movement.

A Recalcitrant State?

Why is it that a country that has a formidable civil society and many traditions of public service has not been able to adopt pro-active measures related to information and communication? Why is it that the state has been forced to concede to the demands for community radio and people's right to information only after substantive lobbying by the community radio movement in India and by being shamed into acquiescing to the need for a right to information act after it became a nation-wide movement? There are no easy answers to these questions. However, this reticence suggests that for all India's emergence as a global economic power and its recognition for its many democratic traditions, it continues to be troubled and sometimes addled by its inability to conceive, establish and execute projects that further substantive rights for the majority of its citizens. The fact that the only state in India that has been able to grant land rights and improve access to Dalits and adivasis is West Bengal (Bakshi 2008) would seem to suggest that India has a long way to go before it becomes a truly democratic nation.

In fact, given the new balance of politics and power between the centre and the states and the emergence of a new elite representing the new sources of power in the various states, it is more than likely that India's myriad socio-economic problems will become exacerbated in the future. The growth of the Naxalite movement throughout India is an illustration of people-based solutions to the perceived inertia of the state to contribute to the development of its people.

The Right to Information Movement in India

The second example of a people-based resistance movement, directed towards claiming people's right to know, is the Right to Information Movement. Access to knowledge and information can lead to social change. Right to information (RTI) policies that have been enacted in different parts of the world have recognised the value of citizen's rights to information as critical to the fulfilment of citizenship. The right to information, as it is well known today, can become the basis for the enjoyment of other human rights. It is essential for the making of transparent and accountable government. It enables citizens to be involved in 'governance', decision making, the making of social policies and in the exercise of substantive democracy. It is also recognised that for it to work, the right to information must be enshrined in law. As the Article 19 document The Public Right to Know: Principles on Freedom of Information Legislation (1999: 1) describes it:

> Information is the oxygen of democracy. If people do not know what is happening in their society, if the actions of those who rule them are hidden, then they cannot take a meaningful part in the affairs of that society. But information is not just a necessity for people—it is an essential part of good government. Bad government needs secrecy to survive. It allows inefficiency, wastefulness and corruption to thrive. RTI allows people to scrutinise the actions of a government and is the basis for proper, informed debate of those actions. Most governments, however, prefer to conduct their business in secret.

The Article 19 document referred to here highlights nine principles that define the core of the Right to Information:

- Maximum Disclosure
- Obligation to Publish
- Promotion of Open Government
- Limited Scope of Exceptions
- Processes to Facilitate Access

- Costs
- Open Meetings
- Disclosure takes Precedence
- Protection for Whistleblowers.

Access to information and its affordable use is universally recognised as a key precursor to development and social change.

Information and Politics

There are, of course, numerous meanings ascribed to information—technical, economic and social—although in the era of information technologies, information has become reified as a panacea for the world's problems. The raw material for information technologies is information, discrete bits of information that are manipulated to make it productive. Digitalisation has enabled convergence and the common language of the digital covers a multitude of uses—from the SMS texts that we send to vote in our preferred winner of a Reality TV contest to the deep manipulations of information that have led to blurrings between human biologicals and human biological information. Information has many sides to it and many uses and its meanings are clearly linked to context. It is interesting to note that one of the election promises of the DMK government in Tamil Nadu during the last state elections was a television for all families without television—a promise that it has tried to keep, although not without its attendant problems—faulty sets, poor connections, along with favouritism and corruption in the sourcing of such sets. What this example reveals is a regional state government's belief in television as an important channel for the negotiation of citizenship, access to mediated culture as a vital element in modernising local publics and television as an important conduit for information that can make a difference in one's quality of life. The fact that access to television was made on a par with access to subsidised rice at 'a rupee a kg' reveals the extent of what some would term populist prioritisation. However, there is more to do this given that in both intended and unintended ways television has begun to impact on Indian society at a level of complexity that is only beginning to be explored (See Mehta 2008). There is, of course, a propaganda angle to this. There is recognition that television can be used as a formidable propaganda tool, especially in an election year.

Information Making a Difference

As against information as propaganda, it can also be used by citizens to make a difference in their lives. The most potent example of information making a difference in people's lives is the story of the right to information movement in India. In this context, information is not seen as a unit or resource that can be manipulated through external means but as narratives and discourses that can be acted upon in real time by real people and as windows of opportunities for furthering local aspirations, goals and lives. Information, in this context, includes access to intangibles such as information on minimum wages that can result in access to tangibles such as grain and essential oils available through the public distribution system (PDS). In other words, 'information' in this context is not an abstraction or just data but is a vital input in human development and social change and in the creation of environments supportive of local needs and aspirations. There is little point in access to information if the larger environment—for example, the local development machinery—blunts and dilutes development and limits social change. If the RTI brings about transparency and allows access to resources, it can lead to substantial improvements in one's quality of life. In this sense, the RTI needs to be seen as being on a par with the water that we drink and the air that we breathe, the public's right to the local commons.

In the context of the RTI in India, 'information' includes all public directives related to development that have been articulated by the state and central governments and that are available as legal documents, planning documents related to development, budgets and the records of development actions in the field. The right to information movement demands access to these documents, its public scrutiny and the right of citizens to demand explanations for and redressals of situations characterised by gaps between the proposed development activities and its actual manifestations. This movement needs to be seen against the background of a state that continues to play a role as a much-reduced, although still dominant, contributor to development expenditures through a myriad number of projects—from welfare-based rural employment projects to the public distribution system that enables all citizens access to essential food grains and oils. Seen against the life of a rural labourer—the state's myriad development projects are essential to his/her survival—be it agricultural subsidies, access to subsidised local health care or to subsidised essential grain. In the context of class/caste-based oppressions throughout India that severely limit life chances, this welfare system, at least in theory, provides the means for the majority of India's poor to have at least one meal a day—for instance, through the mid-day meals scheme—and provide options for at least minimal employment. However, it is widely known that the vast development expenditures at central and state levels that have run into the billions of dollars have been expended within a finely graded system of corruption that has been responsible for scams of monumental proportions that have led to various rungs of bureaucracy benefiting from development expenditures at the expense of the people that were the projected beneficiaries.

The History of the Right to Information Movement in India

From a citizen's perspective, the fact that the key impetus for a struggle that eventually led to the enactment of a national RTI legislation and numerous state-level legislations began at a grassroots level, specifically via a peasant's movement in the state of Rajasthan, the Mazdoor Kisan Shakti Sangathan (MKSS), a movement committed to land, livelihood and wage rights, is little short of remarkable. The MKSS was officially formed in 1990 by local activists including Aruna Roy, Nikhil Dey and Shankar Singh in Devdungri, a village in the state of Rajasthan. Initially, their advocacy focussed on struggles for minimum wages, land and women's rights mainly with landless labourers and initiatives related to making the Public Distribution System, accountable. Their own spartan lifestyles, their life lived with people and their refusal to accept international or government funding for their work placed them in a different category from the average NGO employee in India who is, for the most part, beholden and captive to the exigencies of foreign or state funding. Very early on in this work, they realised that the key obstacles to development at village level is the lack of information on a variety of entitlements to rural people, in the area of employment, rural infrastructure such as dispensaries, clinics, schools, roads and irrigation, along with information on the many government initiatives related to poverty alleviation. They launched a campaign based on consultation, street-based discussions and popular theatre performances throughout the state. In 1994 and in the face of official recalcitrance and unwillingness to cooperate with people's demands, the MKSS decided to organise public hearings (*Jan Sunwais*). These hearings took the form of an audit of local level development projects, especially the social audit of 'employment muster rolls' and expenses related to public works and wages paid to workers. This led to the demand for all copies of documents related to public works to be made public. However, local government officials were not, in the beginning, cooperative and, in fact, launched their own counter-campaigns against the right to information movement.

These hearings, however, took a life of its own. As more and more people throughout the state began to hear the literally hundreds of stories of corruption, they became empowered to act on this information. In district after district, these hearings exposed the vast gaps between official expenditures on development projects and the actual expenditures. These hearings unearthed evidence of widespread corruption and the systemic links between local officials and politicians who were also involved in a variety of scams. This evidence discussed at the public hearings led to non-violent civic actions, boycotts and sit-ins at government offices that was systematically used to wear down the opposition and elicit a response from the government. These local resistances reinforced what the public already knew, the fact that there was gross misappropriation of funds—wages paid to fictitious workers, even to people who had died years back recorded in local employment registers, and incomplete public works projects such as roads and buildings that were listed as complete when these were either partially complete, abandoned, non-existent and often made from sub-standard building material. In a public hearing held in Janawad Panchayat in Rajsamand District, on documented public works worth Rs 65 lakh (USD 144,444) in November 2000, it was 'established that no less than Rs 45 lakh (USD 100,000) of this sum had gone into fictitious, untraceable projects' (Muralidharan 2001).

In 1997, after many protests and hearings, the state government in Rajasthan announced the right of all people to demand and receive photocopies of all public works projects undertaken by local development authorities (the Panchayat). An additional focus was on the Public Distribution System that is mandated to provide subsidised 'rations' including grains and oils, the provision of which has notoriously been based on for 'leakages'—the selling of subsidised grain in the 'black' market and non-availability, when in actual fact, these products were being hoarded—and the substitution of inferior grain and dubious types of cooking oil that were hazardous to local health. This movement spread to other districts in Rajasthan and spilled over into neighbouring states. While corruption was among the initial issues that was exposed, the need for transparency, accountability and openness led to the scrutiny of higher levels of government funding, policies supportive of secrecy and to the demand that institutions that were previously outside the purview of public inspection, be open to such social audits. In 1997, after an epic 52-day sit-in (*dharna*) at the capital city of Jaipur, the then deputy chief minister announced that all local village government institutions were required to give access to information on expenditures, muster rolls and other documents. This eventually led to the Rajasthan government passing a right to information law in 2000. However, most importantly, the success of this movement in Rajasthan and the enormous benefits that it generated became the basis for a national movement focussed on pressurising the government to enact a national Right to Information law. In 1997, the National Campaign for the People's Right to Information was established. In 2002, the then central government introduced the Freedom of Information Act. This was amended by the present government to become the Right to Information Bill (2004). One of the consequences of this movement is the enactment of the Right to Information Bill (RTI Act 2005) that has influenced and in turn been moulded by prior right to information legislations in a number of states in India, including Rajasthan, Madhya Pradesh, Maharashtra, Goa, Tamil Nadu, Karnataka, Delhi and Andhra Pradesh.

Caveats

However and in spite of these welcome measures, this opportunity for popular participation in democratic governance and social change has been seriously compromised by a number of caveats and over-bureaucratised enforcement procedures that do have the potential to stymie the pace and nature of change. While the 2002 Bill included under its remit central, state, district and local level records and information and an enforceable penalty clause, the 2004 Bill has limited the right to information 'to only information available with the Central Government and Union Territories' and has diluted the effectiveness of the penalty clause for those who refuse to be transparent. The 'exceptions' listed in the schedule of the Right to Information Bill (2004) including intelligence and security organisations established by the Central Government and the exclusive focus on 'Public Authority' rather than both public and private sector.

The exemption of the private sector and voluntary agencies from the purview of this act is problematic given the fact that these two sectors are intricately involved in the life of the nation. Scams are not unknown in the private sector and include the accounting scandal at Satyam computers (94 per cent of the cash on the company's books was fictitious), the fourth largest software company in India that employs 53,000 people, operates in 66 countries, serves 185 Fortune 500 companies including GE and is the official IT service provider at FIFA 2010 and 2014. Not only were their auditors the global firm Pricewaterhouse, they were, in 2008, given the global award for excellence in corporate governance by the World Council for Corporate Governance (WCFCG) (BBC News 2009)! The accounting scandal at Satyam computers was preceded by other financial irregularities within Satyam, known to the World Bank. The Bengaluru-based IT-BPO Union had asked the government to investigate the World Bank ban on Satyam although it was informed by India's premium software body NASSCOM that this was an internal affair of the company and that, as such, unions did not have a right to query it (*Economic Times* 2009). The unravelling of reputable firms such as Satyam poses a number of questions to their auditors and to the regulatory system in India.

Companies such as Satyam that were a part of the new and progressive India were supported by the political system and by a board of directors who had both international and national standing and who were power-brokers in their own right. The Satyam scandal is a telling inditement of global and Indian capitalism and reveals the deep and enduring links between the market, finance capital, real estate, the political class and the regulatory system. There is absolutely no compelling reason to not make available corporate accounts to public scrutiny, given that in this case, the futures of 53,000 employees are at stake. Similarly NGOs, charities and mission agencies, for example, involved in post-Tsunami work in India, have spent millions of dollars on rehabilitation projects although it is widely known that there are major issues with accountability and leaching of funds. I have, in my work on Christian missions in India (Thomas 2008), observed that the commodification of Christianity is undergirded by family-based company structures that resist any form of accountability.

The Tamil Nadu state government's implementation of the RTI provides an example of the gaps between principle and practice, gloss and essence. While the Tamil Nadu government was the first to legislate an access law in India, namely The Tamil Nadu Right to Information Act (1997), it contained 21 exemptions including the following:

> [2e] [I]nformation whose disclosure would harm the frankness and candour of internal discussion, including:
>
> (i) proceedings of Cabinet and Cabinet committees;
> (ii) internal opinion, advice, recommendations, consultation and deliberation;

(iii) projections and assumptions relating to internal policy analysis, analysis of alternative policy options and information relating to rejected policy options;
(iv) Communications Between departments, public bodies and Confidence in regulatory bodies

While the Tamil Nadu state government has appointed a State Information Commission and three Information Commissioners, there is a significant absence of urgency in the commission's attitude towards the adjudication of RTI related disputes. As a report in the *Hindustan Times* notes (*Hindustan Times* 2007), 'In the more than one year of its existence, the commission found 96 cases where PIOs (Public Information Officers) had illegally denied information. Despite pronouncements of Rs. 25, 000 penalties against errant PIOs, not one errant PIO has been fined till date…'

Resisting the RTI

While the history of this movement in India certainly provides insights into local grassroots-based social change, its subsequent iterations throughout India have not been without significant limitations. In fact, what is clear from contemporary operationalisations of the right to information in India is that it poses the most formidable challenge to the status quo ever faced by development functionaries in India. Throughout India, RTI activists who have attempted to access information on public works have been threatened, jailed, abused and even murdered. Aruna Roy and Nikhil Dey (2008), writing in the *Indian Express* (June 14), describe the murder of a right to food activist, Lalit Mehta, in Jharkhand. He had attempted to access information on the expenditure records related to the National Rural Employment Guarantee Act—NREGA (2005)—for researchers who were keen on verifying official records against available information by local employees involved in rural development. Lalit was murdered on 14 May, a day before the planned social audit. But as they point out:

> It is not just Lalit Mehta. There are reports of threats to activists seeking information from different parts of the country. In Rajasthan, Social Audit teams have faced planned attacks in the districts of Banswara and Jhalawar in the last six months. According to K.N.Tripathi, member of the State Employment Guarantee Council of Jharkhand, Somay Gagarai, the District Convenor of the Congress for NREGA West Simbhum was killed about two months ago, for trying to access facts on

NREGA expenditure in his Block, through an RTI application. Twenty-six days after Lalit's murder, Kameshwar Yadav, a CPI Liberation NREGA activist was killed in Giridih District, Jharkhand for similar reasons. In Orissa's Koraput District, Narayan Hareka, Naib Sarpanch and member of the Orissa Adibasi Manch, was run down by a tractor on his way home, after he had spent a day trying to get NREGA information from the Block Office. (Roy and Dey 2008)

The monitoring of the national implementation of the NREGA by the Right to Food campaign via social audits conducted throughout the country provides extraordinarily textured data on the gaps between policy and practice in the implementation of this initiative. Their website carries the results of a number of social audits carried out in the different parts of the country. While it is clear that that the RTI has certainly empowered people to demand their rights and has triggered an array of advocacy groups and actions at local levels, the scale of corruption is immense and it will take many years before people benefit from the RTI. A social audit of the National Rural Employment Generation Scheme (NREGS) carried out by another campaign, the Poorest Area Civil Society (PACS) Programme in Chitrakoot, Uttar Pradesh, revealed:

[L]arge scale irregularities in every stage of the implementation of the NREGS: maintenance of documents, registration of households, issuing of job cards, response to demand for work, payment to workers, allotment of work for people with disability, allotment of work up to a maximum of 100 days per household in a year, involvement of gram sabhas in preparations of work plans, technical estimation and issue of work order by due process. Constitution of vigilance allotments, appointment of a mate at work site, provision of facilities at work site, planning and supervision of work.[3] (emphasis in the original)

The report describes irregularities with the registration process:

The audit revealed that friends and relatives of the gram pradhan were registered in large numbers; also, people who did not qualify for the NREGS. The friends and relatives did no labour work. They were land holders and rich people who owned their own farm land, tractors, etc. On the other hand a large number of BPL (below poverty line) families were not even registered. (See Endnote 3)

The availability and access to such reports and the public shaming of corrupt officials often acts as a deterrent. With the public availability of such information, business cannot be as usual and politicians who either turn a blind eye to the corruption or are beneficiaries of the system are forced to be accountable for their lack of action. The agenda of the Right to Food campaign is much larger than the monitoring of the NREGA and includes the monitoring of the government's key poverty alleviation schemes. As it is reported on their website:[4]

> The campaign has already taken up a wide range of aspects of the right to food. Sustained demands include:
>
> 1. a national Employment Guarantee Act,
> 2. universal mid-day meals in primary schools,
> 3. universalisation of the Integrated Child Development Services (ICDS) for children under the age of six,
> 4. effective implementation of all nutrition-related schemes,
> 5. revival and universalisation of the public distribution system,
> 6. social security arrangements for those who are not able to work and
> 7. equitable land rights and forest rights.

One of the key issues is the proper and effective implementation of government schemes and the accounting of expenditures. The campaign recognises the fact that the proper use of allocated budgets and the democratic extension of services can play an important role in reversing poverty ratios in the country. It recognises the fact that the RTI is critical to the enjoyment of constitutional guarantees, including the right to life and civil liberties. Such extensive and intensive monitoring that includes social audits is a major means used to advance the right to know, which in itself is an essential aspect of the right to information. What such campaigns reveal is the extraordinary momentum that right to information legislations in India have unleashed. Backed by citizen and consumer movements, NGO coalitions and in some cases by state-related bodies, this movement does have the potential to contribute towards lasting social change.

Conclusion

In spite of major issues with the implementation of the RTI in India and repeated hurdles, there is no denying the fact that this movement has the potential to democratise access and lead to a lowering of poverty indices. That this movement is being resisted and that ordinary people are being empowered to battle for their right to know are aspects of this on-going struggle. What is important is that a momentum for social change has been created through the right to information movement. The fact that advocacy related to this right is not a stand alone project but is linked to the fulfilment of the food security, employment and health needs of India's millions of marginalised people is what makes this movement unique. In contrast, the community radio movement, while developing in fits and starts, continues to be shackled by the state. While community radio can play an invaluable role in the validation of cultures and identities and in mobilising for social change, in the present context of globalising India characterised by the retreat of the welfare state and growing massive gaps between the rich and the poor, it can become a critical ally to the right to information movement. As I have observed in a review (Thomas 2009) of the book on community radio in India *Other Voices* by Vinod Pavarala and Kanchan K. Malik (2007), 'Community radio could quite easily become an ally of the Right to Information movement in India, but it could also become prey to special interests. That really is the quandary facing the movement in India' (Thomas 2008: 401).

Notes

1. 'Policy Guidelines for Setting up Community Radio Stations in India'. Available at http://mib.nic.in/informationb/CODES/CRBGUIDELINES041206.doc (Accessed on 22 May 2008).
2. Mana News, *Radiophony*. Available at http://www.radiophony.com/html_files/mananews.html (Accessed on 21 June 2009).
3. 'Social Audit Reveals Blatant Fraud in UP'. 2000. Available at http://www.empowerpoor.org/statestoriesdetail.asp?report=593&state (Accessed on 21 May 2009).
4. Right to Food Campaign: A Brief Introduction to the Campaign. Available at http://www.righttofoodindia.org/campaign/campaign.html (Accessed on 21 May 2009).

References

BBC News. 2009. 'India IT Firm Faces Scandal Probe', *BBC News*, 8 January. Available at http://news.bbc.co.uk/2/hi/business/7817449.stm (Accessed on 21 May 2009).

BBC Online. 2006. 'Anger as India Shuts FM Station', 30 March. Available at http://news.bbc.co.uk/2/hi/south_asia/4860162.stm (Accessed on 21 May 2008).

Bakshi, A. 2008. 'Social Inequality in Land Ownership in India: A Study with Particular Reference to West Bengal', *Social Scientist*, 36 (9–10), September–October: 95–116.

Boal, A. 1979. *Theatre of the Oppressed*. London: Pluto Press.

Brecht, B. 1983. 'Radio as a Means of Communication: A Talk on the Function of Radio', in A. Mattelart and S. Siegelaub (eds), *Communication and Class Struggle: 2. Liberation,*

Socialism, pp. 169–171. New York/Bagnolet: International General/International Mass Media Research Centre (IG/IMMRC).

Canclini, N. G. 1993. *Transforming Modernity: Popular Culture in Mexico*. Austin, Texas: University of Texas Press.

Downing, J. and T. V. Ford. 2000. *Radical Media: Rebellious Communication and Social Change*. Thousand Oaks, London, New Delhi: Sage Publications.

Economic Times. 2009. 'Government could have Probed Satyam Affairs Earlier: IT-BPO Union', 9 January. Available at http://economictimes.indiatimes.com/Infotech/Software/Govt_could_have_probed_Satyam_affairs_earlier_IT-BPO_union/articleshow/3952525.cms (Accessed on 21 May 2009).

Fredrikse, J. 1982. *None but Ourselves: Masses versus the Media in the Making of Zimbabwe*. Johannesburg: Raven Press.

Freire, P. 1972. *Pedagogy of the Oppressed*. Middlesex: Penguin Books.

Geertz, C. 1973. *The Interpretation of Cultures*. New York: Basic Books.

Hegde, R. 1986. 'A Case for a Second Channel for TV and Radio Broadcasting', *Seminar*, 41: 49.

Hindustan Times. 2007. 'RTI Unwelcome in Tamilnadu say People's Groups', *Hindustan Times*, 23 July. Available at: http://www.hindustantimes.com/storypage/storypage.aspx?id=486e8514-9f53-47fc-b060-8a38c31682f5&MatchID1=4500&TeamID1=2&TeamID2=6&MatchType1=1&SeriesID1=1122&MatchID2=4490&TeamID3=8&TeamID4=10&MatchType2=2&SeriesID2=1121&PrimaryID=4500&Headline=RTI+unwelcome+in+Tamil+Nadu (Accessed on 21 May 2009).

Laclau, E. and Mouffe. 2001. *Hegemony and Socialist Strategy: Towards a Radical Democratic Politics*. London/New York: Verso.

Lakshmi, R. 2003. 'Community Radio Gives Villagers a Voice', *Washington Post*, 17 September, p. 17.

Martin-Barbero, J. 1993. *Communication, Culture and Hegemony: From Media to Mediations*. London, Newbury Park, New Delhi: Sage Publications.

Mehta, N. 2008. *India on Television: How Satellite News Channels have Changed the Way we Think and Act*. New Delhi: Harper Collins Publishers, India/the India Today Group.

Muralidharan, S. 2001. 'A Forceful Assertion', *Frontline*, 18(9), April 28–May 11. Available at http://www.flonnet.com/fl1809/18090850.htm (Accessed on 9 September 2007).

National Rural Employment Generation Act (NREGA). 2005. Available at http://rural.nic.in/rajaswa.pdf (Accessed on 14 April 2010).

Pavrala, V. and K. K. Malik. 2007. *Other Voices: The Struggle for Community Radio in India*. New Delhi: Sage.

Pinglay, P. 2005. 'Reaching out through the Skies', *Frontline*, 22(9). Available at http://www.hinduonnet.com/fline/fl2209/stories/20050506001309000.htm (Accessed on 21 May 2009).

Raman, A. 2008. 'Radio Bihar Calling', *Outlook*, 17 March: 12–14.

Ramanujan, A. K. 1973. *Speaking of Siva*. Middlesex: Penguin Books.

Rodriguez, C. 2001. *Fissures in the Mediascape: An International Study of Citizen's Media*. Cresskill, New Jersey: Hampton Press.

Roy, A. and N. Dey. 2008. 'Attacking the Right to Ask', Indian Express.com, 14 June. Available at http://www.indianexpress.com/news/attacking-the-right-to-ask/322527/ (Accessed on 21 May 2009).

RTI Act. 2005 Available at http://rti.gov.in/rti-act.pdf (Accessed on 14 April 2010).

Scott, J. C. 1990. *Domination and the Arts of Resistance: Hidden Transcripts*. London, New Haven: Yale University Press.

The Public Right to Know: Principles on Freedom of Information Legislation. 1999. Article 19, June, London. Available at http://www.article19.org/pdfs/standards/righttoknow.pdf (Accessed on 21 May 2008).

The Right to Information Bill: Arrangement of Clauses. 2004. Available at http://www.humanrightsinitiative.org/programs/ai/rti/india/national/rti_bill_2004_tabled_version.pdf (Accessed on 21 May 2008).

The Tamilnadu Right to Information Act. 1997. (As introduced in the assembly), Available in pdf form at http://www.humanrightsinitiative.org/programs/ai/rti/india/legislation/tamilnadu_rti_act.pdf (Accessed on 21 May 2009).

Thomas, P. N. 2003. 'Broadcasting and the State in India: Towards Relevant Alternatives', *Gazette*, 51 (1): 19–33.

———. 2008. *Strong Religion, Zealous Media: Christian Fundamentalism and Communication in India*. New Delhi: Sage Publications.

Thomas, P. 2009. Book Review—V. Pavarala and K. K. Malik. 2007. *Other Voices: The Struggle for Community Radio in India*. New Delhi: Sage Publications. In *Asian Journal of Communication*, 18(4): 400–401.

TRAI. 2004. 'Recommendations on Licensing Issues Related to Community Radio Stations', December 2004, TRAI. Available at http://www.trai.gov.in/Recommendations_content.asp (Accessed on 22 August 2007).

Venkateshwarlu, K. 2002. 'Community Radio has Villagers Excited', *The Hindu Online*, 6 October. Available at http://www.hinduonnet.com/thehindu/2002/10/06/stories/2002100600691200.htm (Accessed on 11 May 2007).

Yadav, Y. and S. Palshikar. 2008. 'Ten Theses on State Politics in India', *Seminar*, 591, November: 14–22.

11

Beyond the Dominant Paradigm of Communication Rights: Operationalising Communication Rights in India

Countries in the South Asian region, despite achieving economic growth over the last decade, continue to face issues related to poverty. While the state and civil society in these countries have invested in a myriad anti-poverty effort, there are serious question marks over the long-term impact of development. In the case of Sri Lanka, the ethnic conflict between Tamils and the majority Sinhala is a dominant reality and this is shaped by chauvinisms on both sides. In the case of India and Nepal, the resistance to poverty has also been shaped by a thriving Maoist movement that is currently rooted in the most prosperous as well as the most desperate contexts in India and whose representatives are now part of the ruling government in Nepal. As we rightly celebrate the successes of community radio in Nepal, for instance, we do need to also ask the question as to whether community radio made any difference to the rise of Maoism. This movement, which the current Prime Minister of India, Manmohan Singh, has described as the number one internal security threat faced by the country (Zissis 2007), poses a number of vexing questions to civil society advocates. First, it gives the lie to V. S. Naipaul's (1998) progressive descriptor of India as a land of a 'million mutinies', given that these mutinies have not amounted to sustainable social change in the lives of the majority people. Second, it forces advocates of social movements to consider the limits to identity politics that is divorced from the politics of basic wants. In other words, in countries that face issues related to basic needs, progressive identity movements simply have to acknowledge the primacy of food, shelter, employment and a living wage. Third, it encourages us to consider and address the fissions and fractures that have driven civil society, so much so that they can be blamed for presiding over an under-development that has been caused by the capitalisation of civil society. Civil society's extractive politics, one can argue, has taken out more than it has given back. The multifarious nature of development supported by INGOs and NGOs, inter-governmental agencies, quasi-governmental initiatives, religious missions, global social movements, philanthropic bodies and the development industry, has given rise to a billion dollar industry in South Asia. While there certainly are numerous civil society initiatives that have contributed to a breaking down of the poverty cycle, there are many more whose involvement in the industrialisation of development has contributed to an exacerbation of the divides in South Asian societies. This goes for Information and Communication Technologies (ICTs) projects, gender projects and host of other major and minor civil society initiatives meant to further 'democracy' in South Asia.

The Operationalisation of Communication Rights

The operationalisation of communication rights is, in my way of thinking, the most critical issue facing the communication rights movement today. Operationalisation, in this context, refers not just to the practicalities, the 'doing', the shaping and implementation of projects, there is also, as part of the operationalisation process, the need to critically assess contemporary reflections on communication rights, the political economy of this enterprise and explore the gaps between theory and practice. At the heart of the struggle to define communication rights is the need to acknowledge other transcripts of communication rights shaped and inflected by local meanings and knowledge, needs, expectations, contexts and institutions linked to 'traditional' forms of civil society. It impels us to consider the question as to whether Hegel, Marx, de Tocquville and Locke's contributions to the understanding of civil society is all-sufficient to an understanding of civil society in Kantipur in Nepal or Villipuram in Tamil Nadu, India. Moreover, it forces us to critically examine the limits to exogenously funded strategies of dominant civil society, be it the 'progressive' sort or otherwise. In the words of Wickramasinghe (2005: 483):

> Civil society—if one agrees to use this term to describe the social and political spaces that express the desire for emancipation and betterment of communities—does not lend itself to external manufacturing. It cannot be

> created *via* blueprints from offices in Washington or London. It is in their attempt to wed theory and practice that donors have effectively stripped the notion of civil society of any substantive meaning.

For those of us who have been involved in communication rights, as advocates, activists and theoreticians, an issue that has persistently vexed us has been our collective inability to globalise the communication rights movement. This concern has been debated and discussed at a variety of fora although very few practical initiatives have resulted from it, with the exception, perhaps, of the Communication Rights in the Information Society (CRIS) project and post-WSIS, Tunis initiatives that have stemmed from it. James Boyle's (1997: 2) online treatise 'An Environmentalism for the Net' explores what it would take for people to acknowledge the worth of a political economy of intellectual property and the nature of the contemporary 'intellectual land grab' towards a global cultural politics supportive of the public domain, particularly on the internet. In Boyle's words:

> [R]ight now, we have no politics of intellectual property—in the way that we have a politics of the environment or of tax reform. We lack a conceptual map of issues, a rough working model of costs and benefits and a functioning coalition-politics of groups unified by common interest perceived in apparently diverse situations.

One Communication Rights or Many?

Some of us involved in communication rights in the CRIS and post-WSIS era may opine that Boyle's agenda is exactly what the movement has striven to clarify and that unlike, say, three decades ago, the communication rights movement today is on firmer ground. The CRIS campaign's *Assessing Communication Rights: A Handbook* (2005), for example, provides an accessible introduction and framework to an understanding of the theory and practice of communication rights. However, it can be argued that its trajectory and discourse is firmly located within a legalistic, UN-inspired framework of human rights and an evolving understanding of communication rights that is linked to the globalisation of the public sphere and civil society's (meaning NGOs) role in establishing the spaces for democratic communications. Is this an all-sufficient framework for dealing with communication rights and are the contexts of contemporary communication rights as is stated on page 29, Corporate Media Dominance, Identity and Culture, Copyright and the Public Domain, Universal Service and ICTs and Civil Rights in the Digital Environment sufficiently universal? Or is there a need to recognise multiple scapes of communication rights?

While there is an absolute need to reclaim the space to communicate by a range of sectors in society affected by corporate media dominance, these are by no means universal issues faced by all and sundry. If one were to explore communication rights in, say, a village in Central India, would local people connect to the issues highlighted on page 29 of the CRIS document or to issues shaped by context, traditions, needs and locality? I am not for a moment suggesting that traditional communication rights issues are not relevant in the context of globalising South Asia. The concentration of media ownership, enclosures around knowledge, and affordable access and use remain critical issues in this region. I would, however, suggest that there are audiences who are affected by these issues and audiences that are not. Landless labourers in Nepal and Bangladesh and displaced Tamils in Sri Lanka are faced with a different set of communication deficits than those faced by urban dwellers.

The stories related to a range of domestic deficits rarely feature in the global media given the dominant accent on India's economic growth. However, religious, sectarian and political conflicts continue to shape India; poverty is on the increase and the gaps between the rich and the poor have widened dramatically during the last decade. Farmer suicides have become a reality all over the country because of indebtedness and the failure of agriculture as a way of life. Can a singular, universal framework for communication rights be the only solution or is there the need for diverse context-specific frameworks for communication rights that are needs-based and that emerge from bottom-up, participatory deliberative processes? And if the latter option is the only clear option, what would its objectives be—the valourisation of voice, structural change, media reform and the opening up of space for public domain access? Should communication rights be defined as a set of stand-alone issues or should it be linked to very specific social contestations? How would the CRIS discourse on communication rights work in South Asia? And as importantly who should be involved in defining communication rights?

NGOs have more often than not been involved in setting civil society agendas in South Asia and there have been serious questions levelled at the efficacy of myriad NGO networks sustained by a bewildering range of agendas to contribute to sustainable development. This critique has come from the established Left in India (See Karat 1984), and also from social movement activists and scholars, who are witness to the gaps between NGO activities and the various expressions and modes of international development on the one hand and the people that they serve on the other.

Civil society fundamentally relates to associational ways of life, although there are theorists such as Partha Chatterjee (1998: 60) who insist that it should only be applied to describe associational life that emerged from Western societies and that are based on 'equality, autonomy, deliberative procedures of decision-making, recognised rights and duties of members and other such principles'.

The issue then is—how does one validate other understandings of communication rights that are context-based, along with the methods of mobilisation and advocacy and evaluation and assessment that are outside the formal structures and practices of development? Dervin and Huesca in a 1997 article introduce the notion of 'verbing' as the basis for a dialogue of knowledges that is a requirement for communicative understanding. Is this dialogue of knowledges an option in the context of communication rights today? While there are, as always, exceptions to this rule, for the most part, the only dialogue is between communication rights experts and the representatives of NGOs whose agendas arguably are, at best, only tangentially related to that of the local people. Notwithstanding the fact that community radio is an important tool for democratisation in South Asia, the question—whose agenda is community radio?—can lead to interesting debates about the merits and demerits of exogenously-induced change.

There is a dominant paradigm of communication rights that I must confess, I do identify with, although I have increasingly felt the need for definitions and frameworks for communication rights that are inflected by needs, locality, context and local knowledge. As Nancy Fraser (2003: 105) has observed in her critique of the public sphere, '...a multiplicity of publics is preferable to a single public sphere both in stratified and egalitarian societies'. While her conceptualisation of societies as stratified and egalitarian is open to contestation, her argument in favour of a larger, more inclusive understanding of democracy needs to be heeded.

This chapter will offer an alternative perspective on communication rights in South Asia. Beginning with a critique of civil society in South Asia, it will explore the limitations of exogenously-led development, before exploring examples of communication rights movements in India.

Financing Civil Society

Seira Tamang (2003), in a critique of civil society in Nepal, makes the point that financing democracy has serious limitations, given that it results in NGOs creating frameworks for democracy and not the large number of local associations that have traditionally provided a range of services for ordinary Nepalis and who, for all practical purposes are 'civil society'. As Tamang also points out, NGOs tend to be closer to their transnational funders than the people; 'for many, villages are not the area of operation... this has resulted in altering priorities from domestic needs to those that reflect the priorities and agendas of foreign assistance programmes.' The global access and democratisation enterprise is transnational and involves a range of actors from the World Bank, to UN agencies, ecumenical mission organisations to philanthropic organisations such as the Ford and Rockefeller Foundations. While there certainly are major ideological and operational differences and objectives between agencies involved in development and social change, these institutions are recognised today as the makers and sustainers of global civil society and are involved in the transfers of large amounts of money, given that it is used to maintain 'civil society' in the South, most often through their support for NGOs and social movements. In other words, one can argue that the development enterprise today, consisting of NGOs, consultancies, the professionalisation of development, the accent on objective reports and planning tools such as log-frames, transnational agencies and the causes that they espouse and the meanings that they invest in, are a continuation of the project of Orientalism, except that this project is carried out, most often, through the benign arm of development rather than through the overt imposition of superiorities, either through education or the barrel of the gun. Interestingly enough the critique of NGO-led civil society has not only emerged from the established Left in South Asia but also from the political right. While such critiques have certainly been motivated by self-interest, it does bring to the fore the need to assess the market orientation of NGOs, irrespective of their credentials in the enterprise of emancipation.

Stirrat (2000: 40–41), for example, maintains that every consultancy is a cultural performance—

> Like the rest of the development industry short-term development consultants attempt to present their culture as objective and acultural even to the extent of remodelling 'other cultures' to fit the categories of their own. Thus, while it is misleading to characterise development agencies or individual consultants as agents of imperialism or neo-colonialism, there is a sense in which there is an imperialism of thought, particular cultural models and categories being imposed upon and often accepted in the developing world.

Stirrat's observations indirectly acknowledge the role playing by language in the reinforcement of dominance in the public sphere.

Thomas Babington Macaulay's (1957) Education Minute (1835), that he introduced to the Parliament in India in support of English education, was meant to establish a class of 'Indians in colour and blood but English in tastes, in opinions, in morals and in intellect', a task that has largely succeeded. One can argue that the dominant enterprise of development is precisely linked to extending the primacy of a singular, development contract and its associated ways of doing. The language of development is, as Luis Beltran once famously described in his critique of the dominant paradigm of communication and development, based on 'alien premises'. It is through the language of development that these alien premises are expressed and institutionalised. Neela Chandoke (2005: 337) reiterates the importance of language as an the issue with her observation that:

> To 'lack voice'...is to lack linguistic and epistemic authority in the public domain, which is arguably governed by a rule-bound set of languages, that of political modernity. To put it otherwise, the marginalised by definition do not participate in the construction of what counts as 'reasonable', or indeed what counts as appropriate and legitimate knowledge in the public domain of deliberation.

Who, therefore, should be involved in defining communication rights—the experts or those who experience a range of communication deficits in their daily lives?

This inability to define their own developmental futures has led to growing gaps between the English-educated elite and the vast majority of South Asians. These contradictions are real and their effects are being felt in the growing divides between metropolitan South Asia and the hinterlands, and is expressed in the gaps between growth and poverty, between modern civil society and traditional civil society (Edwards 2004; Khilnani 1997). It is a clash of meanings, expectations and visions of the future and the dominant paradigm of development and social change has certainly contributed to the reinforcement of these divides. Both religious fundamentalism and insurgencies are in their own ways, a response to the modern state and modern civil society's inability to accept the worth of traditional civil society or protect opportunities for traditional ways of life.

Stirrat and Henkel (1997), drawing on Marcel Mauss's classic essay on 'The Gift', draw a contrast between traditions of reciprocity that exist in traditional societies (such as the potlatch) with the political economy of giving in contemporary development:

> Frequently the gift—the money, the equipment, and so on that the donors pay for through their pure gifts—never actually reaches the people to whom the donors think they are giving. Rather, it ends up supporting a range of people and organisations that are encouraging others to be empowered and independent. Second, no matter how apolitical and, in a sense, otherwordly the development NGOs may try to be, they are inevitably involved in the mundane world of power, patronage, and inequality.

One can argue that contemporary support for communication rights in the South, be it through the Ford Foundation, the Soros Foundation, World Association for Christian Communication (WACC), Association for Progressive Communication (APC) and other agencies, leads to the furthering of a specific construct of communication rights that may or may not be representative of, or for that matter conversant with, local communication deficits. There is also the added issue related to a small body of funding agencies cornering the market for communication rights. This is a serious and much larger issue that affects the very nature and sustainability of national and international media reform. Do communication rights NGOs located in the South represent local communication interests or do their rationales merely link them to the dominant political economy of communication rights? If their agendas are not linked to locality, there is a danger that they will remain irrelevant.

Lamia Karim (2004: 312), in a perceptive essay on NGOs and militant Islam in Bangladesh, has observed that local feminist struggles are ultimately ineffective if they are not based on the possibilities of liberation available in the local context:

> For many Bangladeshi women secularism does not have any relevance, and Islam is seen as a religion of social justice and equality for the poor. Thus, critiques of society have to come from within an Islamic interpretive framework. There are Muslim feminists who have begun to reinterpret the Quran in Islamic terms, arguing that Islam grants equality and justice to women.

Local forms of civil society are best placed to provide answers to local needs for emancipation. As Rashiduzzaman (1998: 4) has observed, 'Bangladesh civil society had non-governmental, voluntary and self-sustaining relationships and organisations long before the plethora of new NGOs arrived there. Such community-based arrangements and traditional leaders included the information council of elders (often known as the panchayats), the shalish, the religious trusts.' In South Asia, there are numerous context-specific associational ways of life that are rooted in locality and that are a response to local needs. These traditional organisations have been marginalised in the context of NGO-focussed development, a marginalisation that has led to increasing conflict between local people and NGOs all over South Asia.

While liberal advocates of communication rights are certainly well-meaning, access and affordable uses of convergent technologies to ICTs and the use of community radio are, by their very nature, laudable ideals, aimed at decreasing the gaps between technology and knowledge, rich and poor and increasing empowerment. This dominant discourse of communication rights often fails to recognise that the discourse of access and empowerment are themselves richly textured, woven with meanings that legitimise the enterprise of contemporary development. Access is, of course, a major plank for a variety of ICTs projects in South Asia although one can argue that a large percentage of these projects are silo projects that are unrelated to each other and that simply do not acknowledge the local political economy (See Thomas 2008) and issues related to culture and society. There is a fervent hope that ICTs will lead to the dissolution of social barriers, a way of thinking that is reminiscent of earlier ways of thinking, related first to radio and then to television. E-governance projects that are meant to increase government control over information flows, pilot projects that do not make a dent to the feudal economy and real commercial pressure from Microsoft and other software and hardware companies, are all realities that continue to be under-theorised in the context of South Asia. Such realities, directly and indirectly, call into question the dominant epistemology of communication rights and its links to the discourses of development, democratisation, civil society, the public sphere and social change that are key aspects of the contemporary understanding of communication rights.

I will, in the next section, highlight two examples of the communication rights movement in India. First, I will deal briefly with the free software movement in India and its attempts to create a nation-wide movement in favour of non-proprietory software and open source as the basis for extending access and affordable use. Second, I will explore what can be described as an example of the Indian tenor of empowerment by reference to public hearings, and its role in the valourisation of Voice in the context of the right to information movement in India. While the free software movement is involved in advocating the use of software platforms and local solutions to problems of access, the right to information movement, as has been described in the preceding chapter, is involved in extending accountability and transparency and is at the cutting edge of improving the quality of people's lives in India. These two examples are not, by any stretch of the imagination, the only examples of localised communication rights in India. A case can also be made for women and media, intellectual property and community radio movements, although it is arguable as to whether these movements are national in scope and sufficiently independent. The IP movement certainly does have interesting local iterations including the advocacy work carried out by the Alternative Law Forum in Bengaluru.

The Free Software Movement in India

India's position as a globally significant hub for software manufacturing and exports has certainly contributed to the establishment of a vibrant free software movement. The existence of large numbers of software engineers and exposure to the international and national politics of software, the presence of a strong NGO movement and dedicated NGOs including Bytes for All, think-tanks such as the Centre for Internet and Democracy, research centres committed to free software such as the Delhi-based Sarai network, keystone centres such as the Indian Institutes of Technology, the Indian Institute of Science, Tata Institute of Fundamental Research, Open Source Software Resource Centre (OSSRC) and the Department of Information Technology (IT) and Ministry of Communication and Information Technology funded National Resource Centre for Free/Open Source Software (NRCFOSS) have played no small part in the making of this movement. The Indian government's commitment to IT-based solutions in development including e-governance, tele-centres, its dedicated IT ministries and the various IT-based solutions explored by the various state governments along with the understanding, both at central and state levels, to explore non-proprietory options regarding software, also contributed to the development of this sector. Abdul Kalam, the ex-President of India remains a keen supporter of this movement. India's plural political environment, in particular the active support extended by Left-oriented governments, have also played a key role in the extension of this movement. One can argue that it is government support that has been absolutely critical to the large-scale implementation of free software projects. The government of Kerala has been a vocal supporter of this movement and has invested resources and personnel in the development of this movement in Kerala.

At the heart of this movement is a commitment to digital pluralism and open standards that allow users the freedom to utilise software code free of royalty, legal and technical constraints. The commitment though is wider and includes the creation of digital democracies based on environments that enable all people, irrespective of their status or abilities (including, for example, the visually impaired and reading disabled), access to technologies and platforms that can be used to make a difference in their lives. Given the global impact of the digital on people's lives—at work and in the context of leisure—access and affordable use of software is increasingly defining a person's quality of life. The fact that proprietory software limits such open uses is an issue that all government's committed to development need to face up to. Not only are there significant savings related to using free software, but its deployment is bound to increase access and affordable use of software solutions in a variety of contexts. As Javed Tapia, director of Red Hat India notes in an article in Red Hat magazine:

> In education, India has 888,000 educational institutions and 350 million children in the age group of 6–19. In the area of e-government, India has to reach out to its one billion plus population at the lowest possible cost. At the individual level, India's per capita income is Rs 20,862 ($474), while PC hardware costs Rs 10,000 ($227) and software costs approximately Rs 11,000 ($250). This means that the cost of hardware and software is more than the annual income of most Indians! (Tapia 2006)

Free software does not, as it is implied, involve zero cost. Rather, free software implies the freedom to run a programme for any given purpose, adapt a programme to one's needs, improve and re-distribute copies. Users of free software, for example, large organisations do have to pay for their purchase of Linux or Apache but have the freedom to adapt it to the companies needs. Sunil Abraham (2008) from the Centre for Internet and Society makes the point that what is at stake is the availability of choice for users. The global dependence on products such as Windows, which is license-based and is based on the control of knowledge production, access and use, needs to be changed. As he observes:

> Corporations have a right to sell products based on proprietory standards just as consumers have a right to choose between products that use open standards, proprietory standards, or even a combination of such standards. Governments, however, have a responsibility to use open standards, especially for interactions with the public and where the data handled has a direct impact on democratic values and quality of citizenship. In developing countries, governments have greater responsibility because most often they account for over 50 per cent of the revenues of proprietory software vendors.... (Abraham 2008: 22)

There are literally hundreds of Free and Open Source Software (FOSS) groups spread all over India, who are involved in adapting Linux and other open source platforms to local needs. Major engineering colleges have also begun courses in Open Software. Red Hat Linux, a company based on Linux solutions is established in the major cities in India and has increasingly begun to support both industry and government. IBM too has made major investments in FOSS. In fact, given the present global economic downturn, FOSS-based solutions are bound to become even more widespread. Throughout India, government departments have begun to migrate at least some proportion of their work on to FOSS platforms. The state of Tamil Nadu in Southern India, for example, plans to adopt open source platforms mainly because of security issues and the high costs of maintaining the Windows platform. While much of on-going government work in Tamil Nadu is carried out on the Windows platform (as is over 70 per cent of software deployed in companies in India), the fact that this government is opting for mixed solutions is a welcome sign and signal that the days of a single-platform monopoly may be broken in the next few years. Uma Shankar, the manager of the Electronics Corporation of Tamil Nadu (ELCOT) in an interview on ZDNet Asia in 2007, has stated that the government planned to deploy FOSS in 10,000 cooperatives and train 30,000 government officials in Linux and FOSS. Microsoft, as Uma Shankar notes, is trying its best to counter this movement:

> Not surprisingly, Microsoft is not resting on its laurels. Umashankar said an official from the software giant's Indian office offered Elcot a discounted price for Windows XP, at 7,000 rupees (US$157) per copy. However, the deal fell through when Umashankar was only willing to shell out 300 rupees (US$6.73). (Tan 2007)

Access, affordability, localisation, the provision of solutions across a number of sectors—in government, industry and the NGO sector—and advocacy efforts aimed at convincing the Government of India to not capitulate to the demands to incorporate software patenting in the Indian Patent Act, are some of the issues that this movement is currently involved in.

The key state in India that is at the forefront of the FOSS movement is Kerala. It is, therefore, not entirely surprising that Richard Stallman, the founder of the Free Software movement, is a frequent visitor to this state located in southern India. V. Sasi Kumar (2007), a leading advocate of FOSS in India, in an online article entitled 'Free Software in Kerala', provides an extensive introduction to this movement and has observed that the success of the movement is linked to Kerala's commitments to social change:

> Government officials and other Free Software supporters in the state of Kerala believe that Free Software meshes particularly well with Kerala's long tradition of democracy, equity and public action. Just as Kerala is often held up as a model of equitable social and human development in the region, Free Software supporters there believe they can leverage the inherent freedoms of Free Software to evolve an equitable Knowledge Society based on software independence and self-reliance. (Sasi Kumar 2007)

The Government of Kerala has embarked upon an extensive project related to IT education in schools based on FOSS and will soon become the first state in India to exclusively use free software in its schools (Sasi Kumar 2007). This is one example of an extensive FOSS-based approach adopted by the government at various sectors of local and state government. Kerala's IT mission established the Society for Promotion of Alternative Computing and Employment (SPACE) in 2003. This organisation has played an important role in the distribution of specific, applications-based free software.

Localisation is a key objective of FOSS. Local language-based software solutions are bound to play an important role in extending the FOSS movement and in the Indianising of Linux-based solutions. Organisations, such as Red Hat, have played an important role in localising applications and operating systems in five languages—Hindi, Bengali, Tamil, Punjabi and Gujarati—and there are moves to include eight more languages, including Kannada, Malayalam, Marathi, Assamese, Marathi, Oriya, Sinhala, Telugu and Urdu. The government too has played an important role in localisation processes and are involved in creating local language CDs released with a General Public License (GPL).

This movement does illustrate the growth of a successful communication rights movement that is beginning to have both an extensive and intensive impact. It also illustrates the fact that the success rate of localised communication rights movements is better than global advocacy movements such as the Communication Rights in the Information Society (CRIS) Campaign that was linked to the United Nation's (UN) World Summit on the Information Society (WSIS). The free software movement has been successful precisely because it has explored localised solutions to real deficits faced by people.

The *Jan Sunwai* and Empowerment

The second example of a successful communication rights movement is the right to information movement in India that has been covered extensively in the preceding chapter. What I would like to focus on in this section is not the movement per se, but on an indigenous pedagogical device used by this movement to mobilise, radicalise and give voice to marginalised people who, traditionally, had been expected to remain silent, even in the face of the most atrocious atrocities committed by the forward castes and the wealthy. Public hearings played an important role in creating popular understandings of the Right to Know.

The strength of the right to information movement in India includes the following. It is an indigenous social movement that was a response to felt needs. It started as a grassroots movement supported entirely by voluntary, local contributions and it employed familiar pedagogical tools like the *Jan Sunwai* (public hearings), that were used to strengthen and valourise Voice.[1] The *Jan Sunwai* is often used by traditional organisations in India such as guilds and associations of small traders and manufacturers to make themselves accountable to their public. Carino (2008: 136), for example, has pointed out the role of these hearings in generating publicity and attracting community support for associations that are faced with difficulties. As pointed out in the Lokniti Newsletter (2005):

> The Jan Sunwai is an empowering process in that, it not only does away with civil society structures that are stacked against the marginalised but also inverts power equations in favour of the marginalised, by making them the centre of the discussion. There are no experts and 'hence on chance of objectification of the victim' and the 'victim represents his case without any technical assistance'.

In the words of the Dalit intellectual Gopal Guru,

> The *sunwai* is a public hearing but it is different from legal and procedural hearings instituted by the state which by its official, legal, and almost pompous nature, place the victim at an inherent disadvantage. The *sunwai* restores to a person his place in the system by allowing him to represent himself and make himself heard.[2]

Most importantly, the *Jan Sunwai* is a mechanism that affirms Voice and strengthens self-confidence, often in contexts where caste and class collude to silence people. In the context of the RTI movement, these public hearings allowed local people to examine both the information and dis-information on local development, the collusions, the silences, the corruption and the political economy of under-development. In Mohanty's words (2006: 20)

> The term *jan sunwai* is taken literally, and it implies that the power, legitimacy and sanctity of the forum will emanate from the people, not any judge or panel; and that it is a hearing and not a court or agitational body. The decision of

the assembled collective to pose certain sets of questions would determine the priorities of the hearing. It did not pass a verdict or punish the guilty. It is out to shame those government officials, in connivance with suppliers and contractors, who made money illegally from the public works.

15 *Jan Sunwais*, organised in advance, became critical to the empowerment process in Rajasthan. These public hearings were complemented by *dharnas* (sit-ins) at the office of the Chief Minister and local government in the face of official inaction on the evidence of corruption. The *dharna* as non-violent civil resistance also became the space for celebrating solidarity. There were instances when the *dharnas* stretched over days in the context of stalemates. As one report states:

> [T]he dharna...witnessed an unprecedented upsurge of homespun idealism in the small town of Beawar and the surrounding countryside. Donations in cash and kind poured in daily from ordinary local people, including vegetables and milk from small vendors, sacks of wheat from farmers in surrounding villages, tents, voluntary services of cooking, serving cold water...and cash donations, even from the poorest...Even more significant was the daily assembly of over 500 people in the heat of the tent, listening to speeches...Active support cut across all class and political barriers. Rich shopkeepers and professionals to daily wage labourers, and the entire political spectrum from the right wing fringe to communist trade unions extended vocal and enthusiastic support.[3]

Given the long drawn-out nature of the *dharnas*, there were a number of focussed cultural events—plays, music, devotional singing, question and answer sessions—that were used to strengthen solidarity, awareness and involvement. The intentional use of local culture and popular involvement in the creation of these skits, dramas and music were critical to the making of this movement. As one report clearly states:

> The essence of communication for social change should also be one which is specific to the local area. For example in Rajasthan, MKSS has used the local deity and his 'bhopa' (witch doctor), as a mode to communicate important issues to the people tend to take whatever the bhopa said seriously and therefore this forms a good technique to present serious issues. (Mohanty 2006: 6–7)

These hearings took the form of an audit of local level development projects, especially the social audit of 'employment muster rolls' and expenses related to public works and wages paid to workers. This led to the demand for all copies of documents related to public works to be made public. However, local government officials were not, in the beginning, cooperative and, in fact, launched their own counter-campaigns against the right to information movement. However, these hearings took a life of their own. As more and more people throughout the state began to hear the literally hundreds of stories of corruption, they became empowered to demand their right to know. In district after district, these hearings exposed the vast gaps between official expenditures on development projects and the actual expenditures. These hearings unearthed evidence of widespread corruption and the systemic links between local officials and politicians, who were also involved in a variety of scams. This evidence discussed at the public hearings led to non-violent civic actions, boycotts and sit-ins at government offices, which was systematically used to wear down the opposition and elicit a response from the government.

Rural–Urban Mobilisation

The cross-sectoral mobilisation of people was one of the strengths of the RTI movement. The inability of communication rights advocates to create and forge rural–urban solidarities and with other movements has hampered the growth of this movement. The RTI movement in Rajasthan, for example, actively expanded the social movement to include the urban middle classes. The Jan Nithi Abhyan was an attempt to broaden the struggle and to create alliances in the city with students and journalists in the wake of local elections in Rajasthan.[4] This urban group participated in the struggle for information rights precisely because they understood and recognised the links between the RTI, enabling local environments and the quality of life.

Conclusion

In conclusion, I think that it is necessary that any framework of communication rights for the twenty-first century recognises the existence of multiple social imaginaries, societal and cultural formations, civil societies and traditions of hope, that are outside of mainstream understandings. While I am certainly not advocating the return to a parochial theorising based on the all-sufficiency of 'Asian Values', pan-Africanist discourses and the like, I would like to think that the valuation given to grand projects such as democracy, freedom and identity, needs to be reality-checked against the persistence, even deepening of older problems, such as poverty and struggles related to basic wants within a context characterised by uneven economic globalisation. The communitarian theorist Charles Taylor (2002: 91) identifies the problem as the inability of Western theorists to think of traditions and solutions to modernity outside of a single, universal framework:

> Is there a single phenomenon here, or do we need to speak of *multiple* modernities, the plural reflecting the fact that non-Western cultures have modernised in their own ways and cannot be properly understood if we try to grasp them in a general theory that was originally designed with the Western case in mind.

Communication rights needs to be de-centred and localised. As the example of the FOSS and right to information movements in India clearly illustrate, people's recognition of the links between access to software and social change and local information deficits and poverty, became the basis for significant, nation-wide movements that continue to make a difference in the lives of citizens of India.

Notes

1. 'The Grassroots Struggle of Rajasthan'. Available at http://foi-asia.org/India/Rajastanstory.pdf (Accessed on 12 February 2008).
2. Guru, G. 'Jan Sunwai: A New Instrument of Democracy in India', *Democracy Asia.* Available at http://www.democracy-asia.org/casestudies_studies_gopal_guru.htm (Accessed on 11 February 2008).
3. History of the Mazdoor Kisan Shakti Sangathan (MKSS). Available at http://www.mkssindia.org/node/3 (Accessed on 23 June 2007).
4. Ramkumar, V. 'Beyond Democratic Rights and Electoral Reform Campaigns: Challenges Facing Non-Party Political Movements'. Available at http://www.freedominfo.org/features/20040630-beyond.htm (Accessed on 11 February 2008).

References

Abraham, S. 2008. 'Open Standards', Global Information Society Watch, pp. 20–22. Available at http://www.giswatch.org/gisw2008/thematic/pdf/OpenStandards.pdf (Accessed on 21 March 2008).

Boyle, J. 1997. 'A Politics of Intellectual Property: Environmentalism for the Net'. Available at http://www.law.duke.edu/boylesite/Intprop.htm (Accessed on 15 February 2008).

Carino, L. V. 2008. 'Collective Governance: An Alternative Model of Third Sector Governance', Chapter 8, in S. Hasan and J. Onyx (eds), *Collective Governance: An Alternative Model of Third Sector Governance*, pp. 131–150. New York: Springer. Available at http://www.springerlink.com/content/x1221g6k71411531/fulltext.pdf (Accessed on 23 March 2009).

Chandoke, N. 2005. 'Exploring the Mythology of the Public Sphere', in R. Bhargava and H. Reifeld (eds), *Civil Society, Public Sphere and Citizenship: Dialogues and Perceptions*, pp. 327–347. New Delhi: Sage.

Chatterjee, P. 1998. 'Beyond the Nation State? Or Within?', *Social Text*, 56, 16(3): 57–69.

Communication Rights in the Information Society (CRIS). 2005. *Assessing Communication Rights: A Handbook*. London: CRIS Campaign.

Dervin, B. and R. Huesca. 1997. 'Reaching for the Communicating in Participatory Communication: A Meta-Theoretical Analysis', *Journal of International Communication*, 4(2): 46–74.

Edwards, M. 2004. *Civil Society*. Oxford: Polity.

Fraser, N. 2003. 'Rethinking the Public Sphere: A Contribution to the Critique of Actually Existing Democracy', in C. M. Elliott (ed.), *Civil Society and Democracy: A Reader*, pp. 83–105. New Delhi: Oxford University Press.

Karat, P. 1984. 'Action Groups/Voluntary Organisations: A Factor in Imperialist Strategy', *The Marxist*, 2(2): 51–63.

Karim, L. 2004. 'Democratising Bangladesh: State, NGOs and Militant Islam', *Cultural Dynamics*, 16(2/3): 291–318.

Khilnani, S. 1997. *The Idea of India*. New Delhi: Penguin Books.

Lokniti Newsletter. 2005. 'Case Studies', 8 November. Available at http://www.lokniti.org/lok_nov05_newsletter.pdf (Accessed on 23 March 2008).

Macaulay, Thomas Babington. 1957. 'Minute of 2 February 1835 on Indian Education', *Macaulay, Prose and Poetry*, selected by G. M. Young, pp. 721–24, 729. Cambridge, MA: Harvard University Press.

Mohanty, B. K. 2006. *The Growing Role of Civil Society Organisations in Contemporary India: A Case Study of the Mazdoor Kisan Shakti Sangathan*. Kolkata: Centre for Studies in Social Sciences.

Naipaul, V. S. 1998. *India: A Million Mutinies Now*. London: William Heineman Ltd.

Rashiduzzaman, M. 1998. 'The Civil Society and the NGOs in Bangladesh: Need for a Realistic Paradigm'. Available at http://www.ashanet.org/madison/docs/mail/asha/0221.html (Accessed on 19 February 2008).

Sasi Kumar, V. 2007. 'Free Software in Kerala', 31 August. Available at http://swatantryam.blogspot.com/2007/08/story-of-free-software-in-kerala-india.html (Accessed on 3 April 2008).

Stirrat, R. L. 2000. 'Cultures of Consultancy', *Critique of Anthropology*, 20(1): 31–46.

Stirrat, R. L. and H. Henkel. 1997. 'The Development Gift: The Problem of Reciprocity in the NGO World', *The Annals of the American Academy of Political Science*, 554: 66–80.

Tamang, S. 2003. 'Civilising Civil Society: Donors and Democratic Space in Nepal', *Himal South Asia*, July. Available at http://www.himalmag.com/2003/july/ (Accessed on 10 November 2005).

Tan, A. 2007. 'Indian State goes for Open Source, ZDNET Asia', 12 January. Available at http://www.zdnetasia.com/news/software/0,39044164,61981452,00.htm (Accessed on 3 April 2008).

Tapia, J. 2006. 'What does Open Source mean in India', *Red Hat Magazine*, 15 January.

Taylor, C. 2002. 'Modern Social Imaginaries', *Public Culture*, 14(1): 91–124.
Thomas, P. N. 2008. 'Bhoomi, Gyan Ganga, e-governance and the Right to Information: ICTs and Development in India', *Telematics and Informatics*, 26, 1.
Wickramasinghe, N. 2005. 'The Ideal of Civil Society in the South: Imaginings, Transplants, Designs', *Science and Society*, 69 (3): 458–486.
Zissis, C. 2007. 'Terror Groups in India', Council on Foreign Relations. Available at http://www.cfr.org/publication/12773/terror_groups_in_india.html (Accessed on 10 February 2008).

Index

About the Author

Pradip Ninan Thomas is Joint-director of the Centre for Communication and Social Change at the University of Queensland. He was previously Director of Research at the School of Journalism and Communication, UQ and prior to that was Director of Research at the then London-based communication rights organisation, World Association for Christian Communication. He has written extensively on issues related to the political economy of communication. He has co-edited the volume *Who Owns the Media: Global Trends & Local Resistances* (2004) and *Intellectual Property Rights and Communications in Asia* (2006). Recent publications include *Strong Religion/Zealous Media: Christian Fundamentalism & Communication in India* (2008) and the co-edited volume *Indigenous Knowledge Systems and Intellectual Property in the Twenty First Century* (2007).